Capri – The Island Revisited

John Clay MacKowen's classic text,
with comprehensive new material based
on current findings and research

Editor
Anna Maria Palombi Cataldi

*Full Professor of English Literature, Department of Modern
Philology, University of Naples, Federico II
Italy*

BEACONSFIELD PUBLISHERS LTD
Beaconsfield, Bucks, UK

First published in 2012

This book is copyright. All rights are reserved. Apart from any fair dealing for the purpose of private study, research, criticism or review, as permitted under the Copyright, Designs and Patents Act 1988, no part of this publication may be reproduced, stored or transmitted, in any form or by any means, without the prior permission in writing of the publishers. Enquiries should be addressed to Beaconsfield Publishers Ltd at 20 Chiltern Hills Road, Beaconsfield, Bucks HP9 1PL, UK.

books@beaconsfield-publishers.co.uk
www.caprirevisited.com

© Centro Caprense Ignazio Cerio, Capri, Italy 2012

The individual named contributors to this work hereby assert their right as set out in sections 77 and 78 of the Copyright, Designs and Patents Act 1988 to be identified as the author of their chapter or chapters wherever this book is published commercially and whenever any adaptation of it is published or produced.

A CIP catalogue record for this book is available from the British Library

ISBN 978-0-906584-63-7

Cover photography by Antonio Federico, Capri, Italy
Cover design by Oxford Designers & Illustrators, Oxford, UK
Phototypeset in Century Old Style and Times by Gem Graphics, Trenance, Newquay, Cornwall, UK
Printed and bound in the UK by Halstan Printing Group, Amersham

For Norman Douglas

a humanist, a scholar, and a profound cognoscente of Capri literature, who expressed the hope that one day J.C. MacKowen's *Capri* would be republished.

Acknowledgments

The Editor and the Publishers are indebted to many different people for making it possible for this story to be told. We would like to express our thanks in particular to the following persons:

The contributors to the modern part of this book, who took MacKowen's material on Capri and extended it to take into account the wealth of new information that has emerged in the light of research, historical study and archaeological findings since his day. Angela Federico, who translated their chapters from Italian into English and whose command of both languages has produced a text of great clarity. Antonio Federico, whose photographs, including the two used on the cover, have added welcome immediacy to the book. Carmelina Fiorentino, not only a contributor herself, for the coordination of all the detail that arises when the work of so many different hands needs to be brought together into a single volume. Dr Vittoria Fiorelli, for her many insights that we were able to use in the book.

Mr Michael F. Howell and Colonel J.L. Hendrickson USAF (retired) of Jackson, Louisiana, who gave us generously of their knowledge of MacKowen's Confederate background as well as much significant information on the events of his last years in Louisiana and his ultimate violent death. The Head and staff of the Special Collections Department, Louisiana State University, Baton Rouge, for permission to draw on and reproduce material from MacKowen's personal papers. Dr Bruce Raeburn, the Director of Special Collections at Tulane University, who facilitated our enquiries into the details of the survival and safe-keeping of the two cases of rare books that MacKowen donated to H. Sophie Newcomb Memorial College, now a constituent part of Tulane University, and for allowing us to reproduce the frontispiece of one of the earliest items from that donation. Ann E. Smith Case, University Archivist of Tulane University, Mary Allen Johnson, Archivist of the Newcomb Archives, Newcomb College Institute of Tulane University, and Sally Main, Senior Curator of the Newcomb Art Gallery of Tulane University, whose knowledge and sustained enthusiasm were crucial to us as we worked our way into the ramifications of our search. Professor Elio Palombi, who confirmed from his reading of the MacKowen collection record that these books are bibliographic treasures of the greatest rarity.

Acknowledgments

We would also like to express our thanks to many other friends and colleagues whose help has played a much appreciated role in shaping the final form of this book:

The Adelson Galleries, New York, for allowing the reproduction in black and white of J.S. Sargent's colour painting 'Rosina', and Elaine Kilmurray, Research Director of the John Singer Sargent catalogue raisonné. Osvaldo Brunetti, Rosa Sessa Maresca and Annamaria Vivo, for relating to us further details about MacKowen, and their recollections of his daughter Giulia Cimino Maresca and the Casa Rossa. Franco Cerrotta, Mayor of the Municipality of Anacapri, for allowing the reproduction in black and white of E.A. Sain's colour painting 'Wedding on Capri'. Anna and Bianca Cuomo, for allowing us to read and quote from the unpublished diary of their grandfather Vincenzo Cuomo, and for allowing us to reproduce MacKowen's medical degree certificate, restored and digitised by Tom Wachtel. Simona D'Angiola, for permission to quote from her study of schooling on Capri, currently in press. Levente Erdeös, for information about Arthur King and Axel Munthe. Serena Lucianelli and her colleagues at the Manuscript and Rare Books Section of the National Library, Naples, for their valuable help. Sergio Rubino, for allowing the reproduction in black and white of his colour painting 'The Casa Rossa'. Maria Luisa Saggese Laviano, former notary on Capri, for consulting the deeds of sale at the Conservatoria dei Registri Immobiliari di Napoli concerning MacKowen's properties. Pasquale Saraceno, for drawing our attention to Dr Ferdinand Bergamo's 1879 report on the unremitting burden of work carried out by the island's women and its toll on the health of so many of them. Gordon Galsworthy, our typographer, whose mastery of his craft is evident throughout the pages of this book.

Preface

[MacKowen, J.C. An American.] His book on Capri, published 1884 in Naples, is so scarce and so informative that it deserves to be reprinted – this time, let us hope, with an index.

Norman Douglas wrote these words in 1952 in the Notes to his last work, *Footnote on Capri*. The book in question, John Clay MacKowen's *Capri*, came up in a chance discussion some sixty years later between the Centro Caprense Ignazio Cerio and Beaconsfield Publishers, and it was agreed that the book's evergreen and spirited insights would fully justify its republication for a modern readership. It was also agreed that its interest to the reader would be even greater if the story could be brought up to the modern era in the light of new archaeological findings, new historical studies and current research.

A number of specialists who know the island well came together to contribute additional material in their own fields of geology, palaeontology, archaeology, ancient and modern history, and social history, referring back wherever relevant to the original chapters, and their work constitutes the second part of the present book. Each of the new chapters has a full set of notes and there is a consolidated bibliography for further reference. There is also, as Norman Douglas wished, a comprehensive index.

MacKowen lived on Capri from 1877 to 1897. He was a medical doctor, a wealthy man in his own right, and a cultivated person with an ample overview of the literature and history of the island from classical times. He explored its archaeological and natural riches tirelessly, including many trips by boat to all its hidden coves and grottoes, and from this he elaborated evocative hypotheses regarding the island's geological and historical past. The style of his writing is fluent and clear and often quite poetic, and his work makes for fascinating reading – some of it seen now to be erroneous but much also that is just as true today, and all through the eyes of a knowledgeable and acute observer.

An unexpected bonus brought into view by the new material is a great deal of hitherto unknown information about MacKowen himself, and this proved to be worth telling for its own sake. He had interrupted his undergraduate studies at Dartmouth College on the outbreak of the American Civil War to enlist in the Confederate Army, rising to the rank of Lieutenant Colonel of cavalry, and was awarded two silver swords for gallantry. After a period in

Preface

San Francisco he qualified in medicine in Munich and practised in Rome for some years before settling in Capri. He was a contemporary on the island of Axel Munthe, with whom he shared a fiercely competitive interest in recovering artefacts from its abundant historical past. The two men detested each other, and on one occasion an argument about a newly unearthed statue let to a challenge to a duel, though it never took place as they were unable to agree on the choice of weapon.

He was a commanding and easily angered man who alienated the people of Capri and its sister community Anacapri alike. He tried for years to have a tunnel entrance to the Blue Grotto constructed down from land that he owned but was thwarted by furious public hostility, above all by the boatmen who earned their living ferrying the increasing numbers of tourists to the grotto by sea. He lived with a local woman and their daughter Giulia in the Casa Rossa, a former watchtower he had bought in the centre of Anacapri, filling it with fine examples of classical statuary, paintings, oriental furniture and antique arms, as well as a large collection of rare books and fine bindings that he, as an avid bibliophile, had collected during his lifetime.

The received legend about his death has always been that he left Capri finally at the end of 1897 to return to his native Louisiana, taking with him two large chests containing his precious collection of books. The story went that on the evening he disembarked in New Orleans he got into an argument with a freed slave about the Civil War, and that the man shot him dead. Further, that the books disappeared without trace that same night. This is often found in the available literature, but is also not true.

His return to Louisiana was in fact uneventful. In due course he donated his bibliographic treasures to a women's college that is now a constituent part of Tulane University, and here they are to be found in the safe keeping of the Rare Books Collection of the university's Howard-Tilton Library. He did nevertheless die a violent death – shot four years later by a State Senator over an unglamorous boundary dispute – and he now lies in the family grave in the Old Jackson Cemetery, Jackson, Louisiana.

This book, in both its parts, is a valuable contribution to our knowledge of Capri and also of one of its most remarkable personalities in the last years of the nineteenth century. Its publication could never have been possible without the felicitous intuition, enthusiastic research and scrupulously painstaking organisational support of John and Irmgard Churchill.

A.M.P.C.

Contents

Acknowledgments	iv
Preface	vi

John Clay MacKowen's *Capri*

1	Geological	1
2	Topography and Climate	10
3	History	14
4	Why Tiberius came and remained in Capri	24
5	History during the Middle Ages and Modern Times	41
6	Habits and Customs	75
7	Description	90

Capri – The Island Revisited

8	An Adventurous Life *Anna Maria Palombi Cataldi, Full Professor of English Literature, Department of Modern Philology, University of Naples, Federico II*	121
9	The Geology of Capri: a noble endeavour *Filippo Barattolo, Full Professor of Palaeontology, Department of Earth Science, University of Naples, Federico II*	151
10	It all began with Cave-dwellers: MacKowen and the ancient history of Capri *Eduardo Federico, Assistant Professor of Ancient Greek History, Department of History, University of Naples, Federico II*	161
11	John Clay MacKowen: an archaeologist in Capri *Rossella Zaccagnini, PhD, Archaeologist, Specialist in Ancient Topography*	168
12	From Capri to the Mainland: an island on the fringes of a capital *Anna Maria Palombi Cataldi*	179
13	Looking Beyond: MacKowen and the habits and customs of the island *Carmelina Fiorentino, Librarian, Biblioteca Caprense Ignazio Cerio, Capri*	187

Bibliography	200
Index	207

Chapter 1
Geological

The island of Capri is composed of limestone from the Tertiary period with a small deposit, here and there, of sandstone. The limestone strata dip from south to north at angles varying from 25° to 70°. From the Faraglioni to the Punta Ventrosa the dip varies from 25° to 35°, at the Green Grotto it is about 40°, at the Marmolara and under the Lighthouse it varies from 60° to 70°.

In Capri are a great many caves, and as these are not only interesting, on account of their beauty of colour and form, to the artist and the lover of Nature, but also to the geologist, the antiquarian and the historian, it is necessary, in order to explain many things in the history of Capri, to understand how these caves have been formed.

Great caves can only occur in a limestone formation, and they result from the chemical fact that the carbonates of lime and magnesia are soluble in water containing carbonic acid. This acid abounds in atmospheric air and is one of the products of the decomposition of animal and vegetable waters, so that rainwater which has percolated the soil has usually been enriched with it from both sources. With carbonic acid as the active agent and water as the carrier, we are able to account for the disappearance of strata however thick, and whether above or below ground. Above ground the result is a lowering of the general level, the deposition of a residual stratum of clay (a constituent, in a finely divided condition, of the valley limestones) and the formation of valleys, where special causes have favoured the disintegration of the stone. 'Hard' water flows away and a clay soil is left behind. Below ground, on the other hand, the result is a cave, if there be a fissure in the strata through which the acidified water may make its descent. In the course of time this fissure is worn larger, and the entering water dissolves and bears away with it, bit by bit, the stratum through which it passes, flowing out at some lower level with its burden of lime and magnesia, but leaving the clay behind to plague the cave visitor.

Earthquakes – the subsidence and upheaval of the island – have furnished the fissures in Capri, through which acidified rainwater has filtered and produced a very large number of caves. The action of seawater, through the beating of the waves, has come to the assistance of rainwater, and when acidified rainwater, coming from landwards, had made a hole in the face of the cliff which fronted the sea, and not too high above the sea-level, the beating of the waves enlarged this entrance so much that easy access was given to the cave, which had already been formed by centuries of work through the carbonic acid. If the seawater could reach the floor of the cave, the residual clay was washed out leaving a clean floor of limestone, or, if the sea were shallow at the mouth, this floor would be covered with pebbles and sand washed up from the bottom of the sea and dashed in by the waves when the sea was agitated. There are a few caves in Capri formed exclusively by the action of acidified rainwater, but the most of them are formed by the combined action of rain and seawater, though quite a number of small caves can be attributed to the boring action of the continual movement of the sea. Through the caves and holes formed by the action of the sea alone, or by the combined action of acidified and sea water, Nature has written the history of Capri's emergence from the sea, its subsidences and later upheavals.

A series of large caves, about seven hundred feet above the present water level, proves that when Capri emerged from the bottom of the sea, the island remained at that level for many thousands of years; these caves are the Cocuzza, the Grotto dell'Arco, the grottoes under the Castiglione and Tiberio, and one or two others under Monte Solaro, which last can only be seen partially as they have been almost destroyed by the undermining effect of the waves. After remaining a long time seven hundred feet below the present water-level, Capri emerged gradually to its present level, but this island, in common with the whole coast of the Bay of Naples, has continually risen and sunk.

Across the Bay, at Pozzuoli, is the temple of Jupiter Serapis, the columns of which have the lower twelve feet smooth, and then for nine feet above this they are perforated by boring shells; and remains of the shells (a species now living in the Mediterranean) were found in the holes. The columns, when submerged, were consequently buried in the mud of the bottom for twelve feet, and were then in water nine feet deep.

Geological

The pavement of the temple is now submerged, and five feet below it there is a second pavement, proving that the sinking had taken place before the temple was deserted by the Romans. The upper pavement is now a few feet under water, and the older pavement five feet below it was undoubtedly, at the time when it was built, so high above the water level that worshippers could pass over it, undisturbed by the beating of the highest waves. The lower pavement must have been at least ten or fifteen feet above the present water level, and the ground, on which was built this temple, stood about twenty feet higher out of the water than it does now.

In the Grotto dell' Arsenale, on the southern side of Capri, was dug up two or three years ago a beautiful pavement of richly coloured marbles, which formed the floor of two rooms built in this grotto. These richly decorated rooms were probably inhabited by some official of the Roman fleet, stationed at Capri during the time of Tiberius, for the name of the grotto most probably has come down to us from the old Romans, who used it as a storehouse or arsenal for naval supplies. But the island of Capri has sunk, like the temple of Serapis in Pozzuoli, some twenty feet below the ancient water level, and this grotto could neither be used today as an arsenal nor as a habitation, because the sea, during a scirocco or southerly wind, dashes into it, and has carried in a large mass of stones and sand, which covers the old pavement to the depth of four of five feet.

The remains of the ancient sewer of the old town of Capri at the Marina Grande, and the ruins of the ancient landing-place at the Tragara, all under water, seem to prove that Capri was higher out of the water, at the time when these ruins were built, than at present. At the Baths of Tiberius remains of an ancient villa can be seen, on a calm, sunny day, under the water at a distance of fifty feet or more from the shore. We know from Horace that the Romans were in the habit of building their palaces in the water, and it is possible that the parts of these ruins which are farthest from the shore were built originally in the sea, but one large room now in the water was originally built on dry land. The southern wall of this room stands on the edge of the water, while the eastern and western walls run out into the sea to join the northern wall, which stands in water ten feet deep. Through this northern wall runs a sewer made to carry off the waste water; this runs under the level of the old pavement, and could never have been built to allow the seawater to run into the room, as the level of the antique pavement is now above the sea-level, therefore it could have been used only as a sewer; but in order to prevent the waste water from returning into the palace through the rush of the waves, this pavement was doubtless built much higher above the water level than it is now.

Another proof that the part of the villa near the shore, but in the water now, was originally built on dry land is that in some places the foundations were laid on rocks which protrude two or three feet above the water level, and on breaking away the hard cement and masonry, which cover the surface of these rocks, it is found to be smooth and has the yellow colour of the pozzolana earth, which abounds in this vicinity. When the foundations of the villa were excavated, the pozzolana which covered these rocks was removed; the masons commenced building these foundations just as the Capri mason of today does. They first threw water on the surface of the rocks until it was completely wet, and then placed mortar, on which they commenced the walls. The water thrown on the rocks did not wash them clean, but there remained some of the pozzolana, which having attached itself to the surface by centuries of contact had become almost as hard as the rocks themselves and had discoloured their surface. This pozzolana can be found today under the masonry. If all these rocks, at the time when the foundations were built on them, had been near enough to the sea to have been exposed to the action of the waves, they would not only have been washed clean of the pozzolana, but would have been roughened and seamed, but on the contrary they are smooth and show no sign of having been exposed to the boring beats of the waves. As these rocks, which jut above the water level, are now from one to forty feet distant from the shore, it is a legitimate conclusion that in the times of Tiberius a part of the villa, which is now in the water, was on dry land, and that necessarily the island stood higher out of the water than it does today. In the semicircular room of these Baths exist two pavements, the one superposed on the other, showing, like in the temple of Serapis, that the island had

Geological

commenced to sink before this palace was abandoned, and therefore that the sinking was gradual, to such an extent that the palace was not completely destroyed.

A line of holes, running around the island, and varying from twelve feet at the Punta Carena to twenty-two feet at the Punta di Massullo above the present water line, proves that the island has been submerged, and that this line of holes was once the water level. The holes are undoubtedly due to the boring action of the waves, and as they do not extend far into the rock, it is a proof that the island remained only a few centuries at that level, and then commenced to emerge again. At the present water level there is a similar line of holes bored into the rock and running around the island, but as these holes appear to be shallower and smaller than those in the line above, they prove that the island has remained a less time at its present level than it did at the level of the upper line of holes. As there is little or no difference between the depth of these holes in the Blue Grotto (or in the other grottoes, where the face of the rock is protected against the disintegrating action of the elements) and of those outside, it is a proof that these holes are not of very ancient formation.

At the Baths of Tiberius the highest part of the southern wall of the room partly in the water stands about sixteen or seventeen feet above the present water level. The top of the western half of this wall is rounded off in such a manner as to show that it is due to the beating of the waves, while the eastern half, which is a little higher, is hollowed out at the level of the line of holes running around the island; the hollowing out is due to the action of the sea water when this wall was fifteen or sixteen feet lower in the water than it is now. We have here a proof that the water level has been sixteen feet higher at this point since the time when this palace was built, and this fact, coupled with the fact that there is a very small difference in the depth and size of the holes in grottoes and on the outside, proves that there has been a subsidence and emergence of the island since the times of Tiberius.

We have seen that the temple of Serapis at Pozzuoli has subsided about thirty-five feet since it was first built and has emerged again about fifteen or sixteen feet. The Baths of Tiberius are almost opposite the temple of Serapis and seem to have undergone exactly the same vicissitudes, viz. that they have sunken and have risen again about fifteen or sixteen feet. These facts make it very probable that when the island of Capri sunk, the whole coast of the Bay of Naples sunk also, but the eastern end of the island of Capri has emerged twenty-two feet, while the western end has emerged only twelve, showing a difference of ten feet. The mainland seems to have done the same, for on the coast of the Bay of Salerno, between the Punta di Campanella and the village of Positano, a similar line of holes exists, which runs progressively higher as it goes to the east.

It would be an interesting subject for a geologist to study the subsidence and emergence of the coast of Magna Grecia, as it is very probable that this form of the convulsions of Nature has had a great effect in destroying the climate and soil of what once contained the most delicious and refined cities of the world, and in turning the celebrated rose gardens of Paestum into malaria breeding wastes. It is sufficient for us to know that the eastern end of the island of Capri is still submerged about thirteen feet, and the end about twenty-three feet below the water level of the times of the Caesars. As an illustration of the manner in which land emerges from the sea, the following description by Professor Palmieri is given: 'Whilst I was studying several phenomena produced by the eruption of Vesuvius in 1861, a rock on the shore and completely out of the water was pointed out to me. On this rock, during the past summer, bathers were covered with water when sitting down. I suspected that this was one of those cases, so often cited by writers on Vesuvius, of the retiring of the waters of the Bay. I took a boat and was rowed along near the bank. Here the shore consists of vertical masses of lava, which flowed down in 1794. I saw on these vertical masses a line of algae and shell fish, about a metre and a half above the sea level. As these fish attach themselves to the rocks always under the sea level, and as this line was parallel with the water's surface, it seemed as though the sea had really sunken. But on rowing to the east and west of Torre del Greco I saw that this line of shell fish gradually descended until it reached the water's edge. From this fact I concluded that the ground, on which the town of Torre del Greco is built, had risen above

Geological

the old level, and this accounted for the retiring of the water of the Bay.' When this upheaval took place, nearly all the houses in Torre del Greco fell down, and as there was no sensible shock of earthquake, the people of the town could not understand how this destruction was caused, until Professor Palmieri explained it by the phenomenon of the earth's upheaval.

At the western part of the Grande Marina is the Cloaca of the ancient town of Capri, described by Strabo. This town was built up around the present church of San Costanzo. Wherever a peasant may dig in this neighbourhood, he finds walls of houses, broken bits of cooking and household utensils, and all the remains of a destroyed town. Many sewers have been found, and they all lead to this Cloaca. The present mouth of this old sewer is some thirty feet from the sea, and on the interlying shore, as well as in the water, are fragments of masonry which formerly served to continue it to the Bay. This Cloaca, which formerly must have dipped from south to north at an angle of from two to ten degrees, to carry off the sewerage of the town into the sea, now dips from north to south at an angle of about twenty-five degrees.

This reversal of the dip is due without doubt to an earthquake or some violent convulsion of Nature. As we regard the island from the Bay of Naples, it is evident that the part lying between Monte Solaro and Monte San Michele has, at some bygone period, dropped down, leaving the perpendicular cliffs of these two mountains standing like two walls. There appears to have been two sinkings, the first of which must have occurred between Monte Solaro and the Castiglione, either when the island was still under the sea or shortly after it emerged above the water level, because the Grotto dell'Arco has been washed out by the action of the waves since the first sinking. Though this subsidence, on the south side of the island between the Castiglione and Monte Solaro, occurred ages ago there are signs that the subsidence on the north side, between San Michele and Monte Solaro, has taken place in comparatively recent times, that is, since the building of the Cloaca of the ancient town of Capri. There is a shelf at the foot of Solaro, which has broken, jagged points of rock which stand up like minarets; these minarets are of such a slender make that, had they been long in their present position, they would have inevitably toppled over, and they look as though they had been formed by breaking off from the rock immediately around them when it subsided, and not as though they had been thrown into their present position from above.

Back of Lady Grantley's house is a large bowl-formed depression, caused undoubtedly by a sinking of the ridge on which the carriage road runs, which connects Capri with Anacapri, while the earth to the south of this depression remained at its old level. On account of the reversal of the dip of the Cloaca on the north side of the island, and this bowl-formed depression on the south side, it seems certain that the north side, between Mounts San Michele and Solaro, has dropped down since the building of the Cloaca. To what depth it subsided, it is impossible to say exactly, but a rough calculation may be made from these two factors, viz. the angle of twenty-five degrees of the reversed dip and the distance of the Cloaca from the top of the ridge; this distance is about 750 metres. From these we deduce that the ridge was formerly three hundred metres above the sea level, and as it is now only 150 metres, the ridge must have sunken at least about 150 metres at the second sinking.

Generally speaking, all over the island on top of the limestone is a deposit of volcanic cinders, over this is a deposit of pozzolana, also of volcanic origin, and over this a deposit of humus.

On the south of the road leading from Capri to Anacapri, and immediately under the Castiglione, is an old Greek cemetery. The bodies were buried at a depth of eight or ten feet below the surface. Under these graves the owner of the ground has excavated some twenty or thirty feet to procure pozzolana and cinders, which are valuable for building purposes. At the distance of twenty-five feet below the surface, among the cinders, were found the trunks, branches and roots of bushes, which were carbonized; these bushes had all the appearance of having been alive at the time when the cinders were thrown on them, as the trunks were in a vertical position, the roots perforated the earth under the trunks, and the branches were spread out as usual in growing bushes. It is probable that these cinders arrived on the island so hot that they reduced to coal not only the trunks and branches but also the roots. The mass of cinders was not of sufficient depth to exclude the damp and prevent the percolation of water, which would naturally have caused the wood to decay; therefore it may be presumed that the carbonization was due to the effect of heat brought by the cinders. It may be questioned whether cinders carried through the air from Vesuvius, or from the now extinct volcano of Epomeo on the island of Ischia, could arrive in Capri so hot as to produce such a carbonization; it is more probable that these hot cinders came from the immense crater which is now the Bay of Naples. The old Greeks called the present bay 'The Crater', as though there might have been a tradition among them that it was the mouth of an extinct volcano.

Chapter 2
Topography and Climate

Capri has the shape of an old cavalier's boot, and Nature in a lavish mood has given it even a spur. It is distant from Naples about seventeen miles, from Cape Misenum and Ischia about fourteen, from Sorrento about seven, and from the Punta di Campanella about three. Its greatest length is about three miles and a half, its greatest breadth about one and a half, and its circumference is about nine. It is forty and one half degrees north of the equator, and nine seconds west of the Royal Observatory of Naples.

Jean Paul thought that the profile of Capri resembled a sphinx, and Gregorovius compared it to 'an ancient Sarcophagus whose sides were adorned with snaky-haired Furies; above lies Tiberius'. The island, from the Bay, is not unlike the head and neck of a huge crocodile; Anacapri forms the head and Capri the neck. The climate is mild in winter, and cool in summer. The presence of the sea tempers the atmosphere to such an extent that on the north side, at the Grande Marina, the orange and lemon trees remain uncovered during the whole of the winter. But in the town of Capri, which is only a few hundred feet above the water, such trees are provided with coverings, even though on the southern slope, as hoar frost is not uncommon every winter, and ice is formed in the houses sometimes, when the winters are very severe. The prevailing winds during the months of November, December and January are southerly and are warm and moist; during the latter part of January, in February and March the north wind, which is dry and cool, is the prevailing one. During the summer months the northwest wind, which is cool and refreshing, prevails. The west wind, which may blow at any season of the year, produces the greatest storms and the highest waves. The rainfall is very little, and cisterns are built in every available place to catch the rainwater. Occasionally it has been found necessary to bring water for drinking purposes from the mainland, and two or three years ago the Italian government was obliged to send steamers regularly from Naples to Capri to furnish the islanders with water for domestic purposes.

Topography and Climate

This dearth of water comes from the fact that the hills of the island are so low that they do not stop the rain clouds which pass over Capri, and pressing against the sides of Vesuvius, Somma and Sant'Angelo, their contents fall on the cities and towns which line the coast of the Bay. This want of rain has a good climatic effect, because the rainy season in Capri is much dryer than in any other resort of Southern Italy. The declivity of the streets and the hard limestone rock, which does not absorb the wet, like tufa, cause the rain to run off quickly, and in the course of an hour after a rain the streets are completely dry. Sloppy, muddy, or damp walks do not exist in Capri. The rainy season commences usually in the second week of September with a copious downpour of several days, accompanied by thunder and lightning. These last two clear the atmosphere of electricity, and then come the bright, pleasant days of autumn with its wine and oil-making, its quail shooting and the variegated colours of vines and trees. November, December and the first half of January are the rainy months, during which the air is moist and warm. The latter part of January, February and March are cold, with occasional rains, but in April the island puts on its spring dress. The dry and warm season commences with May, and lasts through June, July and August; very little rain falls during this time, and sometimes three months pass without a single raindrop. This is the most delightful season of the year in Capri; the Maestrale or northwest wind commences about ten in the morning and blows strongly until about five in the afternoon, so that the coolest part of the day is from midday until about three. For boating and bathing, the weather and the water furnish facilities and temptations which are excelled nowhere.

The indigenous flora is very rich, comprising more than eight hundred varieties; of these, the most common are the myrtle, the laurel, and oak, though the latter is fast disappearing on account of the scarcity of firewood.

During the whole year the air of Capri is remarkably pure and bracing. It is like being aboard a large ship, which never rocks nor plunges, and which affords beautiful, pleasant walks over vine, orange, fig and lemon-clad terraces; these mingle their odours with the sea breeze and furnish pretty contrasts of colour with the ever-changing blues of the sea in the background. The bright skies, the soft air and the beautiful, diaphanous sea make Capri a favourite resort for wearied men of letters, for students, artists, lovers of the beautiful in nature and for travellers seeking relief from museums, churches and picture-galleries. As a station for invalids, Capri is especially adapted to those who suffer from chest diseases, or nervousness. To those who suffer from insomnia it has afforded great relief, as there is something very calming and soporific in its air and quiet life. But, aside from its claims to the notice of the suffering, there is a charm in the beauty and quiet to be found here, close to the gay restlessness of Naples, and in the track of vessels which sail to all parts of the world, which have induced, for more than a century, many persons of cultivation and refinement to make their homes here. A journey to the centres of western or eastern civilization, which are all easily accessible from Capri, can be undertaken at any time, when the Lotos-eating influence of the island is disturbed by a wish to see the eager life of busy crowds in Europe, or the rich costumes and picturesque bazaars of the Orient. Such a journey only makes the traveller return to the island, to find a greater joy in the quiet content which comes over him the moment he puts foot on the shores of this magic land. The traditional Englishman, who came here to pass three days and has remained forty years, is pointed out to the visitor with pride by those, who, like him, have caught the Capri fever and have made their homes in this midway station between the busy eagerness of the West in its devotion to the worship of Almighty Money, and the lazy fanaticism of the East, to escape the wearying restlessness of our nineteenth century life:

> In the afternoon they came unto a land
> In which it seemed always afternoon,
> There is a sweet music here that softer falls
> Than petals from blown roses on the grass,
> Or night-dews on still waters between walls
> Of shadowy granite, in a gleaming pass;
> Music that gentlier on the spirit lies,
> Than tir'd eyelids upon tir'd eyes;
> Music that brings sweet sleep down from the blissful skies.

Topography and Climate

Here are cool mosses deep, And thro' the moss the ivies creep.
With half shut eyes ever to seem
Falling asleep in a half dream!
To dream and dream, like yonder amber light,
Which will not leave the myrrh-bush on the height;
To hear each other's whisper'd speech;
Eating the Lotos day by day,
To watch the crisping ripples on the beach,
And tender curving lines of creamy spray;
To hear the dewy echoes calling
From cave to cave, thro' the thick-twin'd vine,
Only to hear and see the far-off sparkling brine
Only to hear were sweet, stretched out beneath the pine.

Chapter 3

History

Capri, or Crapi as it is called in the Neapolitan dialect, was called by the Greeks Kapreas, Kaprie, Kapriae, Kapria, Kaprea, and lastly Kapraia. As the Greeks were here many years before Rome was founded, and as Greek was the language of the island when Augustus first brought it to public notice, we must naturally look to the Greek for the derivation of the name. The Greek word 'capros', meaning wild boar, suggests that the name was given by the Greeks, either because these animals were found here by them, or because they imagined that the shape of the island resembled, at the time when they settled in it, that of a wild boar. Strabo used this name in his *Geography*, which was written before the time of Augustus, and the Romans took the name from the Greeks, calling the island Capreae. The Romans used the plural number, as though they wished to show that there were two or more islands. There are some writers who derive the name from the Latin 'capra', a goat, or 'caprea', a wild goat, but this derivation is ridiculous. There are others, who go farther back than the Greeks, and seek to derive the name from the Phenician or Hebrew word 'capraim', which they interpret as two towns, founding this derivation on the fact that Strabo in his fifth book says, 'Anciently Capri had two towns but afterwards only one'. From the fact that the island is divided into two sections, Capri and Anacapri, and as all philologists are agreed that the prefix Ana (meaning upper) of Ana-Capri (meaning Upper-Capri) is Greek, it is certain that the word Anacapri has come down to us from the Greeks. This fact excludes not only the derivation of the name from the Latin Capra or Caprea, as it is very improbable that a Greek adverb would be joined to a Latin proper name after the island had come into the possession of the Romans, but would make it improbable, though not impossible, that a Greek word should have been prefixed to a Phenician. When we remember that all the cities and islands of the Bay were Greek at the time of Strabo, and had Greek names, why should Capri form an exception to this rule when, from the rugged formation ot the island, and the prolific growth of oaks, which are indigenous here, Nature seems to have especially fitted it as a home for the wild boar, from the number of caves and abundance of acorns, which furnished food and shelter to these animals?

The first probable mention of Capri is by Homer in the Odyssey. On leaving the island of Circe (most probably Ischia) and on his way to Sicily, Ulysses passed the island of the Sirens. It is generally supposed that Capri was the island alluded to under this name, as it was the first shore which would be passed by Ulysses on his way to Scylla and Charybdis. Pope's translation of the passage is as follows:

> Next where the Sirens dwell, you plough the seas.
> Their song is death, and makes destruction please.
> Unblest the man whom music wins to stay
> Nigh the curst shore and listen to the lay.
> No more that wretch shall view the joys of life,
> His blooming offspring or his beauteous wife!
> In verdant meads they sport; and wide around
> Lie human bones, that whiten all the ground;
> The ground polluted floats with human gore,
> And human carnage taints the dreadful shore.
> Fly swift the dangerous coast; let every ear
> Be stopped against the song! 'tis death to hear!

Those who make Capri the scene of the Sirens' songs consider the 'human bones that whiten all the ground' to have been the white limestone rocks strewn along the shore of the Piccola Marina, in sight of which Ulysses must have sailed as he passed to the south of Capri on his voyage; and as a proof of this the Piccola Marina retains today the name of La Sirena. Any historical fact deduced from the poems of Homer would be necessarily very uncertain, but this is given for what it may be worth. It is certain that Capri had its cave dwellers and its age of stone, as is proved by the interesting collection of arrowheads, knives and other utensils of stone excavated by and still in the possession of Doctor Cerio. These various instruments were made from a variety of stone not found on the island, and at the time when they were made, these cave dwellers either were sufficiently acquainted with navigation to allow them to communicate with the mainland, or Capri was at that time still joined to the mainland. Other excavations in the Grotto dell'Arco, undertaken by Doctor Cerio, brought to light several specimens of pottery, some of which bore the peculiar ornaments so common among the Phenicians. It is very probable that the Phenicians took the place of the cave dwellers, and these in turn gave way to the Greeks. Livy says the Teleboi were the ancient Greek settlers of Capri, and Strabo describes the Teleboi as coming from Acarnania.

On the northwest side of the town of Capri, and serving today as the foundations of the housewalls, is an old Cyclopean wall, which crops out above ground here and there; it is built in the same manner as the Acropolis at Cuma, and it is probable that the Cumans built this, and may have used it as a prison to which prisoners of war or criminals were sent. Traces of this wall have been found in all the space which extends from the hill of San Michele to that of the Castiglione.

The first historical mention of Capri is an account of the visit made to it by the Emperor Augustus, and of the lucky omen which greeted his landing. Towards the end of his reign, when sick in body and wearied of the cares of state, he visited the island. Charmed with the manners of the joyous Greek inhabitants, the healthy air, the wild, picturesque scenery, and the quiet, he proposed to the Neapolitans to give them the island of Ischia, which was his personal property, in exchange for the island of Capri. But Suetonius relates more graphically in his gossipy manner the doings of Augustus: 'In the island of Capri some decayed branches of an old ilex, which hung drooping to the ground, recovered themselves upon his arrival; at which he was so delighted that he made an exchange with the Republic of Naples of the island of Ischia for that of Capri.' Augustus was suffering from the disease to which he finally succumbed, notwithstanding which, he went round the coast of Campania and the adjacent islands, and spent four days in that of Capri, where he gave himself up entirely to repose and relaxation. Happening to sail by the bay of Puteoli, the passengers and mariners aboard a ship of Alexandria, just then arrived, clad all in white, with chaplets upon their heads and offering incense, loaded him with praises and joyful acclamations, crying out: 'By you we live, by you we sail securely, by you we enjoy our liberty and our fortunes.'

At which being greatly pleased, he distributed to each of those who attended him, forty gold pieces, requiring from them an assurance on oath not to employ the sum given them in any other way than the purchase of

Alexandrian merchandise. During several days after, he distributed Togae and Pallia, among other gifts, on condition that the Romans should use the Greek, and the Greeks the Roman dress and language. He likewise constantly attended to see the boys perform their exercises (called Ephebian) according to an ancient custom still continued in Capri. He gave them likewise an entertainment in his presence, and not only permitted but required from them the utmost freedom in jesting, and scrambling for fruit, victuals and other things, which he threw among them. In a word, he indulged himself in all the ways of amusement he could contrive. He called an island near Capri, Apragopolis, 'the city of the Do-littles' from the indolent life which several of his party led there. A favourite of his, one Masgabas, he used to call Ktistes, 'Founder', as if he had been the planter of the island. Observing from his room a great company of people with torches, assembled at the tomb of this Masgabas, who died the year before, he uttered very distinctly this verse which he made extempore: 'Blazing with lights I see the Founder's tomb.'

Then turning to Thrasyllus, a companion of Tiberius, who reclined on the other side of the table, he asked him, who knew nothing about matter, what poet he thought was the author of that verse; and on his hesitating to reply he added another: 'Honoured with torches Masgabas you see', and put the same question to him concerning that likewise. The latter replying that, whoever might be the author they were excellent verses, he set up a great laugh and fell into an extraordinary vein of jesting upon it. Speaking of Augustus' taste in his palaces: 'Those of his own, which were far from being spacious, he adorned, not so much with statues and pictures, as with walks and groves and things which were curious either for their antiquity or rarity; such as, at Capri, the huge limbs ot sea-monsters and wild beasts, which some affect to call the bones of giants and also the arms of ancient heroes.'

This picture of the man who, as Tacitus pithily says, 'had quietly strangled eloquence as well as everything else which marks a free state' is charmingly drawn by Suetonius. This old man, whose successes military, naval and political had broken the power and cowed the hate of his enemies, whose shrewd policy had taught the turbulent Romans that quiet and security in their pleasures and in their pursuit of wealth were better things than liberty, the master mind which controlled the Augustan age with its literature and luxury, and founded fast that empire which to this day has never been equalled, was, after all, human, and in his old age could escape from the flattery and homage of kings, and the cynical pleasures of Rome to delight in the romps of boys, their rough ways and impertinent jokes; and among the rocks of Capri jest with his companions, and pay a tribute of affection and respect to the memory of a faithful friend. In Rome we think of Augustus as the founder of an empire and the destroyer of Rome's liberties, with feelings of admiration at his wonderful knowledge of the human heart, and with feelings of anger and pity for the sublime selfishness, which urged him on to use this knowledge so ruthlessly to destroy an enemy or win a friend as policy dictated. But in Capri Augustus is the amiable, indulgent, kind old man, and we think only pleasantly of him as he yielded to the bright influences of the charms of nature in this 'gem of the sea', and became a Lotos eater for a few days.

To the people of Capri the acquisition of the island by Augustus must have been a great benefit, for it seems that the Republic of Naples did not transfer the old inhabitants to Ischia after Augustus had made the exchange, because Suetonius speaks of the Ephebian exercises, which were kept up according to an old custom among the Capriotes. Workmen were needed to build palaces and lay out gardens and walks, and when Augustus held court here, large sums of money were spent by him and his courtiers. It was no longer necessary for the islanders to trust alone to the sea for a precarious and dangerous livelihood as sailors or fishermen.

The island, called Apragopolis by Augustus, was most probably the present Monacone, and on it still exists an ancient tomb, which may have been that of Masgabas. The palace from which the Emperor saw the gathering around the tomb must have been in the vicinity of the Punta di Tragara.

In the 27th year of the Christian era Tiberius chose Capri as a permanent place of residence (he was then sixty-seven years old), and remained on the island about ten years. During this time he left it only twice, and for a few weeks only. During his second absence, while waiting at Misenum for the sea and wind to go down so as to enable him to return to Capri, he died.

History

Tacitus describes his arrival as follows: 'Tiberius, having dedicated temples in Campania, ordered that no one should be allowed to disturb his quiet, and placed sentinels to prevent access to him. He disliked the mainland and the colonies so much that he shut himself up in the island of Capri, which is distant three miles from the Cape of Sorrento. Capri pleased him because it stood alone and had no ports, small ships could land only with difficulty, nor could any vessel approach without being signalled. In winter, sheltered by the mountains against the cold winds, the air is mild, and in summer the west winds keep it cool. The view over the water and along the coast, at that time not deformed by the eruption of Vesuvius, is most beautiful. It is said that Capri was settled by the Teleboi. Tiberius occupied his time in building twelve country palaces, in giving his attention to the affairs of state, and in plunging into the greatest excesses of ease and lust.'

Suetonius dwells more at length on the personal habits, tastes and fancies of Tiberius. He says, 'After the loss of his two sons, of whom Germanicus died in Syria, and Drusus at Rome, he withdrew into Campania. After he had gone the round of Campania and dedicated the capitol at Capua, and a temple to Augustus at Nola, which he made the pretext of his journey, he retired to Capri; being greatly delighted with the island, because it was accessible only by a narrow beach, being on all sides surrounded with rugged cliffs of a stupendous height, and by a deep sea. But immediately the people of Rome being extremely clamorous for his return, he crossed over again to the continent, and gave all people free access to him; so much the more, because at his departure from the city, he had caused it to be proclaimed that no one should address him, and had declined admitting any persons to his presence on his journey. Returning to the island, he so far abandoned all care of the government that he never filled up the decuriae of the knights, never changed any military tribunes, or prefects, or governors of provinces, and kept Spain and Syria for several years without any consular lieutenants. He likewise suffered Armenia to be seized by the Parthians, Moesia by the Dacians and Sarmatians, and Gaul to be ravaged by the Germans, to the great disgrace and no less danger of the Empire. But, having now the advantage of privacy and being remote from the observation of the people of Rome, he abandoned himself to all the vicious propensities which he had long, but imperfectly, concealed and of which I shall here give a particular account from the beginning.

While a young soldier in camp, he was so remarkable for his excessive inclination to wine that for Tiberius they called him Biberius, for Claudius, Caldius and for Nero, Mero. After he succeeded to the Empire, and was invested with the office of reforming the morality of the people, he spent a whole night and two days together in feasting and drinking with Pomponius Flaccus and Lucinus Piso; to one of whom he immediately gave the province of Syria, and to the other the prefecture of the city; declaring them in letters patent to be 'very pleasant companions and friends fit for all occasions'. He likewise instituted a new office to administer to his voluptuousness, to which he appointed Titus Caesonius Priscus, a Roman knight.'

Suetonius gives a detailed account of the refinements used by Tiberius in his voluptuous pleasures while on the island, and dwells on the particulars with so much gusto that we are compelled to think that good, old, gossipy Suetonius was as corrupted in his morals as the rest of his countrymen at that epoch, who delighted in such details and smacked their lips over them. 'A few days after his arrival at Capri, a fisherman coming up to him unexpectedly, when he was desirous of privacy, and presenting him with a large mullet, he ordered the man's face to be scrubbed with the fish, being terrified at the thought of his having been able to creep upon him from the back of the island, over such rugged and steep rocks. The man, while undergoing the punishment, expressed his joy that he had not likewise offered him a large crab, which he had also taken, he ordered his face to be farther lacerated with its claws.'

When Tiberius retired to Capri, he left Sejanus in Rome as his vice-regent. Sejanus, aspiring to the imperial power, induced Livia, the daughter-in-law of Tiberius, to poison her husband Drusus, the son of Tiberius by his first wife. Sejanus then demanded Livia in marriage. Tiberius refused the demand, which so enraged Sejanus that he formed a conspiracy to dethrone him. But the Emperor having all the threads of Sejanus' conspiracy in his hands wrote to the Senate demanding his execution, which immediately ensued. 'Exasperated by the information

History

which he received respecting the death of his son Drusus, he carried his cruelty still farther. He imagined that Drusus had died of a disease occasioned by his intemperance; but finding that he had been poisoned by the contrivance of his wife, Livia, and Sejanus, he spared no one from torture and death. He was so entirely occupied with the examination of this affair for whole days together, that, upon being informed that the person in whose house he had lodged at Rhodes, and whom he had by a friendly letter invited to Rome, was arrived, he ordered him immediately to be put to the torture as a party concerned in the enquiry. Upon finding out his mistake he commanded him to be put to death, that he might not publish the injury done him. The place of execution is still shown at Capri, where he ordered those who were condemned to die, after long and exquisite tortures, to be thrown before his eyes from a precipice into the sea. There a party of soldiers belonging to the fleet waited for them, and broke their bones with poles and oars, lest they should have any life left in them.'

Distrustful and apprehensive of an insurrection at the execution of Sejanus, and at the same time fearing that the Senate might not carry out his orders for the execution, he had ships in readiness to transport him to any of the regions to which he might consider it expedient to make his escape. Meanwhile he was upon the watch, from the summit of a lofty cliff, for the signals which he had ordered to be made if anything occurred, lest the messengers should be tardy. Even when he had quite foiled the conspiracy of Sejanus he was still haunted as much as ever with fears and apprehensions, insomuch that be never once stirred out of the villa Jove for nine months after.

During the whole of his seclusion at Capri, twice only he made an effort to visit Rome. Once he came in a galley as far as the gardens near the Naumachia, but placed guards along the banks of the Tiber to keep off all who should offer to come to meet him. The second time he travelled on the Appian way as far as the seventh milestone from the city, but he immediately returned, without entering it, having only taken a view of the walls at a distance. For what reason he did not disembark in his first excursion is not certain; but in the last he was deterred from entering the city by a prodigy. He was in the habit of diverting himself with a snake, and upon going to feed it with his own hand, according to custom, found it devoured by ants, from which he was advised to beware of the fury of the mob. On this account returning in all haste to Campania, he fell ill at Astura, but recovering a little went on to Circeii. And to obviate any suspicion of his being in a bad state of health, he was not only present at the sports in the camp, but encountered, with javelins, a wild boar, which was let loose in the arena. Being immediately seized with a pain in the side, and catching cold upon his over-heating himself in the exercise, he relapsed into a worse condition than he was before. He held out, however, for some time; and sailing as far as Misenum, omitted nothing in his usual mode of life, not even in his entertainments and other gratifications, partly from an ungovernable appetite and partly to conceal his condition. Meanwhile finding, upon looking over the acts of the Senate, 'that some persons under prosecution had been discharged, without being brought to a hearing', for he had only written cursorily that they had been denounced by an informer, he complained in a great rage that he was treated with contempt and resolved at all hazards to return to Capri, not daring to attempt anything until he found himself in a place of security. But being detained by storms and the increasing violence of his disorder, he died shortly afterwards at a villa formerly belonging to Lucullus in the seventy-eighth year of his age, and the twenty-third of his reign, upon the seventeenth of the calends of April (March sixteenth, 37 A.D.).

Tacitus in his concise manner resumes the life of Tiberius in these words: 'Thus died in his seventy-eighth year Tiberius, the son of Nero, also of the Claudian family by his mother, who was afterwards adopted into the family Livia, and then into the Julian. From his first years his fortune was doubtful, because he accompanied his father into exile. Having entered the family of Augustus as his step-son, so long as Marcellus, Agrippa, Caius and Lucius Caesar lived, he was in continual conflict with them as rivals. His brother Drusus was more in favour with the citizens of Rome. He was at enmity with his wife Julia, because he could neither tolerate her libidinous propensities nor did he dare to put her away. Having returned from Rhodes, he occupied the post of heir-apparent for twelve years, and then that of Emperor for twenty-three. He changed his manners according to the times. During the life of Augustus, when in command of the army or in private life, his reputation was of the best; whilst Germanicus and Drusus lived, he feigned to be virtuous; the good and bad of his character were equally mixed until the death of his mother; as long as Sejanus lived to be loved or feared, he stained his character with execrable cruelty and hidden lust, but when all restraint was removed, he abandoned himself to every wickedness and crime, and to the most shameless lust as was his nature.'

To this masterly summing up of the character of Tiberius by Tacitus, may be placed in contrast the homely gossip of Suetonius, who contents himself with giving us the omens which preceded and presaged the death of the Emperor, among which was: 'a few days before he died, the Lighthouse of Capri was thrown down by an earthquake'. As a sign of the times and as a trait of the manners during the stay of Tiberius at Capri, Tacitus relates: Cocceius Nerva, who remained always near Tiberius, learned in all divine and human knowledge, healthy in mind and body, determined to die. Tiberius remained near him, implored and demanded: 'How is this? What remorse, and what a reputation do you cause me, if you, my dearest friend, without any reason whatever, put an end to your life!' Nerva turned his back on him, and starved himself to death. Those who were well acquainted with him said that seeing the State sunk so low, with mingled feelings of anger and fear he wished to die pure and unstained.

Chapter 4
Why Tiberius Came and Remained in Capri

The relationship which existed between the various members of the Imperial family was so intricate that it may not be considered out of place to recall it to the memory of the reader. Augustus had an only child, Julia, by his wife Scribonia, whom he put away and then married Livia. By Livia he had no children, though at the time when he took Livia away from her husband, Tiberius Nero, she was with child and had already brought into the world a son, Tiberius, who became Emperor; the other son of Livia and Tiberius Nero was named Drusus Nero. Marcellus, the son of Octavia, and therefore nephew of Augustus, was the first husband of Julia, but no children were born from this union, and Julia was married a second time to Marcus Agrippa, by whom she had three sons, Caius, Lucius, and Posthumous Agrippa. After the death of Marcus Agrippa, Julia married Tiberius and one child was born to them, but died shortly after its birth. Tiberius married for his first wife Agrippina, the daughter of Marcus Agrippa and step-daughter of Julia. By Agrippina he had a son, Drusus, and Agrippina was pregnant a second time when he was obliged to put her away and marry Julia, who was his mother-in-law by marriage.

Capri and Tiberius are two names so intimately connected, and his stay in Capri has interested students of character, of psychology and of history so much, that a digression on the subject of his stay here may not be considered out of place. Suetonius says, 'His infancy and childhood were spent in the midst of danger and trouble; for he accompanied his parents everywhere in their flight, and twice at Naples nearly betrayed them by his crying, when they were privately hastening to a ship as the enemy rushed into the town; once, when he was snatched from his nurse's breast and again from his mother's bosom by some of the company, who on the sudden emergency wished to relieve the women of their burden. Being carried through Sicily and Achaia, and entrusted for some time to the care of the Lacedaemonians, who were under the protection of the Claudian family, upon his departure thence, when travelling by night, he ran the hazard of his life by a fire, which suddenly bursting out of a wood on all sides surrounded the whole party so closely that part of Livia's dress and hair was burnt.

Tacitus, describing his life among his adopted relations, says, 'Having entered the family of Augustus as stepson, as long as Marcellus, Agrippa, Caius and Lucius Caesar lived, he was in continual conflict with them as rivals.' From these glimpses into his early life, the period which was 'father of the man', we see that, as an infant, he was exposed to many dangers from which he was extricated by the courage and devotion of his mother. When he became a member of the Imperial family, he was continually insulted and maltreated by his adopted cousin Marcellus, the nephew, and by his stepsons Caius, Lucius and Agrippa, the grandsons of Augustus. They looked on Tiberius as an interloper and made a common war against him. But Tiberius had a protectress in his mother Livia, who always lent a willing ear to his boyish complaints against the rudeness of Marcellus, and took his part bravely against the whole Imperial family, yet with a woman's fine tact, so as not to offend the susceptibilities of Augustus. There grew up between Livia and Tiberius a relation so strong that the protectress was a rival in power to the mother. From his earliest youth he looked up to her as something more than a mother, as one who, with her position, shrewdness, tact and courage, was a power in the Roman state, which could make and unmake princes and kings at her will. At the triumph of Augustus for the victory of Actium, which made him virtually master of the world, Livia took good care to place Tiberius on the left-hand horse of the victor's chariot, and to obtain for her son the highest place of honour in the games celebrated. Through her ambitious tact Tiberius was kept constantly before the eyes of the Romans in a conspicuous position. He was a boy of talent and courage, for, 'when he was only nine years of age, he pronounced a funeral oration in praise of his father upon the rostra', and he fulfilled the duties of his high position in a worthy and honourable manner.

Livia was a mistress in statecraft, and among the celebrated women who are renowned in history as rulers, her name, if not the first, stands among the first. But when women sacrifice everything to ambition, and unsex themselves so far as to lay aside the gentle qualities, which cause even the most cynical men to look back on their mothers as examples of the purity, self-sacrifice and untiring devotion, which they deny to the rest of the human race, such women are never happy in their domestic life. Among the many new vices and crimes introduced among the Romans by their conquest of the East, and intimacy with its luxury, was domestic murder, and Livia has the infamous distinction of having first committed this crime, and of accustoming the Romans to this manner of removing obstacles. She was the evil genius of Tiberius, of the Caesar family, and of the Roman people. This Imperial Becky Sharp, who was vile enough to pander to the most brutal tastes of Augustus in order that she might retain her hold and control his mind, would not shrink from any act which she thought might increase her power in the state.

In the Museum at Naples there are five busts or statues of Tiberius in the hall of the Caesars. Four of them stand on one long pedestal to the right on entering, and the other stands opposite, placed side by side with a bust of Marcellus. The contrast between the thoughtful, studious, intelligent and unhappy expression of face of Tiberius, and the arrogant, pleasure-loving and pampered look on the face of Marcellus is striking. On the large pedestal is a statue of Tiberius wearing the chlamys and bearing a cornucopia in his left hand. There is a look of budding, manly dignity in the face, but there is something about the forehead and eyebrows, which shows that he has not yet escaped from the bickerings and rivalry of an unhappy household. There are determination and force of character about the mouth and chin, and his full lips show that he is a youth of strong affections without sensuality or brutality. The body and limbs are well-formed and graceful, and the whole statue gives an impression of so much character and intelligence, that among an assemblage of youths of his own age, we feel sure that he would soon assert himself and become a leader.

Another statue of him represents a young soldier with the determined and self-reliant look which presages the successful general. He has commenced his career among genial comrades, and in the active life of the camp has left behind him the little jealousies and bickerings of his domestic life. He has in his face none of the mildness or duplicity which begets the politician, but the manly frankness and vigorous expression of the soldier.

A small bust shows us the happy, married man, and the successful general who has won the respect of Augustus and of the Romans.

Why Tiberius Came and Remained in Capri

Suetonius says, 'He married Agrippina, the daughter of Marcus Agrippa and granddaughter of Caecilius Atticus, a Roman knight, the same person to whom Cicero has addressed so many epistles. After having by her his son Drusus, he was obliged to part with her, though she retained his affection and was again pregnant, to make way for marrying Augustus' daughter Julia. But this he did with extreme reluctance; for, besides having the warmest attachment to Agrippina, he was disgusted with the conduct of Julia, who had made indecent advances to him during the lifetime of her former husband; and that she was a woman of loose character was the general opinion. At divorcing Agrippina he felt the deepest regret; and upon meeting her afterwards he looked at her with eyes so passionately expressive of affection that care was taken she should never again come in his sight. At first, however, he lived quietly and happily with Julia; but a rupture soon ensued, which became so violent that after the loss of their son, the pledge of their union, who was born at Aquileia and died in infancy, he never would sleep with her more. He lost his brother Drusus in Germany and brought his body to Rome, travelling all the way on foot before it.'

In these words Suetonius tells the ruin of the inner life of Tiberius. Livia had waited many years, hoping always for children by Augustus, but when she knew that this was an impossible hope, her scheming mind formed a plan only possible to be carried out by an intellect so clear and a character so unprincipled as her own. The first act was to force Tiberius to divorce Agrippina, with whom he was very happy, and marry Julia. Suetonius uses the words 'Tiberius was obliged to part with Agrippina'. What means Livia used to induce her son (who loved her not only as his mother, who had risked her life several times to save him, but looked up to her as his best guide and friend) to put away a woman whom he dearly loved and respected, to marry a prostitute whom he despised and disliked, may be easily imagined. From his earliest years, on account of the wandering life and the absence of his father, she had been everything to him, and when she used all her influence to cause him by one act to destroy his self-respect, to mutilate his affections and sacrifice his manhood, the struggle must have been long and severe; but the victim could not see the depth of the pit prepared for him, and he allowed his affection and respect for his mother to triumph over his love for Agrippina and his own better judgment. Unfortunately for Tiberius he was a man of strong feeling, and his love for his mother and brother amounted to fanaticism, as witness his following his brother's dead body on foot from Germany to Rome. It is easy to understand, from their peculiar domestic relations, why these three should have been bound more closely together than mother and sons usually are, but though Livia, thanks to this fanatical affection, gained her point and brought about the desired marriage, yet she strained her hold on the respect and affection of Tiberius to such an extent that, when he found out what misery his second marriage caused him, his fanatical love was turned into a fanatical hate of his mother.

In those days men and women loved and hated with a strength and expressed their thoughts with a force unknown to our modern civilization. Though Augustus had usurped all the powers of the Republic, and had a Roman Senate ready to obey any wish of his, yet to the populace were allowed many liberties of speech in the theatres and at the games, which he never dared to take away. It is easy to imagine the number and quality of satirical bon-mots not only recited in public places and in a gross form, but circulated in a quiet manner and in elegant dress among the courtiers of Augustus – all at the expense of the Imperial cuckold Tiberius, who had been too successful in his military and civil life, and whose strong character would not allow him to curry favour with the mob, or flatter the poets and wits who made public opinion at court. His enemies took good care that these shafts should reach their victim, and the effect on one whose nature was sensitive, impulsive and strong must have been terrible. Julius Caesar had put away his wife because 'the wife of Caesar must be above suspicion', and Augustus had put away his wives and taken other men's wives to suit his pleasure, but here the case was reversed, and while Julia was dragging her husband's honour and good name through the mud by her notorious profligacy, all the lampooners, satirists and wits of Rome were exercising their abilities at the expense of Tiberius. He answered the gibes of his enemies by a separation from Julia; but a strong feeling of resentment against his mother and his persecutors, and of shame, grew on him and he determined to escape from them by leaving Rome. Neither the earnest entreaties of his mother, nor the complaint of his father-in-law, made even in the senate, that he was deserted by him, could prevail upon him to alter his resolution. Upon their persisting in the design of detaining him, he refused to take any sustenance for four days together. 'At last having obtained permission, leaving his wife and son at Rome, he proceeded to Ostia without exchanging a word with those who attended him, and having embraced but very few persons at parting.' (Suetonius)

Tiberius had become a power in the state, had entered the city with a public ovation and had been consul twice, but he shrunk now from public observation and buried himself in Rhodes, where he occupied himself with literature. What occurred between Tiberius and his mother, or whether he even took leave of her before his departure, is not known. She had not as yet commenced the murders of the heirs to Augustus, though to allay the anger of her son and regain his lost confidence and love, she may have been urged on by these impulses as well as by ambition to remove, as soon as possible, every obstacle in his way to the post of Emperor. It is almost certain that she did not confide her plans to her son, because the historians of that time do not accuse him of complicity with her, and directly accuse Livia of these domestic murders. He remained eight years in Rhodes, and during this time Augustus caused his divorce from Julia to be granted by the Senate. His continued absence brought his name and power into disrepute, and to such an extent 'that the people of Nismes pulled down all the images and statues of him in their town' (Suetonius); and to illustrate the manners of that time as well as the feelings of his stepson Caius, upon mention being made of him at table, one of the company said to Caius, 'I will sail over to Rhodes immediately, if you desire me, and bring you the head of the exile', for that was the appellation now given him. (Suetonius)

Becoming tired of his self-enforced idleness, and fearing that his enemies might procure his death, he determined to return to Rome. On his arrival there he lived the retired life of a simple Roman gentleman, but the deaths of Caius and Lucius induced Augustus to adopt him, and he was called again to an active life. The revolt of the Illyrians and Germans gave him an opportunity to show that he was a great general and to save the Roman empire from complete destruction. After three years hard fighting he vanquished the Illyrians; but Varus had lost everything in Germany. Tiberius marched against the Germans, and after a war of two years brought them again under the Roman yoke. These were the most serious wars since the Punic, as they threatened the very existence of the Empire, and Tiberius was justly regarded as the rival in military skill of any general who had preceded him. He was hailed on his return as the saviour of Rome; the Senate wished to give him the title of 'Invincible'; and Augustus, who was never generous in his compliments to him, wrote that all those likewise who were with him acknowledge that this verse was applicable to him: 'One man by vigilance restored the state.' 'When I hear and read that you are much impaired by the continued fatigues you undergo may the Gods confound me if my whole frame does not tremble! So, I beg you to spare yourself, lest, if we should hear of your being ill, the news prove fatal both to me and your mother, and the Roman people should be in peril for the safety of the Empire. It matters nothing whether I be well or no, if you be not well, I pray heaven preserve you for us, and bless you with health both now and ever, if the Gods have any regard for the Roman people.' (Suetonius)

Not only did Augustus write privately to Tiberius in this high strain of praise, but he also 'swore publicly in an assembly of the people that he adopted him for the public good.' (Suetonius) These successes silenced his enemies, but the honours won by his ability and courage were wrung from the Senate and the people almost against their will, for Tiberius, though a great general and administrator, had none of the winning ways and affable manners which cause popularity. He possessed a dignity of character and brightness of intellect which marked him as the most prominent man of his time, and as the able successor of Augustus. His successes gave him the confidence of the army, but his strict discipline and severe punishment of any offence had alienated their affections, therefore, though the deaths of Lucius and Caius, and the disgrace and banishment of Agrippa to Sorrento made Tiberius the most probable successor to the Imperial power, yet it would require no little ability, in the face of so many difficulties, to seat himself, without civil war and popular uprisings, in the post of Emperor. Augustus died and before dying either gave an order, or Livia forged one, for Agrippa's death, and he was immediately despatched. Tiberius, to whom the Centurion commissioned to do this deed reported that the order for Agrippa's death had been obeyed, sternly rebuked him

Why Tiberius Came and Remained in Capri

and said that he would be held responsible for this action. But as he was never punished, it is probable that either Livia alone added this murder to that of Agrippa's brothers, or did it in connivance with Tiberius. The writers of those times, however, consider that Livia was responsible for the murder.

On becoming Emperor great fears were entertained of mutiny among the soldiers, who made exorbitant demands, and of tumults among the people; but Tiberius by shrewd state-craft silenced his adversaries, and fixed himself firmly in power. Once in this position, he came to an open rupture with his mother whom he had hated from the moment she had extorted his divorce from Agrippina and his marriage to Julia. 'She having frequently urged him to place among the judges a person who had been made free of the city, he refused her request, unless she would allow it to be inscribed on the roll that the appointment had been extorted from him by his mother'. (Suetonius) This was probably a taunt thrown at Livia to recall her unfortunate success in bringing about his miserable marriage with Julia. But Livia, who had had the courage and duplicity to pay a Roman noble a heavy sum to induce him to see, and to swear that he saw, an eagle fly out from the funeral pyre of Augustus and ascend to heaven; who based on this eagle the foundation of a new religion, which was organized with the greatest pomp and ceremony to pay divine honours to the new god Augustus; and which enabled its high-priestess, Livia, to enjoy higher earthly honours than any woman had ever before enjoyed in Rome; this shrewd, quick-witted, far-seeing, unprincipled murderess had also foreseen that some day an open rupture might occur between her and her son, and she was prepared for it. 'Enraged, Livia brought forth from her chapel some letters from Augustus to her, complaining of the sourness and insolence of Tiberius' temper, and these she read'. (Suetonius)

The kindly, affectionate relations of mother and son had long ceased between Livia and Tiberius, but on his return from Rhodes they mutually used each other for the advancement of their ambitious plans. Livia feared the advent to power of Caius, Lucius or Agrippa, for her power would not only be gone, but even her presence in Rome would not be allowed, therefore she murdered them, and hoped, by obtaining the post of Emperor for her son, to retain her place as a power in the state, and control him as she had controlled Augustus by making herself useful and necessary to him. Tiberius, though he probably had no hand in these murders, was willing to profit by them, and when his mother originated her stupendous scheme of inventing a new god and a national religion, he did not oppose it, as he hoped by this means to exercise a greater influence over the Romans. From this habit of mutually assisting one another in political matters, though their rupture was an open one, and though no attempt was ever made by either to bring about a peace, yet they tacitly agreed not to interfere with the political plans of each other. Tiberius was on terms of peace with the high-priestess Livia, but against his mother he could not restrain the resentment and hate which had been silently growing since his married happiness had been destroyed. The high priestess and widow of Augustus could be formidable, even to the Emperor: her affable manners, engaging person, long continuance in power, habit of ruling and thorough knowledge of the prominent men of Rome gave her not only the second place in the Roman state, but made her a rival of Tiberius. It was the policy of Tiberius not to carry on a political war with her, and Livia had nothing to gain by warring against him; thus these two lived in Rome.

The ambition of Livia was satisfied with the religious pomp and Imperial splendour which surrounded her, but the misery of Tiberius sought relief by quitting Rome, which was made hateful by his mother's presence. He was now sixty-seven years old, and his successful career as a soldier and statesman had fixed him firmly on the throne. He had built a camp within the city walls and had quartered the Pretorian guards in it; he could rely on the fidelity and valour of these troops, and was free to choose any place as a residence which might suit his fancy or his wants. He wished a place near enough to Rome that, at any time when his presence might be required, he could make his appearance suddenly, and from which he could make his mother and the Romans feel that he was cognizant of every movement on their part, and if necessary could use quickly all his power to counteract any attempts against him. He sought also a beautiful, healthy residence, where he could surround himself with the comforts and luxuries which his old age demanded. In addition to all these requirements, it was necessary that the position should be capable of defence against

Why Tiberius Came and Remained in Capri

attack, or any outbreak on the part of the people or of the army, and from which, in case of the worst, he could escape with a fleet to some distant province, which, he thought, might remain faithful to him. The island of Capri was the only place which united these many requirements, and he took up his permanent residence here in the twenty- seventh year of the Christian era.

Roman society by this time was thoroughly corrupted. The conquest of Asia and Africa had introduced the vices and crimes of the licentious, supple, soft-mannered Eastern. For some time the bold, rough, warlike Romans could not habituate themselves to the refined voluptuousness and domestic murders of the Orient, because the presence on their borders of such formidable enemies as the Germans and Illyrians obliged them to be soldiers and accustom themselves to the hardships of war. But Tiberius had so effectually crushed these two enemies, and organized so well camps, fortifications and a civil administration among them that they, as well as all the powerful nations of the North, felt themselves powerless against the might of the Romans. Augustus by a long, prosperous rule had habituated the Roman people to a certain amount of luxury, and, as Rome had become the world capital, poisoners, panders, catamites, eunuchs and other instruments of a refined licentiousness and of a perverted civilization streamed towards Rome. They found willing pupils among these sons of the valiant strong, old soldiers who had conquered the world, because the Romans still had such bodily strength that they could indulge in every new excess invented by the pleasure-loving Oriental, and they had so much wealth, and their tastes had been so corrupted that they welcomed every inventor of a new pleasure, however infamous, as a benefactor.

Therefore during the reign of Tiberius the robust Romans plunged into excesses, which frightened even their teachers, whose bodily powers had been weakened by generations of the luxury and effeminacy common to warm climates. As an example of the corruption which marked the beginning of Tiberius' reign, Suetonius says: 'Women who were suspected of illicit connections, divesting themselves of the rights and dignity of Matrons, had now begun a practice of professing themselves prostitutes, to avoid the punishment of the laws; and the most profligate young men of the senatorian and equestrian orders, to secure themselves against a decree of the Senate, which prohibited their performing on the stage or in the amphitheatre, voluntarily subjected themselves to an infamous sentence by which they were degraded. All these Tiberius banished that none, for the future, might evade by such artifices the intention and efficacy of the law.'

During the first years of his reign, though he introduced many civil and military reforms, yet all his attempts to prevent the growing laxity of manner were futile. Considering that the corruption was due to the influx of Eastern habits and religions, 'he suppressed all foreign religions and the Egyptian and Jewish rites, obliging those who practised that kind of superstition to burn their vestments and all their sacred utensils. He also expelled the astrologers; but upon their suing for pardon and promising to renounce their profession, he revoked his decree'. (Suetonius) But these attempts could not impede the torrent of eastern licentiousness which spread through every class in Rome, and finally the Emperor ceased his struggle against the inevitable. In Rome it was the orgy of the parvenu, 'who had suddenly acquired undisturbed possession of almost unlimited wealth and power; and all moral restraints had been destroyed by the fatal effects of civil wars. A poet summed up the hopes and ambitions of Rome in the celebrated lines:

… Atque duas tantum res anxius optat
   Panem et Circenses.

It is necessary to read the sixth satire of Juvenal to understand the infamy of the women; and his tenth satire to appreciate the vileness of the men of that time, and what he says is not the hyperbole of a poet, but his statements are verified by the writers of those and later times. To the honour of Tiberius it should be remembered that he did everything in his power to improve the public morals; he was better and stronger than the Romans of his time, and Cocceius Nerva, who was his friend and councillor, starved himself to death, affrighted at seeing the state of public morals sunk so low. He never upbraided Tiberius, but knowing the weakness of human nature, and fearing that so much vice might overcome his virtue and taint his hitherto unsullied character, 'with mingled feelings of anger and fear he wished to die pure and unstained'.

Why Tiberius Came and Remained in Capri

No man, however strong in mind and character, can completely resist the influences and manners of his time. Tiberius was no exception to this rule, and though he had shown the noble qualities of courage, of military and civil skill, of forbearance, of kindness and affection, tempered by a certain military severity, yet there can be no doubt that, at times, he gave way to the licentiousness of his time and to the drunkenness which seemed to have been a fault of his younger days. This however was only at intervals, until he went to Capri, but here in his old age when weakened by his infirmities and by his terrible domestic troubles, his moral nature became impaired and he gave way to the baser qualities.

Some men have a restless intellect and a fund of restless energy, which demand that they should work, and work hard to the last. To them, quiet and rest mean misery, and they are compelled to give their attention to something which engrosses their thoughts and energies. Sylla, after he had conquered Marius and murdered all his enemies, finding no one to murder and nothing to oppose him, retired to Baiae to seek rest and quiet for his old age; but his restlessness obliged him to pass his time in all sorts of licentious amusements in the company of buffoons, jesters, and troops of dancing and singing girls. Alexander, finding no more worlds to conquer and forced to be quiet, expended his energies in drunken debauchery. Sylla and Alexander died in the course of a year after they ceased working as soldiers and statesmen, because they attempted excesses which their physical powers would not admit, and were tempted to commit these excesses on account of the want of other work. Tiberius, in the quiet of Capri, still occupied himself with the affairs of state, and the dangerous condition of things in Rome claimed his attention to such an extent that, though he indulged himself both 'in Bacco et in Venere', his restless energies and intellect found such a vent in the management of Roman politics that he was saved from the excesses which brought on the drunken death of Alexander, or the loathsome, mortal disease of Sylla. His indulgences were carried to a refinement which has made his name and that of Capri inseparable, but he kept within the bounds of his bodily powers, and attained an old age so hearty that, when seventy-seven years old and only a short time before his death, he 'encountered with javelins a wild boar, which was let loose in the arena'.

Some writer has said that nations get the rulers which they deserve, and while this saying undoubtedly has much truth in it, other writers go farther and ascribe to a ruler of any certain epoch, noted for its good or bad qualities, all the good or bad qualities of his epoch. There can be no question that the Roman people, on account of the violence of the civil wars of Sylla and Marius, and of the ill gotten wealth obtained by the conquests of Julius Caesar, Pompey, Augustus and Tiberius, had become so corrupted that the reign of Tiberius was an orgy of crime and debauchery. But that we should accept, without farther inquiry, the character ascribed to Tiberius by Suetonius and Tacitus, which makes Tiberius a monster who united all the crimes, vice and excesses of his subjects in his own character, would be a gross injustice to a great statesman and general. The Latin writers and their successors and imitators, the writers of the Latin races, have made a common mistake very often in their descriptions of celebrated characters; they unfortunately are too apt to show one side of a character only.

This one-sided literary method is called the Classical school, and is best illustrated in modern times by Racine and Corneille. These two writers took marble statues of their heroes and brought them on the stage in the full paraphernalia of regal splendour, they never lay aside their crowns, sceptres or magniloquent speech, but remain marble statues to the last with nothing human; and we turn with feelings of relief and pleasure from the high-flown, sonorous sounding periods, and the tiresome, monotonous grandeur of the statuesque kings and princes of Racine and Corneille to the manliness, the homely profanity, the pranks and vulgar wit of Shakespeare's flesh-and-blood kings, princes and courtiers. Shakespeare threw light on his characters from all sides, his kings are not only kings but are men. This one-sided literary method prevailed among the historians of the Caesars, and it is very difficult to obtain a fair judgment of the men described by them. Tacitus, who wrote about sixty years after the death of Tiberius, gives him a most infamous character and ascribes to him only infamous motives. The summing up of the life of Tiberius, at the end of the sixth book of the Annals, unites in him all the wickedness of his time, and this bitter criticism is in strange contrast to the glowing eulogy on the character of Livia, in the beginning of the fifth book. The historian who could apply the words, 'Sanctitate domus priscum ad morem' to the woman who introduced domestic murder among the Romans, was as far from the truth as when he wrote about Tiberius, 'postremo in scelera simul ac dedecora prorupit'. Tacitus rarely or never gives his authorities for his assertions. He has portrayed the character of Livia in most glowing colours, while he has painted Tiberius in the blackest; there is no middle ground, but with a sententious dogmatism which discredits his statements has lauded to the skies, or has damned to the lowest depths, persons who deserve neither unqualified praise nor blame. Suetonius, who wrote twenty years later, on the contrary, continually quotes his authorities, and though in his description of the libidinous side of the character of Tiberius he leaves the suspicion on the mind of a modern critic that he wrote it after consulting a copy of the book of Elephantis (the Marquis de Sade of those times) and that he ascribed to Tiberius every form of refined vice contained in that epitome of obscenity, yet between the lines of the gossipy narrative of Suetonius we obtain a much truer impression of the real character and motives of the Emperor than we get from the Annals of Tacitus.

That a man of Tiberius' ability should commit murder for murder's sake is preposterous, but that he would not hesitate to order the execution of any one who plotted against himself or the state, and that he would mercilessly murder the friends and followers of such a plotter, are beyond doubt. Those were morally diseased times, and the prompt, severe remedies of Tiberius, if they could not cure, at any rate kept down the disease to a certain extent, and allowed the patient to hold on to life until a healthy reaction might set in. He was accustomed to say when speaking of the Romans, 'I have got a wolf by the ears', and he died holding this wolf with the firm grip of a master. But the ferocious wolf, once freed from this grip, gave barks of delight over its dead master, and uttered angry growls of impotent rage at the strong will and severe hand which had controlled its ferocity and taught it that after conquering the world, it was necessary to conquer its own propensities if it wished to retain its supremacy over its hardly won conquests. Tiberius was a political necessity of those times, and long after his death his influence was felt; to his administrative and military ability were due the vitality and elasticity of the Roman Empire, which enabled it to live through the crazy pranks of Caligula, Claudius and Nero, until the Flavian family arose to rescue it from the ruinously disturbed and unsettled condition caused by the short and disgraceful reigns of Galba, Otho and Vitellius.

'During all the time of Tiberius' retirement at Capri, he saw Livia but once and that for a few hours only. When she fell sick shortly after his seeing her, he was quite unconcerned about visiting her in her illness; and when she died, after promising to attend her funeral, he deferred his coming for several days, so that the corpse was in a state of decay and putrefaction before the interment; and he then forbade divine honours being paid to her, pretending that he acted according to her own directions. He likewise annulled her will, and in a short time ruined all her friends and acquaintance; not even sparing those to whom on her death-bed she had recommended the care of her funeral, but condemning one of them, a man of equestrian rank, to the treadmill.' (Suetonius). It was impossible for Tiberius to forgive his mother the cruel wrong she had done him, and he did not attend the funeral. Her friends and partisans, who formed a court around her, did not have the strong political sense which distinguished Livia, and, when her shrewd counsels were withdrawn, instead of keeping still and repressing every open exhibition of their feelings against the Emperor, allowed themselves most probably the luxury of denouncing him both as a man and ruler, and of extolling the great qualities of their mistress whom they considered the builder and support of the good fortunes of Tiberius. But the consideration which the Emperor had shown to the high-priestess and widow of Augustus was not reserved for her friends, and, as men in those days went from words to deeds, Tiberius, probably considering them his own enemies and the nucleus of an opposition which might eventually give him great trouble and cause tumults or outbreaks, destroyed their influence by the confiscation of their property, and imprisonment. Shortly after the death of Livia came the conspiracy of Sejanus, and the terrible truth came to light that his son Drusus, who, he thought, had died a natural death, had been poisoned by his wife Livilla and her paramour Sejanus to allow their marriage. This seems to have been the culminating blow to the domestic happiness of this strong, old man, weighted with the infirmities of years and the chagrins of a ruined

Why Tiberius Came and Remained in Capri

domestic life; it roused him up from his lethargic misery, and he vented his mad rage on all who were connected with Sejanus or Livilla.

Suetonius gives us this picture of his state of mind, after he had put down the conspiracy of Sejanus: 'At last, being quite weary of himself, he acknowledged his extreme misery in a letter to the Senate, which began thus: What to write to you, Conscript Fathers, or how to write, or what not to write at this time, may all the gods and goddesses pour upon my head a more terrible vengeance than that under which I feel myself daily sinking, if I can tell.' Thus his last days dragged on, days of terrible sorrow and jaded pleasures, until death came to relieve him from his misery. His intellect remained clear enough to the last to enable him to cheat his enemies and die a natural death. Seneca, who was thirty-five years old when he died, and who held a high position, wrote: 'That finding himself dying, he took his signet ring off his finger and held it a while, as if he would deliver it to somebody; but put it again upon his finger and lay for some time, with his left hand clutched, and without stirring; when suddenly summoning his attendants, and no one answering the call, he rose; but his strength failing him, he fell down at a short distance from his bed, and died.' The testimony of Seneca is the most reliable which we have, but if he were suffocated by Caligula, as some historians assert, it was one more illustration of the force of his destiny that to his own family he should owe the misfortunes of his life.

In the Museum at Naples there is only one bust of Tiberius as Emperor; his head is crowned with oak leaves and his richly chiseled armour is adorned with bound captives and trophies, recalling his victories over the Rhetians, Vindelicians, Pannonians and Germans. It is the portrait of a man who held in his hands the destinies of the world. Kings came, or sent their sons with rich presents to do homage to him as their lord and master, and his cup of happiness ought to have been full. But on examining the face, what a tale of misery it tells! We shudder as we look at the deep lines, the skin bloated with drunkenness, the eyes with a brooding look, and on watching the flabby and loosely hanging lips we imagine we see them trembling with the tremulousness of the debauchee. The artists of those days were remarkable for their life-like portraits, and the only flattery done to this likeness of Tiberius by the sculptor was to leave out the pimples on the face of his Imperial client. The portrait was made when the Emperor was old, but the artist has put him in the dress of a successful general enjoying his triumphal procession, and in the place of the look of triumph, which should naturally go with the dress, there is a look of intense misery and distrust pervading the whole face. Contact with Livia and Julia robbed him of all tender feelings, poison and murder took away his sons, betrayal after betrayal destroyed any belief in the existence of friendship or of any high and pure motive; for him there were no friends, no loved ones, no honour, no truth and no manhood!

There is a statue of his mother by the side of Tiberius, draped in the graceful folds of a Roman matron's dress and with an expression of quiet, womanly dignity in her beautiful face; but on the opposite side and near Augustus is another Livia, clad in the costume of a priestess, and the priestess, with a scornful smile of triumph on her lips and with the pride of a satisfied ambition lighting up her dainty features, looks over derisively at the subdued face of the beautiful matron.

As we pass through the hall of the Caesars with the gay sounds of Neapolitan life in our ears, and the warm, cheery sunlight flooding the court, we bring back to life these dead men and women, and as the warm life-blood pours into these pieces of marble and brings them before us as they were when they sat before the sculptor, we have a feeling of compassion as we see the happy, affectionate and loved Tiberius stand side by side with the hated old man adorned with the symbols of Imperial power, but in his face are lines which tell of a ruined inner life, and of sorrows which have eaten out his soul; and we have a feeling of abhorrence as we see Livia, the loving, gentle mother, transformed and changed to the honoured old woman, in the dress and with the symbols of a high-priestess, whose joyful face bears no traces of murder and the daring sacrilege which made Augustus a God.

Chapter 5
History during the Middle Ages and Modern Times

After the death of Tiberius we hear but little of Capri from the Latin writers. During the life of Tiberius, Caligula shaved his beard for the first time and assumed the toga at Capri. Suetonius says that after Caligula became Emperor he visited the islands of the Gulf of Naples, and it is very probable that Capri was included during this visit. Vitellius also visited Capri during the life of Tiberius. Statius, who lived during the reign of Domitian, speaks of the lighthouse at Capri, and of its great benefit to sailors and travellers who passed through the Strait. From him we know that the lighthouse, which, according to Suetonius, had been thrown down a few days before the death of Tiberius, had been rebuilt by one of his successors. Dion and other writers inform us that the Emperor Commodus sent Crispina and Lucilla, the one his wife and the other his sister, as exiles to Capri. The island still remained in all probability the personal property of the Emperors until the fall of the Western Empire, and was then joined to the territory of Sorrento under the sovereignty of the Duke of Naples.

The first mention of Capri in Christian times occurs in the sixth century, under Pope Gregory the Great. Saint Gregory wrote to the Bishop of Sorrento, to grant the petition of Lavino, the abbot of a Benedictine hospice or monastery on the island, this abbot having asked permission to depose some relics of Saint Agatha in the church of this monastery. This hospice was dedicated to Saint Stephen and belonged to the monks of Monte Cassino, who very probably came to Capri for the sea-bathing and the good air. It was very probably where the present Cathedral of Capri now stands, as there was an old church here dedicated to Saint Stephen, and on its site was built the present Cathedral of Capri in 1688. Some writers assert that the island became the property of the monks of Monte Cassino, but this statement has been called in question. In 812 a fleet of forty Saracen vessels entered the Gulf of Naples and ravaged its cities and islands; and Capri very probably underwent this disaster. About the year 868 the Emperor

Ludovicus took Capri from the Duke of Naples and gave it to the Duke of Amalfi as a reward for valuable services.

From the hill called Tiberius, on looking across the Gulf of Salerno, can be seen the site of a fortress called Acropolis; it was situated about five miles to the southeast of Paestum. The Saracens established themselves here in 860, and remained until 915, when they were driven away by the united forces of the Gulfs of Gaeta, Naples and Salerno. This robber colony sent out expeditions by land and sea, which pounced down suddenly on the cities, villages and islands in its vicinity, plundered whatever could be found, and carried off the men, women and children, who were sold as slaves on the African coast. Against these attacks, all along the coast and on the island, were built small towers, which are commonly called Martello towers, because when the approach of the Saracens was discovered, the alarm was sounded by beating with a Martello or hammer on a piece of metal, and the inhabitants in the vicinity could thus gain a place of refuge. In Capri, which from its position was more exposed to these attacks than any other of the islands, not only were there towers, but the fortresses of Barbarossa, Castiglione and Solaro were built as places of refuge. In 920 a bloody naval battle was fought between the Neapolitans and Saracens, in which the latter were badly beaten. One of the Saracen ships took refuge at Capri, whereupon the Capriotes attacked the vessel, captured it, and killed every man aboard. In the 12th century King Roger of the Norman dynasty conquered Amalfi and Naples and joined them to his kingdom, but, as the chronicles relate, the people of Capri did not wish to submit to the new king, and, when attacked by Roger's forces, finding themselves too weak to withstand the Norman troops, retreated to the castle of Barbarossa, where they held out and withstood a siege, but capitulated shortly after on account of the want of provisions. Under the Hohenstaufen kings no particular mention of Capri is made, but during the reign of the unfortunate Conradin the body of San Costanzo, the patron saint of Capri, was transferred to Monte Vergine from Benevento, to which latter place the monks of Monte Cassino had carried it from Capri. Tradition says that the body of San Costanzo was borne miraculously by the waves and wind in a barrel to the shores of Capri from Constantinople, where he was formerly bishop and suffered martyrdom. The exact date of this event has

History during the Middle Ages and Modern Times

never been determined, but the barrel was opened, the body was taken out and was then deposited in the church of San Costanzo on the island, and remained there until the monks of Monte Cassino carried it away to Benevento.

A piece of marble was dug up some years ago near the foundations of the monastery of San Francesco, and is now in the possession of Mr. Haan. On this marble is an inscription cut in Gothic letters, and as these letters have the same form, and bear a great resemblance in every way to the letters cut on the tombs of the Anjou kings in the church of Santa Chiara, at Naples, it is a proof that this monastery or hospice existed during the Angiovine reign, which commenced in 1266. The monastery of San Francesco was situated on the north side of the island, near the water at the eastern extremity of the Grande Marina.

After the Sicilian Vespers in 1282 the Kingdom of Naples was ruled by members of the house of Anjou, and that of Sicily by the Aragon kings. Under Charles second of Anjou war broke out between him and King James of Sicily. During this war Capri was attacked by a Sicilian fleet of twelve galleys under Bernardo di Serriano, who captured the island, and leaving a small garrison, attacked and captured also the island of Procida; but both islands were restored to Charles soon after the making of peace. Under his successor Robert, who commenced his reign in 1309, Capri must have possessed more mouths than could be fed, as the obstructions to the exportation of grain from the mainland to the island were rescinded, and the Capriotes were allowed to import eight thousand tomoli of grain yearly. As there was a scarcity on the mainland during these years, the amount allowed to be exported to Capri must have been in some proportion to the number of the inhabitants. As there are about forty-three and a half kilogrammes to the tomolo, this would give a total of three hundred and forty-six thousand kilogrammes, and as an adult in these warm climates eats about a kilogramme of bread daily, for bread was then and is now the principal food, this would give a population of less than one thousand; but taking into account the women and children, who would eat less, it is probable that the number of inhabitants at that time was about fifteen hundred.

During the reign of Joanna first, Giacomo Arcucci, Count of Minervino and Altamura, the secretary and chamberlain of the Queen, founded the monastery called Certosa, and by a deed dated May first, 1371, the Queen granted a considerable tract of land on the island to this Carthusian monastery, whose construction commenced that same year. Some years after the monastery was finished, Arcucci incurred the enmity of Charles third, Queen Joanna's successor, and was stripped of all his honours and wealth, so that he was compelled to come poor, old and disgraced to seek shelter, and end his days in this same monastery, where he died on the 22nd of November 1386. To the honour of the monks they gave him a kind reception and did everything in their power to lighten the burden of his declining years and disgraced old age; after his death they gave him a sumptuous funeral and erected in the church of the monastery a handsome marble tomb to his memory. Under Ladislaus, who commenced his reign in 1386, the Capriotes frustrated a mutinous attempt of the soldiers of the citadel, who had arranged a plan to assassinate their commander and flee from the island. On account of this gallant deed the King exempted, by a diploma dated 1408, the islanders from the payment of all taxes or exactions of any kind. A garrison of soldiers was stationed here to hold in check the Saracens and signal their arrival to the mainland, as these robbers were accustomed to visit Capri and ravage it, as well as Ischia, before commencing operations on the mainland. About this time the men of the island were formed into a species of military organization against the Saracens, and as it lightened the cost of the defence of the island to the King, he was disposed to grant corresponding privileges and exemptions to the Capriotes. These privileges were confirmed by Queen Joanna second, the successor of Ladislaus.

During the war between Renato, the last King of the Anjou dynasty in Naples and Alfonso of Aragon, King of Sicily, a priest of Capri went to the camp of Alfonso at Capua, and offered the allegiance of the Capriotes to him. Alfonso accepted the proffered allegiance and sent six galleys to take possession of the island. A short time after, a vessel came from France with eighty thousand scudi for Renato, and the Captain doubting nothing landed at Capri for some reason, whereupon the vessel and treasure were captured and the money was sent to Alfonso. This capture was very damaging to Renato, as he was waiting for the money, with which he intended to pay off his dissatisfied troops; but it encouraged Alfonso, and he renewed his efforts to capture Naples, so that on the 2nd of June 1442 he entered the city, and the reign of the Aragon dynasty commenced. Under the Aragon kings several decrees relating to Capri were issued. They are of little interest, as they only confirmed former privileges or exempted the islanders from some new taxes. One decree gave special rights to the Capriotes for the fishing of the 'aguglia' or garfish.

During the reign of Frederick, the last of the Aragon kings, in 1496. the people of Anacapri petitioned this monarch for redress against the many wrongs inflicted on them by the people of Capri. This was the official commencement of a quarrel between the two communes, which had probably already existed for a long time and has not abated to this day. Among the grievances set forth in their petition were the following: the people of Capri were more numerous than those of Anacapri, and for this reason the seat of government was at Capri, but this had a bad effect on the interests of Anacapri, because influences were brought to bear on the Governor of the island by the people of Capri, among whom he lived, which injured very seriously the interests of the Anacapriotes; therefore the petitioners humbly besought his Majesty to allow them to rule their own affairs, and that the rights of Anacapri should be made equal with those of Capri. By a lengthy decree of the 24th October, 1496, the King conceded to the Anacapriotes all the rights petitioned for; he separated the government of the two communes, and, to awe the Capriotes into good behaviour, ordered that all questions between the two communes or individuals thereof should be transferred to the courts at Naples.

Under the Spanish viceroys terrible days were in store for Capri. In 1535 the famous Saracen Admiral of Solyman's fleet captured the island. It is a tradition among the inhabitants that Barbarossa completely destroyed the walls and houses of the old town of Capri, which was at the Grande Marina and near the present church of San Costanzo. He also destroyed the most formidable fortress on the island, which, since that time, has borne the name of Barbarossa. So great was the destruction that many of the inhabitants left the island, and it became greatly depopulated.

There is another tradition, which says that Barbarossa pillaged Sorrento and carried away twelve thousand men and women into slavery, but Capri was saved by a miracle wrought by San Costanzo, the patron saint of the island. The tradition, as it exists on the island now, is that an old woman, early in the morning before daylight, was spinning thread with her distaff, when suddenly the distaff cried out: 'The Saracens are at the Piccola Marina!' The old woman looked around everywhere in the room to find the person who had spoken, but could find no one. The distaff then repeated its first exclamation, and the old woman went out of the house, and saw that Capri was in flames and beset by the pirates. But suddenly San Costanzo appeared, and ordered the flames to become extinct, and the fire went out. He also caused a panic among the Saracens, who retreated immediately to their ships. It is possible that Barbarossa, having a large fleet, made Capri his headquarters, whence he could easily and quickly make an attack on any village of the Bays of Naples and Salerno, and could then retire in safety with his booty and captives to Capri, where he was in no fear of pursuit or surprise. After this expedition of Barbarossa, by an edict from the most celebrated of the Spanish viceroys, Pietro di Toledo, every one on the island was allowed to keep and carry arms, as an attack from the Corsairs might be expected at any moment.

Capaccio in his History of Naples, printed in 1607, page 552, speaks thus of Capri: 'In this island is the town of Capri, which has a very strong fort, and contains about two hundred inhabitants; there is also the village of Anacapri, which has a population likewise of two hundred souls. The village of Anacapri is built on a high rock, which is approached by a narrow, steep and difficult path, but to the inhabitants this way is easy, and they even carry burdens over it. The inhabitants of this village are either fishermen, sailors or shipbuilders; many of these last find employment in the Royal dockyards at Naples, where they are considered most skillful. On account of their occupations they are necessarily absent a greater part of the year from their homes, and for this cause they petitioned the king not to allow those who are banished to the island to pass the night at Anacapri, as their wives being alone would be insulted; this petition was granted. The people of Capri and Anacapri are enemies, doing out of spite all the damage they can to one another. In a petition, presented by the people of Anacapri to the Emperor Charles fifth, requesting a confirmation of the privileges accorded by the Aragon dynasty, they complained that the inhabitants of

Capri damaged their houses, burned their boats and the products of their fields and drove them away from the fishing of the gar, therefore they prayed that the Governor of the island might live three days in the week in Anacapri, that he should administer justice there and protect them against the Capriotes. The inhabitants are free from all taxes and imposts and are allowed, as a special privilege, to go always armed. They have always been very faithful to the Austrians. They live in the greatest poverty, as they are very often preyed upon by the Turks, who carry away the sailors and fishermen into slavery. On the island are two noble families, the Arcucci and the Faracci.'

In 1656 the Pest broke out in Naples, whence it spread to Capri in the following manner. In Naples a young lady of the noble family of Morcaldi died of the Pest, and the family sent a tress of her hair and some articles of dress to her relatives living in Capri. Through the negligence of the guards the articles entered the island, and carried with them the dreaded disease. At first it attacked only the poorer class, which were more liable to disease on account of their bad nourishment, but soon the air was so vitiated by the number of the sick and dying, that the richer class also were infected. At first the precautions in use at that time were employed to prevent the spread of the people, but physicians and medicines could not be obtained, so the disease spread until the whole island was infected. The only ones who escaped were the monks at the Certosa. On the first outbreak of the disease, they shut the doors of their monastery and refused to have any contact or communication with the outer world. The ravages of the Pest became daily greater, the deaths were so numerous that those who were employed to bury the dead could not complete their labours, and finally the unfortunate dead were left in the places where death overtook them. Every house contained one or more dead bodies, and those who fled from their homes were sometimes attacked by the disease and fell dying in the streets. Some hid themselves in caves, or among the rocks, and either succumbed to the Pest, or to hunger, and were eaten by the starving domesticated animals. When the Pest first commenced its ravages, the sacraments of the church were administered by the priests, but in a short time some of the priests died, and the others, participating in the general fear, shut themselves up in their houses and left the dying to prepare themselves, as best they could, for the other world. Relatives forgot all the ties of affection, and either threw the dead out of their houses, or left them in the place where death overtook them, or, fearing infection from the sick, deserted them and their homes to seek refuge in caves. It happened that many families became extinct, and no relative, however distant, survived to inherit their property. The Carthusian monks appropriated these possessions, and thus acquired a large portion of the island. As no one existed who could make any legal claim to the property, the Capriotes considered it best to allow the Carthusians to hold these properties, hoping that the profits arising therefrom might be applied to the alleviation of the poverty and wretchedness of the survivors. To the honour of these monks it is chronicled that they gave succour to those inhabitants whom age or sickness had reduced to beggary.

Under Charles second of Spain, the old rights and privileges were renewed, but, instead of a civil governor appointed annually, a military officer was sent to rule Capri, and as he knew nothing of the civil law, a judge or assessor (to use the old name) became necessary. In a small island like Capri, where the population was poor and uneducated, it was impossible to find anyone qualified to perform the duties of this office, therefore a Neapolitan was always selected, who did not remove his residence to Capri but remained in Naples. This was a manifest injustice to all the people on the island, because, on account of storms, it was often impossible to appear before the judge on a certain day, when a lawsuit was set for trial, and the expenses of all litigation were trebled. The people also found fault with the personal character of the military governors, who were, for the most part, favourites of the viceroys, who took this means of providing places for men, whose fitness for the office was rarely or never taken into consideration. But there was another evil still greater, as we see from a description of the Bay of Naples by Antonio Parrino, printed in 1727, at Naples, where, on page 127, the following terrible condition of affairs is described: 'Every day many unhappy fishermen are carried away into captivity by the Mahometan corsairs, and especially by Renegades, who come here to inflict every species of barbarous outrage on their native land; among these Renegades is an infamous villain named Coperchiulo.'

Parrino describes Capri and gives some interesting particulars about the island, among these he says: 'For its spiritual needs, Capri has a bishop, who derives the most of his income from the quails, turtle-doves and other birds of passage, which are caught here in great abundance.' (From this fact, the Bishop of Capri was somewhat irreverently styled the Bishop of Quails.) 'The Carthusian monastery, consecrated to Saint James the Less, brother of Saint John the Evangelist, of whom it possesses an arm, was built by Giacomo Arcucci, in imitation of the monastery of San Martino in Naples. Near the monastery of San Francesco on the seashore are four fountains, one of these, they say, is of sea water, another is of running water, the third is called Truglio, and the fourth Marocella. Lately, on the south side of the island, a large quantity of water burst forth. In Anacapri there is the church of Santa Maria Cetrella on top of the mountain, with a hermitage, where lately they found, on exavating, statues and a highly prized pavement composed of rare marbles.' In 1734 the Bourbons ascended the throne of Naples, and under their reign extensive excavations were made in Capri, and many works of art, including statues, bas-reliefs, intaglios, precious stones and, more important than all, pavements well preserved and composed of richly coloured and valuable marbles, were found. Under Charles third of Bourbon the defence of the island was better organized, and guards composed of Capriotes were always stationed near the various landing places; these guards gave the alarm when the Corsairs appeared, and several times it happened that, by concentrating all the troops and arms-bearing Capriotes at one point, the Corsairs were beaten back to their ships. Encouraged by these successes, and the consequent security of property, more attention was paid to the organization of the means of defence, and among other things a large supply of eatables was brought over from the mainland and kept in store, to meet any emergency which might arise from a suspension of communication between the island and the opposite shore through stormy weather, or a blockade.

During this reign several excavations were made, and among others, the foundations of the Villa Jove were cleared from the rubbish surrounding them, and a pretty pavement, now adorning the Cathedral of Capri, was found in a subterranean chamber. By the orders of this King, several remarkably fine columns of giallo antico in the little church of San Costanzo were taken away, and carried to Caserta, where they now adorn the Royal

Chapel of the palace. In 1750 the governor of the island, Don Giuseppe Maria Secondo, gave in manuscript a brief account of Capri; in this document he cited many of the old Latin writers to prove the celebrity of the island, and pointed out the spots where, he thought, it would be best to make excavations. King Ferdinand fourth, the son and successor of Charles, visited Capri frequently for the purpose of quail hunting. He also caused partridges to be raised by the Capriotes, and gave premiums to those who killed the serpents, which destroyed the partridges' eggs. During his visits to the island, the King always stopped in the house called 'Palazzo Inglese'. This house was built about the middle of the last century by an Englishman named Nathaniel Thorold, who was of a noble family, but during the gambling times of the Georges 'had wasted his substance in riotous living' and was compelled to seek a home in foreign lands. He came to Italy and was the first to introduce the salt and dried codfish to a large extent as a common article of food among the Italians. By this commerce he gained a large fortune, and came to spend his old age in quiet among the vines and olives of Capri.

King Ferdinand held several reviews of the local militia, which had been organized exclusively for the defence of Capri and was not subject to military service elsewhere. This fact would seem to prove that the Saracen Corsairs were still in the habit of making raids on Capri, or that their raids were feared even as late as 1780, but Hadrava, who was attached to the Austrian embassy at the court of Naples and accompanied the King on several of his excursions to the island, has given a description of one of these reviews, which proves that this militia was not very effective. 'Every year there is a parade, during which everyone of the arms-bearing population must present himself with his gun, and ammunition consisting of twenty-three balls and a half pound of gun powder. Once I was present at this beautiful ceremony, at which I saw guns without any barrels, which, with the powder and balls, were borrowed from the old men. This review takes place in the spring, usually on the day of San Costanzo, and after dinner – as at that hour the men exhibit more vigour and military ardour.' With such a troop, it was probably good for the island that the Corsairs did not trouble them, and it is a proof that the Capriotes had enjoyed such an immunity from their attacks that they had commenced to neglect all precautions. In 1764 both the towns of Capri and Anacapri had united to send a petition to the King, requesting that the military governor should be replaced by a civil governor, who could administer affairs and dispense justice on the spot, thus putting an end to the expensive and wearisome litigation attendant on the judge's residence in Naples. This petition had been granted by the King, but in 1782 the civil governor was deposed by Ferdinand on account of certain charges brought against him by the people of Capri, who did not wish a civil governor.

Hadrava was with the King when a demonstration was made against this governor, a certain Doctor Marcello de Angelis, and describes it in the following manner: 'The governor and a crowd of Capriotes awaited the landing of the King and his party; the governor had learned a set speech, with which he intended to welcome his Majesty to Capri, but, on the stepping ashore of the King, the cries and laments of the men and women drowned his voice, and finally he was thrust aside by several of the islanders, who drew from their breasts bread, broke it, and exhibited its bad quality to the King. They then poured forth their complaints against the governor, specifying his crimes and tyranny, and implored that they might be freed from this monster in human shape. The King, at the time, took no notice of these complaints, but during his stay on the island made enquiries, and on the day of his departure had the governor arrested, and sent him for trial to Naples amid the hearty applause of the rejoiced people.' The charges brought against him were immoral habits and extortion, and after presenting these charges the people of Capri requested that the military governor should be restored, because, as the petitioners said, the island was so accustomed to military rule, and the people had such military habits that only a military governor could rule them properly. The King granted this petition, and sent an officer whose name was Emanuele Diversi, as military governor to rule the island. The old state of affairs commenced again, the judge lived in Naples, and all lawsuits were carried there to be tried before him. The military governor, instead of receiving his appointment annually, held it for a long time, and this gave rise to serious abuses. Living as he did in Capri, not only did he, by a long residence, form likes and dislikes among the people in the town of Capri, but every influence was brought to bear on him by the population of Capri against the people of Anacapri. In 1783 the town of Anacapri protested against this misrule and petitioned that the civil governor should be sent back again. The town of Capri, on the contrary, considered that military rule was eminently proper and just, and sent a contrapetition for its continuance. The matter came for trial before the court in Salerno, under whose jurisdiction Capri was, and the court decided that not only should a military governor reside on the island, and that he should be appointed annually, but that a civil governor should also be sent there, that he should reside permanently on the island to dispense justice and administer civil affairs, and that all his expenses should he defrayed by the two towns.

In 1775 Doctor Giraldi, an Italian, went to Capri, and caused excavations to be made in several places to the depth of three or four feet, but discouraged on finding very little, he did not prosecute the work. He collected all the best specimens of sculpture and antique remains which had been dug up by the peasants while cultivating their vineyards or planting their orchards. The Doctor carried off a rich booty, and wrote a short description of the island and of his stay on it; the most interesting part of his manuscript was devoted to the flora of Capri.

A few years later Doctor Arcucci wrote and presented to King Ferdinand an account of Capri, in which, for the first time, an attempt was made to point out the sites of the twelve Tiberian villas mentioned by Suetonius. As almost every writer on Capri has fallen into the error of supposing that, because Tiberius had built twelve villas which he most probably reserved for his own use, necessarily every large mass of ruins found anywhere on the island was the remains of one of these villas. Against any such theory as this, it should be remembered that the court of Tiberius was lodged here, that embassies from all parts of the world were received here, that the Emperor kept a large number of soldiers, sailors, dancers of both sexes, actors, catamites and other instruments of pleasure here, and that this large assemblage of persons necessitated a considerable number of large buildings, in which all these persons could be lodged. Earthquakes and time have so far destroyed and disfigured all the ancient buildings that it is impossible to tell for what purpose they were built, and we can only judge that any particular ruin was an Imperial residence because it is situated in some place which enjoys an exceptionally fine view. It should also be remembered that everywhere on the island are found ruins of villas, palaces or large buildings, and that their number far exceeds twelve.

In 1776 the old bishop of Capri died and a new one, Monsignor Gamboni, took his place. Bishop Gamboni was gifted with great intelligence and energy, and did very much for the education of the young. In addition to a seminary for training young men to the priesthood, he established four other schools, one of which was devoted to the study of Agriculture and Naval affairs. Among these schools was also one for girls, where they were taught not only reading and writing, but also how to prepare silk and work it into various shapes, so that it could be sent to market as ribands or scarfs.

During the visits of King Ferdinand to Capri for bird-shooting he was accompanied by several members of the embassies accredited to the court of Naples, and among these was Hadrava, in the Austrian diplomatic service. Hadrava was no hunter, and left the King and his companions to their sport while he wandered over the island, examining the ruins scattered about. One day, on his way up the hill called Castiglione, some peasants drew his attention to a fig tree which had been torn up by the roots through a violent storm; the roots had carried with them sufficient earth to leave a hole about four feet deep, and at the bottom of this hole was an opening through an arched roof. Through this opening could be seen well preserved stucco work attached to the walls. This roused his curiosity, and, giving orders to the peasants to widen the hole, he prepared to descend into this subterranean room, where, on entering, he found a succession of chambers leading the one into the other. The peasants, seeing his eagerness, and excitement at this discovery, proffered their services, in case he might wish to undertake excavations. Hadrava first requested permission from the King, who readily granted it, with the remark 'that in case anything worthy of the Royal Museums should be found, it should be reserved for them'. In the year 1786 Hadrava commenced his excavations on the spot mentioned above, and kept on excavating there and in other parts of the island for about twenty years.

After finishing his excavations on the Castiglione, he excavated the Baths of Tiberius, a part of the Villa Jove, the Lighthouse, and made many partial excavations in various places, to determine the site of the twelve villas mentioned by Suetonius. He found bas reliefs, cameos, heads of statues, vases, an altar, several fine columns with their capitals, both of rare and valuable marbles, but it was his good fortune to find several beautiful pavements, one of which is now in the palace of Capodimonte in Naples and is considered one of the finest and best preserved of all the antique pavements hitherto discovered. Hadrava wrote a series of letters which were published in book form in 1793, wherein he not only gave a detailed account of some of his excavations, but also described the habits and manners of the inhabitants. He was a good judge of character, intelligent and happy in his descriptions, so that these letters are exceedingly interesting, and present a good picture of Capri and its people as they existed a hundred years ago. There was at that time no hotel on the island, though at the Grande Marina one house ambitiously had the name of tavern painted on it, yet there was nothing to eat in it, nor could it furnish a bed to the traveller. Any stranger who arrived brought his provisions with him, and found lodging either in the house of the Governor or in the Palazzo Inglese. There was no butcher, and beef could be obtained only when a cow had the misfortune to fall over a precipice and find an untimely death; whereupon, a herald with a trumpet announced to the people that a cow had been butchered and that the meat was for sale in the Piazza.

The monastery of the Carthusian monks owned not only the whole of that part of the island in the neighbourhood of the Certosa, but had many vineyards and olive plantations in the communes of Capri and Anacapri, as well as possessions on the mainland. There were only fourteen monks in all, and their yearly income was fifty-one thousand francs. The monks distributed, in time of want, flour, bread, and other necessaries to the poor, and defrayed some of the expenses connected with the bishopric. The best bread on the island was baked by them, and a famous liqueur was manufactured and sold in the monastery. The monks grew broad-shouldered and round on the fat of the land, and if they mixed their prayers with many thoughts of the 'inner man', and became gourmets as well as gourmands, let us hope that their capon-lined stomachs had a ready sympathy for the empty stomachs of the poor.

The inhabitants, before the arrival of Hadrava, considered antiquities of but little or no value. Whenever a peasant found a marble column, or statue, he called together his relations, and they pounded it with their hammers, until it was broken into bits sufficiently small to be thrown away or to be used for making walls. At the Marina, fine columns of valuable marble were fixed upright in the ground, and were used for attaching boats. Once, some strangers, who had noticed two large, unbroken columns of precious marble lying near the sea, came with a ship at night, and took them away. The guards, who saw them, drew near and took great interest in the dexterity used to hoist the columns aboard ship. As soon as everything was ready, the strangers wished the guards a pleasant good night, and sailed away. On relating this adventure, the next morning, in the Piazza, many of the Capriotes envied the guards their good fortune at having witnessed the ingenious method of hoisting adopted by the strangers, but never thought that the columns possessed any value.

Hadrava considered Anacapri an Arcadia. There the air was of the purest; old men of ninety, a hundred or even more years, with smiling, contented faces, greeted him pleasantly as he passed through the clean, picturesque streets. The houses were always left open, as no one feared thieves; they gave each other assistance in case of need, and lived together in perfect harmony. There was one thing which impressed Hadrava very much; it was the extreme hatred against the inhabitants of Capri; the Anacapriotes considered the Capriotes to be full of fraud, deceit, malice, and all the other vile qualities which degrade man. There were old persons in Anacapri who had never been to Naples, and even a few who had never descended to Capri. The population of Anacapri was 1,300, while that of Capri was 2,200, making a total of 3,500 inhabitants on the island. As a contrast to this charming picture of the Anacapriotes, the Capriotes are painted in colours not at all flattering, 'Several writers have eulogized these people of Capri, extolling their innocence and simplicity, but my experience has been the contrary. Probably, in times gone by, they were all that their admirers claim for them, but today these innocent islanders, though they have no knowledge of the laws, nor the art of eloquence, possess a wonderful ability in hiding their real pretensions, until an opportunity presents itself, and then, when least expected, find an excuse for eluding their obligations.' Hadrava made excavations only in Capri and never came in close contact with the people of Anacapri; had it been otherwise, probably he would have been as lavish with his blame for the Anacapriotes as for the Capriotes. He says further: 'The commerce of the island is carried on by means of two boats, which leave for Naples every Monday and Friday, but sometimes as many as ten or twelve boats leave Capri together, bound for the different cities around the Bay. The products consist of wine, oil and fruits. Annually there are produced about two thousand butts of wine, and this wine is considered equal, if not superior to the Lacrima Cristi of Portici, or the wine of Piedimonte. The cheapest Capri wine is sold at nine francs the barrel, and the better qualities cost twelve, seventeen or even twenty-five francs. The annual amount of oil produced amounts to six thousand measures, and each measure costs, according to the abundance of the yield, from ten to fifteen francs. Another source of revenue is the quails, doves, and other birds of passage. The number caught varies every year, but the greatest catch in one day was twelve thousand quails, and during the whole time of passage, which does not last more than fifteen days, they have never caught more than a hundred and fifty thousand birds. The fishing is very good, and in 1784 four hundred tons of fish were sent to Naples, exclusive of what was consumed on the island. There is a small gain from the sale of cheeses, manufactured on the island from cows and goats' milk. Many of the males pass the summer fishing for coral near the coast of Sardinia, and when the season is at an end return to their families. However, some of them never return, as they fall victims to the Saracens and are carried off to Africa into slavery. There are two hundred and fifty goats here, which belong to the Carthusian monks, who have the exclusive right to possess them. Fishing nets and silk ribands or scarfs are the only manufactures. The men and old women make the nets, while the girls and young women work up the silk, which is furnished by Neapolitan merchants, but by a hard day's work only five sous can be gained. The Capriotes are fond of holidays, and every church, congregation and chapel has its festa. The festa consists in firing off a mortar several times, and in tapping a fresh butt of wine, which is selected by a vote of the majority of the recognized wine-tasters. At these festas, the men wear long Neapolitan sailor caps of red colour, and the women have their hair put up in nets, and confined by a silver needle run through it; their dresses are ornamented with a broad strip of gold lace, which is sewed on the bodice, but under the arms of unmarried women to

History during the Middle Ages and Modern Times

distinguish them from the married. As a general rule, the women are tall and well made, of a brown or yellow complexion, and have the old, Greek type of face.'

About the beginning of the year 1806 the French entered Naples and forced King Ferdinand to retire to Sicily, where he was protected from molestation by the English fleet. Capri shared the fate of Naples, and a French garrison, under the command of Captain Chervet was sent to take possession of, and guard the island. The French were aware of the strategic importance of the place, and determined to fortify it strongly, as well as provide it with heavy artillery. The English were informed of this determination, and resolved to capture the island. On the 12th of May, 1806, an English fleet appeared unexpectedly at the Grande Marina, and under cover of a heavy fire from the ships attempted a landing. The French, having no artillery, could not respond to the fire of the ships, but Captain Chervet posted his men under the shelter of the houses and rocks near the Grande Marina, and defended his position bravely against the landing party. Towards evening the English effected a landing not far from the Marina, drove the French back, and during the night took possession of the Castiglione, which commanded the town and made the English virtually masters of the situation. Captain Chervet, finding out this move of the English, attacked them vigorously before daylight, but, as he was killed at almost the first fire, the French lost courage and retired. In the morning, the English occupied the town, and the French laid down their arms. The loss of life on both sides was slight. Captain Chervet was buried with military honours, and the French, who were allowed to retain their arms and baggage, were sent to the mainland. Peace and order were restored in the name of King Ferdinand, and, as strict orders had been given to respect life and property, everything resumed its usual course. Sir Hudson Lowe took command of the garrison, and set busily to work to fortify the heights against any future attack on the part of the French. In a short time the hills of San Michele, Santa Maria Soccorso, the Castiglione, Cesina, the Grande and Piccola Marinas were put in a state of defense, and were furnished with cannon of heavy calibre. Stockades were built in Anacapri at the chapel of San Antonio, near the head of the stairs leading from Capri to Anacapri, at Santa Maria Cetrella, at Damecuta, and at several places along the western coast. The English either built very slight fortifications or none at all near the various landing places, because they relied on their fleet. Sir Hudson Lowe, after the fortifications were finished, considered his position impregnable, and with some pride called Capri 'the little Gibraltar'. A civil governor was sent from Sicily by the King, to administer justice and preserve order among the inhabitants. The capture of Capri was considered an important achievement by the English and Sicilians, because, from its position at the mouth of the Bays of Naples and Salerno, the commerce by sea of all the cities and towns on these two Bays was destroyed.

The Ponza islands had always remained in the possession of King Ferdinand, and Capri was valuable as a way station. A fleet of English men-of-war cruised continually in the two Bays, except when it was compelled to seek the open sea on account of storms. Commerce was impeded to such an extent that the French were extremely irritated, and two attempts were made by Joseph Bonaparte to recapture the island, but, on account of the want of secrecy, the English were always acquainted with the French plans and had their fleet in readiness each time, so that they captured or dispersed the Neapolitan ships. Murat, who succeeded Joseph Bonaparte as King of Naples, introduced new vigour into the administration of his kingdom, and, among other things, resolved to put an end to the English rule in Capri. He confided this intention only to his Minister of War, and to an engineer officer who went around the island in the disguise of a fisherman, to find out where landings might be effected. To carry out his purpose, Murat organized a flotilla consisting of one frigate, a corvette, twenty-six gunboats and about one hundred transports. This small fleet, with the troops necessary for the expedition, was kept in constant readiness to make an attack on the island whenever favourable circumstances might permit. On the fourth of October, 1808, everything appeared favourable, as the English fleet was not in sight and the sea was very calm. General Lamarque was appointed commander-in-chief of the expedition, with Generals Montserras, Destres and Prince Strongoli-Pignatelli, assisted by Adjutants Chevardes and Thomas. The soldiers composing the expedition numbered about two thousand, and were picked men from the Carabineers, Grenadiers, the Royal Guard and a Corsican regiment stationed at Salerno. The fleet was divided into three parts; the main flotilla, containing about fifteen hundred troops, sailed from Naples and Pozzuoli and directed its course towards the western coast of the island; a smaller flotilla from Castellamare, with a hundred troops, sailed for the Grande Marina, and another from Salerno, containing about four hundred Corsicans, made its way to the Piccola Marina. Two feigned attacks were to be made, one at the Piccola Marina, and another at the Grande Marina, which would keep the troops under the immediate command of Sir Hudson Lowe at their posts and thus prevent his sending reinforcements to Anacapri, where the real attack was to be made. Colonel Lowe had a regiment of Corsican riflemen in Capri, and Major Hamill commanded a regiment of Maltese troops in Anacapri, the two regiments together furnished an effective force of eighteen hundred men to oppose the French. When Sir Hudson saw that two flotillas were making their way to the Marinas of Capri, he bestirred himself for his defence by placing the artillerists in the forts with the heavy guns, and the infantry at all points which were likely to be selected by the French as landing places. A barricade, formed of a line of boats fastened together at prow and stern, and filled with infantry, was anchored out a short distance in the water at the Grande and Piccola Marinas, and Captain Panettieri, a Corsican, commanded a considerable force at the Punta di Tragara. At Anacapri, from the Punta delle Gradelle to the Punta di Carena, the troops of the Maltese regiment were stationed in small detachments, but the largest detachment remained in the camp, which was on the plateau of Damecuta.

About three o'clock in the afternoon, the various attacking parties reached the island almost simultaneously and commenced firing with their heavy guns, to which the English responded with their artillery. The vessels then approached within musket range, but those at the Piccola and Grande Marinas soon retired beyond the range of the English heavy guns, as they had already accomplished their object, in preventing Colonel Lowe from sending any of his troops to reinforce Major Hamill in Anacapri. When Colonel Lowe saw that the attacks at the two Marinas were only feints, he sent two detachments of a hundred men each, under Captains Shurk, an Irishman, and Susino, a Corsican, to the assistance of Major

Hamill. These two officers had been stationed in Anacapri already, and knew the ground well. As the English had no artillery in Anacapri, the French fleet approached within short range, and commenced a heavy fire, under cover of which, with hooks and ladders, an attempt was made to land. The first who climbed up the rocks were some Grenadiers and Corsicans under the command of Adjutant Thomas, and they were immediately shot down by the Maltese. Among the French Corsicans was a Lieutenant Boccagiamba, who received a mortal wound here, and at the moment when he met his death, his brother, an officer in the Corsican-English regiment at Capri, was fighting the French. The French continued climbing up the ladders, until finally they obtained a foothold on the top of Orica, and succeeded in hoisting their colours, around which a desperate struggle ensued; but the French kept on mounting the ladders and finally drove the Maltese back, up the hill, at the point of the bayonet so that the whole force of fifteen hundred men landed without any further difficulty. The French pushed forward, driving back the Maltese, who kept on firing and retreating up the mountain side, until night came on. The main flotilla, after landing its contingent of fifteen hundred men at Orica, went to seek the Corsican troops who had come from Salerno. Under the cover of night, this detachment lauded near the Blue Grotto, and with a deserter as guide made its way to the top of the stairs leading from Capri to Anacapri; thus cutting off the retreat of Major Hamill's regiment to Capri. After leaving a small body of men to guard the stairs, the French Corsicans attacked the Maltese in the rear, causing great confusion among them. During this attack Major Hamill was killed, which increased the confusion, and the Maltese retreated in disorder to the top of Mount Solaro, where the English Corsicans under Captain Shurk had already taken possession of the fortifications there.

As there was no artillery in these fortifications, and as the French followed up their success by a pursuit, the Maltese, considering further resistance useless, made overtures for surrender. The English Corsicans, taking advantage of the darkness, and of the suspension of hostilities to define the terms of surrender, climbed down the cliffs, and, by a very precipitous and dangerous path, regained their regiment stationed at Capri. On the morning of the fifth of October the Maltese regiment, consisting of eight hundred officers and men, surrendered. They were allowed to march into the French camp in the village of Anacapri with their arms and baggage, and, the same day, were sent to Naples as prisoners of war. The French loss in killed and wounded, during the landing and the fighting which ensued, was very heavy on account of their exposed condition, while that of the English was inconsiderable. While these events were happening in Anacapri, Sir Hudson Lowe was doing everything in his power to strengthen the fortifications of the town of Capri, which possessed at that time, in good condition, a strong wall with towers at intervals. This wall defended the northern and western sides of the town, which were the only ones liable to attack; the fortifications on San Michele commanded the road leading from the Grande Marina; and those of the Castiglione commanded the approaches from the Piccola Marina. There were several stockades on the stairs leading to Anacapri, and these were filled with troops by Sir Hudson Lowe. The French, with great fatigue, succeeded in dragging up Mount Solaro a battery of heavy artillery, which they planted at Santa Maria Cetrella, and with this commenced firing on the town of Capri, within whose walls the English had retreated. But finding that they caused little damage, and desirous of obtaining possession of the island as soon as possible, they determined to descend the stairs and attack the English in their fortifications. The French feared the arrival of the English fleet, which might appear at any time, and would thus not only put an end to all hope of capturing Capri, but they would be at the mercy of the English. Sir Hudson, when he saw the French flotilla approaching on the 4th of October, had sent dispatches to Sicily and Ponza, requesting immediate aid, and, on this account expecting relief hourly, was disposed to hold out to the last. On the night of the fifth of October, the French descended the stairs, and driving back the English made their way to the Marina Grande. They planted a battery of heavy artillery at the Campo Militare and commenced firing on the town. Under the cover of this battery and that of Cetrella the French advanced near to the town wall and, taking possession of the houses in its vicinity, kept up a continual firing with small arms.

 Colonel Lowe acted entirely on the defensive, waiting for the English fleet, which finally appeared on the seventh of October. It was composed of four frigates, two corvettes, three brigs, four bomb-ships, fourteen gunboats and nine transports. These vessels surrounded the island, and cut off all communication with the mainland, but on account of the high wind prevailing, it was impossible to land the troops from the transports. The commander of the English fleet hoped, by depriving the French of ammunition and supplies, to force them to surrender to Sir Hudson Lowe. The wind increased in force, and the English fleet sought the open sea for protection; the French seeing this, and having a flotilla of gunboats with many other boats laden with supplies and ammunition ready at Massa, put to sea and ran over to Capri in spite of the storm. The English vessels endeavoured to intercept them but did not arrive in time, and though the French flotilla was hotly cannonaded, it succeeded in reaching the island safely, where the boats were beached, and their cargoes were discharged. During this time Murat was at the Punta di Campanella, and watched with great interest this successful attempt to supply his troops. The wind increased to such an extent that the English fleet was compelled to seek safety in Sicily, and left the French free to carry on the siege of Capri undisturbed. General Lamarque pushed on the siege with redoubled vigour, hoping to capture Capri before the English could return. A continual cannonade was kept up both night and day, which caused much damage to the walls and houses of Capri, and much annoyance and loss of life to the English. Finally, on the sixteenth of October, Sir Hudson Lowe despairing of succour, and fearing that the French might storm the town, which, on account of the knocked down walls and the small number of English soldiers fit for duty, could easily be taken by assault, hoisted a white flag, and negotiations for the surrender commenced. The French offered favourable terms, which were accepted, and the English marched with flying colours, arms and baggage into the Certosa, which was assigned to them as quarters after the signing of the capitulation. An hour or so after Colonel Lowe had surrendered, there hove in sight a large English fleet, which had been sent expressly from Sicily to relieve the island, but it was too late, and, though the weather was bad, Sir Hudson and his command embarked at the Piccola Marina on English vessels, which set sail immediately for Sicily. General Lamarque, on taking possession of the town, found many cannons and a large supply of ammunition; he restored order, placed Adjutant Thomas in command, and then, with his generals, returned to Naples, where he was received enthusiastically by the King and populace.

The preceding account is taken from English and Bourbon sources, but the French account is somewhat different. General Colletta, a Neapolitan, who accompanied the French, and was both an eye-witness and actor, gives a short account of this expedition in his History of Naples. Colletta received a wound during the fighting, and to him is due the merit of the plan which worked so well in the hands of General Lamarque; for Colletta, disguised as a fisherman, had gone round the island in a boat, and had chosen the point of attack. His account is as follows: 'At midday, on the fourth of October, the island was attacked at three points simultaneously; at the Grande Marina, at the Piccola Marina, and at a point on the coast of Anacapri: of these three attacks, the first and second were only feigned, though, from the number of the boats employed and the vigour displayed, they seemed to be real. The attack at Anacapri was modest in appearance, but was the real one. Here, on the rocks, several of us, officers, landed, and placing a wooden ladder against the steep rock we ascended; then, after climbing over the stones for a little distance, by means of another ladder we succeeded in attaining a level space. To the first succeeded others, among whom was General Lamarque, our commander. At the top of each ladder we planted our flag as a sign of triumph, and our number was more than eighty before the enemy saw us. When we were seen by the English, who were above us on the top of the hill, they seemed timid and irresolute, as though they were waiting for reinforcements from Capri. They fired at us from behind the rocks, but did not dare to come near us. In the meantime our troops kept on landing, until we were five hundred. The sea then became so rough that it was impossible for the others to come ashore; some bold spirits tried it, and were drowned, whereupon the others desisted from the attempt. Not considering our force of five hundred men, of whom seven had been already killed, and one hundred and thirty-five wounded, sufficiently strong to warrant us in advancing, we waited for the darkness of night to hide the weakness of our force. Meanwhile fighting was going on all around the island. Colonel Lowe, a good disciplinarian, but unaccustomed to war, threw everything into confusion by his useless orders. While our vessels were threatening the coast, he ordered his troops to march from one fortification to another without any scope whatever, and the small regiment of Maltese, which garrisoned Anacapri, was not reinforced. Finally night came on, but after a while the moon came out, illuminating the crest of the hill occupied by the English, but leaving us in the shade. As we could see them without their seeing us, many of them were killed or wounded, so that finally they were compelled to retreat, leaving only a few sentinels, some of whom were soon killed, and the rest fled. Our little force was then divided into two parts; one detachment marched to the right, and the other to the left; and in this order we ascended the hill very quietly. We left behind some of our soldiers, who kept on firing, and making as much noise as possible. In a short time, without attracting the attention of the enemy, we gained the top of the hill, and found ourselves only a short distance from them; we then immediately made a vigorous attack with shouts and rolling of the drums, and put them to flight. Most of them were taken prisoners, but some, on account of the darkness, escaped and made their way to the fort on the top of Mount Solaro. During the night the head of the stairs leading from Anacapri to Capri was occupied, and we then approached and surrounded the fort. On the morning of the fifth, at daybreak, a messenger was sent to the fort, who demanded an immediate surrender. After a short parley, during which our messenger insisted on the impossibility of resistance, the surrender was agreed on. Three hundred men gave themselves up to us, and these, added to the four hundred taken prisoners the night before, were sent immediately to Naples. During the same day we posted a battery with which we could cannonade the town of Capri under us, though it was at very long range; everything was put in order, and the other troops landed where we had landed the evening before. We waited for night to descend the stairs leading to Capri, and every moment during the descent expected to be fired on by the English, but Colonel Lowe had shut himself up in the town with all his troops, numbering more than a thousand, and we passed safely down the stairs, which might have been easily defended, and posted our men in such a manner that in the morning we commenced a regular siege. The English fleet, which was in Ponza, had been informed of our attack on Capri, and came to the relief of Colonel Lowe. It broke off our communications with Naples, and made a real or feigned attack on

Anacapri. By a continual bombardment, it interfered with the progress of our siege. The fleet communicated with the besieged town by way of the Piccola Marina. The coming of the fleet only caused us to redouble our efforts to reduce the town, and we moved up our heavy battery within three hundred yards of the town walls. Colonel Lowe was of a timid disposition, and moreover was influenced by several Neapolitans, who had fled from Naples on account of crimes or political offences, and feared to fall into the hands of the Neapolitan police. On this account he hoisted a white flag, and the articles of surrender were signed on the 18th of October. According to these, the town with all its munitions of war was given up to us. The prisoners, amounting to seven hundred and eighty English and Corsicans, gave their parole of honour not to engage in any hostilities against us for the space of one year and one day, and two days after the surrender were allowed to depart on their own ships for Sicily. The criminals and political offenders had embarked on English vessels before the articles of surrender were signed. After the town was given up to us, and before the English had departed, another English fleet laden with soldiers and munitions of war appeared before Capri; but it was too late.'

The account given by Colletta differs in many points from that given first, but such discrepancies always exist, and, in trying to get at the truth, it is necessary to judge of the credibility of the sources from which these two accounts are derived. The first is almost exclusively taken from facts related by the Capriotes to Mangoni, and as the islanders were very partial to the English, because under their rule an extensive contraband trade was carried on with the mainland, it is natural that the sympathies of the Capriotes should have been contrary to the French, who put an end to this trade and thus deprived the islanders of a large revenue. Colletta commenced his history in 1825, and finished it in 1830. Many of the minor details of this expedition had escaped his memory, but in the main he was most probably correct. A man of his high position would not purposely deceive, though it is possible that the bitterness of exile and the persecutions of the Bourbons may have tempted him to exaggerate the gallantry of his friends, who were the enemies of the Bourbons. The English in England were not at all satisfied with the conduct of their countrymen, and while most critics found fault with the fleet, yet it is most probable that the incapacity of Sir Hudson Lowe brought about the loss of the island. Of this siege the only thing which remains at Capri to recall it, is the ruined west side of the Palazzo Inglese, whose walls were knocked down by the French battery at Cetrella, and have never been rebuilt. Tradition says that Colonel Lowe had his headquarters in this house until the French captured Anacapri, after which he left it and took up his quarters within the town.

At Anacapri, in the little piazza in front of the church, a marble tablet was let into the wall, which contained the following inscription: 'To the memory of John Hamill, a native of the County Antrim in Ireland and Major in his Britannic Majesty's late regiment of Malta, who fell while bravely resisting the French invasion of Anacapri, on the fourth of October 1808, and whose mortal remains are deposited near to this place. This tribute of affection and respect has been placed by his kinsman and namesake, October 3d 1831. Requiescat in pace'. Major Hamill's cousins, John and Catherine Hamill, went to Anacapri in 1831, and with the help of the peasants found the remains of their relative, and had them buried in the parish church, as the Hamills were Catholics.

Adjutant Thomas, who was left in command of the French garrison on the island, set about to fortify it in such a manner that the recapture of it by the English would be very difficult. To prevent any approach through the strait, he erected a fort under Santa Maria del Soccorso, and constructed a road from the fort to the top of the hill behind it. At the Grande Marina he built two forts, one to the east on the foundations of the old monastery or hospice of San Francesco, and the other to the west at the Campo Militare, now the villa of Mr. Haan. Ports were also erected by him at the Piccola Marina, at Pino, at Campetiello, at Orica and at Gradelle; and the fort on the Castiglione was amplified. All these were provided with heavy artillery, and well garrisoned. Engineers were sent to the island to furnish plans for a port at the Grande Marina, which was to have been strongly fortified. Plans for new fortifications were also made, but the disturbed state of affairs, consequent on the disastrous campaign in Russia, prevented the carrying out of these intentions. A judge was sent to Capri by Murat, to settle all legal questions, and supervise the execution of the laws. During the French occupation, the monastery of the Carthusians and the two nunneries of Santa Teresa, the one at Capri, and the other at Anacapri, were suppressed, and their property was confiscated for the benefit of the state. The revenue of the lands, which came into the possession of the Carthusian monks by the extinction of whole families through the Plague of 1656, was given to the cathedral of Ischia.

In 1811 a shower of fine ashes fell on the island, brought over by a strong north wind from Vesuvius. In 1815 the Bourbons returned to Naples and the old order of affairs was restored to Capri, viz. a civil and military governor. More attention was paid to the culture of the vine and olive, so that the wine and oil of Capri were reputed among the best in Italy. The various schools which flourished under the fostering care of Bishop Gamboni were shut up, as that intelligent and worthy prelate had been compelled to leave his diocese, on account of the political troubles of 1799, and seek refuge in the north of Italy, where he occupied the high position of Patriarch in Venice. In 1818 the bishopric of Capri was abolished, and the island came under the ecclesiastical jurisdiction of the Bishop of Sorrento. The fishery was not so good as formerly, and the revenues paid to the Cathedral of Ischia formed a heavy drain on the resources of Capri. From these causes many of the inhabitants were reduced to beggary, and went from house to house demanding alms, or pestered strangers who visited the island. The Bourbon kings, who thought more of stamping out liberalism and establishing their divine rights, than of encouraging commerce or manufactures, allowed all the material interests of the Kingdom to decay, and Capri suffered, as did the other communes. In the old nunnery of Santa Teresa at Capri, a hospital for invalid soldiers was established, and though this hospital was transferred to Massa many years ago, still today several of the invalided Bourbon soldiers remain on the island, having taken wives among the Capri women.

Capri was used as a species of Botany Bay by the Bourbons, and malefactors were sent here to expiate their crimes. On this account it was necessary for every stranger, who visited the island, to have a passport from the authorities in Naples, or in Sorrento. The abbé Lamenais, who unfortunately neglected this precaution, was arrested as a suspicious character, was put in prison, and kept there, until his traveling companion could go over to Naples, procure his passport, and return with it to the Governor.

In 1825 there was but little accommodation for travellers, but the wine must have been good, for Mariana Starke in her 'Information and directions for travellers on the Continent' says: 'The most comfortable way of managing the excursion to Capri is to have a ten-oared boat, taking a cold dinner, bread, salad, fruit, plates, glasses, knives, forks etc. but no wine.' In 1826 the German painter and poet, Kopisch, swam into the Blue Grotto, and was enchanted with the beautiful colour of the water, caused by the reflection of the light. He extolled its beauty so much that his description attracted the attention of strangers who visited the island, and they, in turn, spread abroad the report of this natural wonder to such an extent that the influx of visitors has steadily increased yearly; new hotels have been built, and the principal source of revenue to the island now comes from strangers. Mangoni, a Neapolitan priest, published, in 1834, a diffuse though interesting history of Capri, and in his book gives 3,500 as the population of the island, of which 1980 were in Capri, and 1,520 in Anacapri. Alvino, a Neapolitan engineer, passed some time on the island in 1837, and describes the inhabitants as 'sober, hard-working and quiet in their movements, but extremely avaricious. Whenever a stranger is seen, rich and poor, large and small surround him and clamorously beg for money. The women wear gaily coloured gowns, with red or green silk aprons, and bodices adorned with gold braid; the arms of their chemises are tied up with red ribbons. They dress their hair with ribbons, dividing it into two tresses, which are plaited, then rolled up behind the head, and supported by large silver or gilt silver pins. The men wear long trousers, red Neapolitan fishing caps, and go barefoot. The people of Anacapri do not come in contact with the convicts, who remain at Capri, and therefore the manners of the Anacapriotes are more simple and natural; the women are more affable and pleasing, and there are some who have perfect Greek faces. Not only do they dance the Tarantella, but also another dance which they call Trescone or Tarascone. It is a Greek dance, and is danced by four or eight couples, who turn round and round, then all form into a grand circle, snapping their fingers and clapping their hands.' Alvino illustrated his little book with several coloured wood-engravings, and from them a great difference can be seen between the ruins of forty years ago and today. Then, they were in a much better state of preservation than now, for the Capriote destroys, as quickly as possible, every ruin from which he can derive no profit, to prevent strangers from passing through his vineyard or olive orchard, and in case he wishes to mend a broken wall, the nearest ruin is knocked down to procure materials for building.

In 1848 a terrible disaster occurred, which almost ruined the land owners and peasants. A disease infected the vines, and so great was the damage done that in 1850 not a single barrel of wine was made on the island. The old vines were torn up by the roots, and burned, and new ones were planted in their stead, but even these never grew with the vigour, nor produced grapes which had the flavour of those grown by the old vines. To prevent vines from succumbing to disease, a custom has grown up of sprinkling vines and the bunches of grapes, after they are formed, with sulphur, and when the wine-makers on the island make their vintage, they do it so carelessly that a large amount of sulphur goes into the must, and, changing chemically into sulphuretted hydrogen, destroys the bouquet of the wine. Thus Capri wine lost its fame, and as it was very difficult to remove the taste and smell of sulphuretted hydrogen from the wine after it was made, and as it was impossible to persuade the native wine-maker to improve on the methods used three or four thousand years ago, the wine dealers in Naples, to supply the demand for Capri wines, which had taken a foremost rank among the most celebrated of Italy, were compelled to resort to their fabrication. This fabrication of the spurious Capri, principally out of the cheap wines growing in the country immediately north and east of Naples, has grown to such an extent that hundreds of thousands of bottles are consumed yearly in Italy by the unsuspecting traveller, and even by the Italians themselves, while a large amount is exported abroad for foreign consumption. It is only during the last two or three years that any attempts have been made to free the Capri wines from this taste of sulphuretted hydrogen, and give the pure wine its former rank as the first, or among the first, of the Italian wines. All these attempts have been made on the island, and some of them have been successful.

After the annexation of the Kingdom of Naples to that of Italy, criminals were no longer sent to the island, but a company of discipline for soldiers guilty of breaches of discipline was established, and still exists, in the Certosa. As an instance of the political astuteness of the Capriotes, it is worthy of mention that when a vote was taken for the annexation of Naples to Italy, and it turned out to be favorable, the worthy town-councillors, some of whom were Bourbons at heart, instead of giving an order to remove the shield with the Bourbon coat of arms, which was placed above the town-gate, ordered that the shield should be plastered over to hide the fleur de lys, but in such a manner that in case His Majesty, Francesco, should 'come to his own again' some day, the plaster could be easily removed, and the Capriotes could boast that during all the time of his banishment and exile they had remained true to their rightful king. The shield is there today, to prove that the spirit of Macchiavelli hovers over Capri and inspires its inhabitants.

The priestly influence is very strong, and a great deal of good or evil can be done by a good or bad arch-priest, who is the highest ecclesiastical power on the island since the bishopric was abolished. In general, the priests perform their duties well, and in times of epidemics, however loathsome or infectious may have been the disease, they have not flinched from performing the last rites and administering to the poor wanderer into the unknown land the last consolations of his religion. They are ignorant, and therefore narrow-minded, but this ignorance is tempered by a bonhomie which prevents them from doing much harm, and is often the cause of much good. When the ecclesiastical property in Italy was confiscated and sold by the government, only one Capriote was brave enough to risk the excommunication threatened by the Pope to those who dared to purchase property despoiled from the church. What he did not buy was bought up at a nominal price by some one of the laity who represented the Bishop of the diocese (for it was well understood among the Capriotes that no one was to run up the price), and when the Bishop had obtained possession of the property, he sold it again to the Capriotes at its real value, thus pocketing more money than the Italian government. This occurred some years ago, but should another such opportunity present itself today there is no doubt that many buyers would present themselves, in spite of the excommunication; for modern ideas have reached even the peasants of Capri. Doubtless the liberal and enlightened policy pursued by Italian statesmen keeps the priests everywhere in the kingdom from abusing the enormous power placed in their hands by the confiding ignorance of the peasant population, yet great praise should be given to the country priests, who, by their good sense and tact, have prevented any conflict between the state and the peasants on account of religion.

But there is another power at work which is creating among the people a check more durable. Every year some young Capriotes enter the army or navy, they travel about and see the various cities and customs in the whole of Italy; they come in contact with new ideas, and have their minds opened to a larger range of thoughts and impressions; they learn obedience, patriotism, cleanliness and, in case they are unlettered, are taught to read and write. After a peasant's term of service has expired, he returns to his home and astonishes his parents and relatives, who neither read nor write and have never travelled, by his many acquirements. He measures himself with the priest of his own age, or even with one a little older, and finds himself superior in knowledge of the world, of men and of the exigencies of modern life. This undermines the priest's influence by bringing his knowledge and power into disrepute, and the young peasant, who has been a soldier, often asserts himself against priestly influence in a manner which irritates the priest, and excites the horrified admiration of his relatives. A case in point is the following: an old peasant woman, in whose family existed a domestic quarrel, gave so much trouble with her tongue to her opponent that he was compelled, as a last resource, to apply to a priest to silence her. The priest, who doubtless acted for the best, according to his lights, considered that, as domestic quarrels were always the most bitter and often caused great scandal among his congregation, it was his duty to bring about peace, or, at any rate, quiet between the belligerents at any cost. The two opponents were called up, and each was patiently heard; the priest counselled peace and moderation, but the opponents were related to each other as mother-in-law and son-in-law, and on the death of his first wife, the son-in-law had married another woman, who was distasteful to the mother-in-law, and not only did he maltreat his children by his first wife, but even prevented his mother-in-law from seeing her grandchildren; these wrongs had so stirred up the motherly feelings of the old woman that she could not restrain her indignation, but poured forth, in a high voice, a torrent of abuse, which nothing could stop. The poor priest, at his wits' end, determined at all hazards to support his dignity and assert his authority, so he finally said to the woman: 'Keep still, and make peace with your son-in-law! If you do not, you know that Heaven has placed in my hands the power of life and death, and with one word I will kill you. If I hear anything more of this disgraceful scandal, I will speak to Saint Peter about it, he will tap you on the head with one of his keys, and it will kill you instantly; Saint Peter will then shut the doors of Heaven in your face, and you will go immediately to a place of eternal punishment, from which you will never be released.' This complication of evils staggered the old woman, and her lively imagination pictured immediately her horrible death, and her terrible future. The priest knew human nature well, and the realism of his sentence accomplished his purpose, it quieted the old woman, and her fears made her give a reluctant half-promise that she would make peace with her son-in-law.

When she left the priest's presence, she related everything to her relations and friends, who agreed that against the opinion of the priest, it was foolhardy and dangerous to fight, as he would certainly say the fatal word, which would destroy her, body and soul; but one of her relations had been a soldier, and he expressed very strong doubts about the power of any priest over life and death. The old woman was willing to catch at a straw, and finally the soldier's doubts had such an influence on her that she determined to consult some one in whose judgment she had more confidence. As the question was not only a theological one, but pertained to the science of medicine, the soldier advised her to get the opinion of a medical man on the question. Among the foreigners at Capri who have bought property, and are looked on as quasi citizens, is one who is a doctor of medicine, and, though he does not practice his profession, occasionally, out of pure kindness of heart had taken charge of several difficult cases and had cured them. Among his cures had been that of some relation of the old woman, and, as she was very affectionate, this had gained her heart and confidence. To this foreign doctor, then, she went in her trouble, to find out whether he thought it was possible for any one and especially for a priest to cause her death by a single word, and whether, if he had never seen it himself, he had ever heard of such a thing in all the various and many lands through which he had travelled. The doctor quieted her fears, and assured her of the impossibility of such a thing. This not only erased every apprehension from her mind, but, on the spot, she recounted all her domestic trouble, and declared her intention to wage unceasing war with her 'vagabond of a son-in-law'. The doctor did everything he could to quiet the storm he had unwittingly raised, but it was too late, and the domestic trouble was carried into court, to the intense mortification of the priest and the satisfaction of every scandal-monger on the island.

A few years ago evangelical proselytism reached the island and made its headquarters at Anacapri, where the leader of the movement bought the old nunnery of Santa Teresa. What success this new form of worship may have among these people, who have an eye for colour and the beautiful, who rejoice in processions, flowers, wax candles, altars, pictures and incense, remains to be seen.

In comparing the Capri of today with the Capri of a hundred years ago, many changes are worthy of note. The population now is 4,848, of which number 2,827 are in Capri, and 2,021 in Anacapri, showing an increase of 1,348 for the whole island; which is divided between the communes favorably for Anacapri, as it has had an increase of 721 against 627 for Capri. Instead of four hundred tons of fish sent to Naples yearly, not more than twenty-four tons are sent now. The amount of oil produced is more than formerly, as instead of six thousand measures, eight thousand are produced now. The vineyards yield only eight hundred butts of wine in the best seasons, to take the place of two thousand butts formerly made. The silk culture has entirely disappeared, and the amount of dairy produce is about equal to the consumption. The large quantity of fish, caught here formerly, was due to the presence of the Tunny, and either too much fishing, or disease, or catching the fish when they were too young, or all these causes combined have caused the disappearance of the Tunny, as well as the diminution of other species formerly very abundant. That the agricultural products have not kept pace with the increase of the inhabitants is due to several causes. One of these was the confiscation of the ecclesiastical property under the Bonaparte dynasty, and the troubled times which followed on account of the continual wars of that period. Before the confiscation, all the best lands belonged to monks, nuns or priests, but especially to monks, and as these last had very little to do, they gave much attention to agriculture. In case they leased any land to tenants, they were careful to see that it was improved a little every year, and, knowing the character of the land as well as that of their tenants, they had an organized system, which worked well. The confiscation of their lands broke up this system, and the new owners, many of whom did not live on the island, had no time to organize a new system during the troubled times of the Bonapartes, and the return of the Bourbons seemed to paralyze all industrial and commercial enterprise. In addition, other occupations were found more lucrative, among these was coral-fishing, which was no longer dangerous on account of Saracen corsairs; and later came the influx of strangers, who bring now more gain to the island than all the other sources of revenue. Latterly emigration to America carries off many of the strong young men and women. These various causes have produced a decided diminution in the revenues from agriculture and fishing, but Capri becomes richer every year; new hotels and restaurants for the travelling public, and new dwelling houses for strangers, who seek quiet or health by a permanent residence, spring up every year. The increase in the amount of oil is due to the vine disease of 1848, which so discouraged the peasants that they tore up their vines and planted olive trees instead.

Chapter 6

Habits and Customs

The Capriote of today is as avaricious as his ancestor of a hundred years ago. In making a bargain with him it is necessary to stipulate everything beforehand, and when the time for payment comes, if he has to do with a stranger, it is amusing to hear the excuses brought forward for an increase of the sum agreed on; either on account of his old age, or sickness just passed through, and if not his own, then that of some member of his family; or for some little extra service done; or because the gentleman is very handsome, or the lady is very pretty; or because the visitor is English, or American or Russian, and all the English, Americans, or Russians are so very rich that a franc or two more will in no way whatever be felt by their long and heavy purses, or the visitor is a German, and the Germans are so remarkably kind, affable and good-hearted that they, and they only of all the visitors who come to the island, can appreciate the sufferings and wants of a poor man who earns his bread by the sweat of his brow. Or probably the visitor is French or Spanish, and then he is claimed as something approaching a fellow countryman and co-religionist, who comes from a country much richer than poor Italy, where all the people are ground down with enormous taxes, and therefore his well-filled purse will take a pleasure in relieving the burdens of a father of a large family, who will always pray that the Madonna and all the Saints may send down on the head of this good Frenchman or Spaniard all the blessings and good things, which heaven has in store for those who are lucky enough to secure the prayers and blessings of the poor. The innocent, confiding manner, with which all these demands are made, usually disarms the resentment of the stranger, and if he answers all these compliments with the remark that 'a bargain is a bargain', the Capriote, with an imploring shrug of the shoulders, and the pitiable expression of a long-suffering and ill-used man, says: 'As your Excellency pleases, I leave everything to your Excellency's generosity.' This has usually the effect of arousing the stranger's wrath, if he be of a choleric disposition, or the very absurdity of the demand, or the pitiable expression of face, or simply the wish to get rid of him often induces the visitor to give an extra franc, which will be shown later on to his fellows with pride, as a proof of his shrewdness and ability in 'doing' the unsophisticated wayfarer; while the visitor, if he be a humourist, will consider this extra franc the best spent money of his journey, as he has had so much for so little. Men and women, who are well to do, compel their children to run out to the road and demand money from the stranger passing along before their houses.

But these are the bad points of the Capriotes, and they are the remains of former misery, ignorance and consequent want of manhood; any one of them who has been a soldier, and has been taught self-respect, disdains such petty means. The good qualities of the Capriote far outnumber his bad qualities, he is temperate in all things, is neither impertinent, nor impudent, is industrious, is very much attached to his family, is of a peaceful disposition, and, when aroused, never uses a knife or revolver like his countrymen across on the mainland, but resorts to the weapons provided by nature. For the amount of food he eats, it is remarkable what an amount of work he can do, and then he is always ready, and in a good humour. It is pleasant to see the strong, healthy-looking women toiling up the rocky paths, with burdens on their heads, but laughing and chattering with an infectious vivacity, or dividing with one another an orange, or a bunch of grapes, which some bold spirit among them has stolen from a neighbouring orchard or vineyard, and enjoying with infinite gusto the fruit, and the fact that it has been stolen. When we come from crowded cities and countries where civilization makes its iron rule felt, and cramps, or develops our faculties and sensations, as it chooses; we cannot help feeling that, after all, we, who are born to wealth and the joys of a highly civilized life, have not all the good things in this world, and when we return to our ordinary life and surroundings, in the struggle for gain or honour among the educated whose faces are marked with lines of care and thought, or among the lower classes where vice and misery have distorted what was once noble in them, we look back with pleasure and regret to the pleasant picture of the bright, sunny day, the straight backed, handsome women with their burdens and graceful poses, their dark, laughing eyes, their clear, brown, healthy complexions and gay chatter among the narrow and rocky paths of Capri. Most of the men are away from the island nearly

Habits and Customs

the whole of the year, at sea, either coral-fishing, or employed in the coasting trade, or on long voyages, and, for this reason, almost all labour is done by women; so that it is no exaggeration to say, all the houses in Capri have been carried to their present site on the heads of women.

Some of the customs are very characteristic and peculiar, and among these the doings of the midwives are very curious. When called to a patient, she carries the same sort of chair, which was used hundreds of years ago in England, France and Germany. In this chair the midwife places her patient in a sitting posture, and puts in the hands of the suffering woman one or two images of Saint Anna, then, as the pains increase, the midwife and patient both call on the Saint for assistance, cryng out; 'Saint Anna, Saint Anna! do thy work quickly! Saint Anna! I pray thee! quickly! Saint Anna! I vow thee two candles! be quick! be quick!' After a little, the aid of Saint Ciro is also invoked in the same manner, and when the midwife thinks that the parturition is not far off, she takes a basin of water, and puts into it a dried Sempervive plant; she then tells her patient to look at it, and encourages her by saying; 'Look at this rose! it is dry and dead, but in a short time you will see it come back to life, and when it has come back to life the child will be born.' The poor, suffering woman looks with superstitious awe at the plant, as it absorbs the water and swells out until it fills the basin. and with cries to Saint Anna and Saint Ciro, which grow louder and louder, finally a new Capriote gives a faint cry as it comes in contact, for the first time, with the cold, outer air. This invocation to Saint Anna, and the placing of her image in the hands of the patient come from an old Roman custom, which, in spite of the change of religion, holds its own after the lapse of centuries. Instead of Juno Lucina, and the old invocation, 'Casta, fave Lucina! Juno Lucina, fer opem, serva me obsecro!' Saint Anna has taken her place in the Christian calendar; but with that fertile imagination which characterizes the Italian, a saint has been added to assist Saint Anna in her duties and this is Saint Ciro.

According to the legend, as it exists in Capri, and as related by a midwife, whose racy manner is retained as much as possible, the story is as follows: 'Once upon a time, many years ago, Saint Ciro was very friendly with a pious lady who was near her time, and was in great fear lest she might die. The Saint took compassion on her, and told her that he would pray to the

Madonna to be allowed to undergo the pains, which this poor lady would naturally endure. The Madonna granted his prayer, and one morning, when Saint Ciro was saying mass, he suddenly doubled up with pain, threw the chalice on the head of the acolyte, kicked over the altar, and rolled down the steps to the floor of the church, where he lay kicking and crying out. The people in the church thought he was possesed of a devil, and stood around him with grief and consternation depicted on their faces; neither priest nor doctor could give him any relief, when, all of a sudden, the pain left him, and he arose weak and pale but very much relieved; at the same time the pious lady came towards him and showed him a beautiful child, thanking him at the same time for his great kindness in relieving her from so much suffering. Saint Ciro said to her: 'Oh! that was what was the matter with me, was it! You will never catch me praying to the Madonna again, to allow me to undergo the pains of another woman!' But, in remembrance of this event, Saint Ciro is always called in to assist Saint Anna in her difficult duties. As soon as possible after the birth of a child, to remove the danger of its dying without receiving the sacrament of baptism, the midwife with the godmother, both gorgeously arrayed, carry the child to church, and there the ceremony is performed. Sweetmeats are thrown by the godmother to the street urchins, on issuing from church, and when the procession arrives at the house of the parents, a substantial meal awaits both midwife and godmother. In case the midwife thinks there is danger that the newborn child may die before a priest can arrive to baptize it, she performs this rite.

When a young Capriote has bestowed his affections on some maiden, he sends over to Naples and procures a sheet of note paper and an envelope, stamped with as many flowers, transfixed hearts and Cupids as can well be put on them, He then goes to the hunchback, who unites the two qualities of letter-carrier for the stranger, and letter-writer for all the islanders who cannot write; but often, even when the young lover can write, he is diffident of his power to express all his feelings, and on this important occasion the hunchback's services are required. The hunchback concocts an epistle, which savours very much of 'The Complete Letterwriter', only it completely outdoes it, and the swain chooses one of his female relatives, either his mother or aunt, to carry this expression of his love to the mother of his beloved. The messenger dresses herself in her best clothes, puts on all her rings, chains, lockets and other gold or gilt ornaments, and, having first wrapped up the letter in a piece of an old newspaper or her handkerchief to prevent any of the Cupids or transfixed hearts from becoming soiled, proceeds to deliver it. The two old women then sit down, and, after the letter has been carefully unfolded and delivered, drink a glass of wine, and talk on indifferent subjects, until some one can be found who can read the letter; but as it is usually couched in such flowery and high-flown sentences that neither of the mothers understand a word of it, the mother of the young man then explains to the other the cause of her visit, which was already guessed, for the beautifully stamped envelope and the grande tenue of the embassadress have already betrayed the secret of her mission. The matter is then fully discussed. On the one side, Pasquale has been coral-fishing, or has gone on some long voyages, and has laid aside already two or three hundred francs; in another year, or, at the most, in two years more, he will have money enough to buy all the furniture, and, in the meantime, is anxious to send to Carmela, in case her mother has no objections to the marriage, a gold locket, or a gold ring with two hearts joined emblematically on it, and will probably add a gold necklace to this gift before many months. On the other side, Carmela has been carrying stones, lime or other burdens on her head for the last two or three years, and has bought already some house-linen, and has a little money laid up, which will be used for the same purpose; at the farthest, in one or two years, she will have all her own, and the house-linen ready. Then, when the parents of both are dead, their little vineyards and olive orchards will be divided equally among their children, and thus the future will be provided for. Two old dowagers could not discuss and determine the marriage settlements of their children with more shrewdness than these two old peasant women, who have gained almost every penny they possess by the sweat of their brows. Finally, when everything has been fully settled, Pasquale and Carmela become betrothed; there is no ceremony at the betrothal, but Pasquale immediately sends the ring or locket, which is followed by presents of a like nature. The gold is only twelve carats fine, and is not by any means solid, but makes a famous show for the money spent. If any trouble should occur, and Carmela should take it into her head that Giuseppe is richer or handsomer than Pasquale, and Giuseppe wishes to marry her, she may dismiss Pasquale, but must give him back all the finery she has received from him; if Pasquale has a quarrel with Carmela, or, for any other reason, leaves her without explaining himself, to transfer his affections to Mariuccia, then he is very apt to lose all his presents. When a dispute arises as to whose fault has brought about a breaking up of the betrothal, the priest is called in, and his judgment is considered final on the question of the presents.

The betrothed couple are allowed to see each other freely, but a sharp eye is kept on them by the relatives of Carmela. Finally, when Pasquale has purchased a double bed, a dozen chairs, two chests of drawers, three or four framed pictures in flaming colours of San Costanzo and some other saints, he then usually buys an image of the Bambino or Christ-child, which must have its glass case, and occupies in the modern Italian household the same position occupied by Cupid in the old Latin. The parents of Pasquale notify the parents of Carmela that everything is ready on their side. The parents of Carmela then notify in due form the parents of Pasquale that Carmela has everything also ready, and on a certain day all her possessions will be laid out for view, and will then be counted and their value appraised. On the day appointed, the wearing apparel, house-linen and cooking utensils of Carmela are exposed to the view of relatives and friends who come to witness the counting and appraisement. Every article is written down with the price affixed, and Carmela keeps the list with great care so that, in the future, should any question arise she can show that she did not marry empty-handed. Pasquale has rented or possesses an apartment, which usually consists of a large, comfortable room and a kitchen; there, all the possessions of the couple are carried, and in the afternoon of the day before the wedding they receive their friends and relatives. A glass of wine or liqueur is given to each visitor, and a Tarantella is danced.

On the day of the wedding, the bride and groom, dressed in their best, walk in procession, followed by the invited relatives, friends and 'compare', or best man, to the church, where they are married a second time, for the civil marriage has already been performed by the mayor at the municipality, either the day before, or a few hours before the religious ceremony. After the marriage, and on the way back from church, friends await the

Habits and Customs

procession and throw grain mixed with flowers on the heads of bride and groom. Flowers betoken wishes for happiness, and grain augures a fruitful union; it is an old Latin custom, and a very pretty one. If the bride be in a condition which does not correspond with the virgin white of the orange-blossoms on her head, then her enemies throw white and black beans on her, or before her, and sometimes, to such an extent that the streets become slippery and dangerous to those walking in the procession. On leaving the church, the compare, who has a bag filled with coppers or sweetmeats, throws them among the children, who attend outside the church door; the children then follow or procede the procession, as it is the custom to throw sweetmeats to them, when grain and flowers are thrown at the bridal pair. The procession proceeds to the house of the parents of the bridegroom, where a dinner is served, which, if not of the best according to Capri tastes, meets with severe criticisms from the assembled guests, because each one of them has sent a present to the married couple, and expects a return in the shape of a tickled palate and full stomach. The bride sits at the head of the table, and the compare, who always pays for the gold ring of the bride, has the seat of honour at her right, while the groom sits at her left, and the invited guests, according to their rank, are seated in the vicinity of the married couple. The young men have provided themselves with sacks of sweetmeats, and during the meal throw them at the young women, the prettier the girl, the more sweetmeats she receives in her face, or on the head; she throws them back, and a general war ensues, which is sometimes annoying to any gentleman or lady who may be among the guests; for the sweetmeats are hard, and the young men and women have strong arms, and hurl their sweet missiles with a force which is supposed to be in a ratio to the intensity of their affections; but as their aim is not always of the surest, many of the sweetmeats strike the gentler guests in the face, or on the head, and, if they have the good sense to throw off their dignity for a short while, and mix in the contest, they will soon be promoted to the post of honour, and become marks at which showers of projectiles will be directed. The father, mother, brothers, sisters and cousins of the groom wait on the table, and a destruction of comestibles goes on, which would excite the envy of a Gargantua. A hilarity, always tempered with the gentilezza of the Italian, accompanies the feast from beginning to end, but when dozens and dozens of bottles of wine have been absorbed, and stomachs are filled to repletion with eatables, then the fun arrives at so high a pitch, that only the quick springs and dizzy whirls of the Tarantella or Trescone can satisfy the animal spirits of the guests. Between the dances a song or two is sung, whose allusions would shock the prudery of our civilized, nineteenth century, but in this assembly are received with a jovial smile, and hearty applause. But, in the course of the evening, the strongest legs get wearied and the sleepiness, which comes from well filled stomachs and unaccustomed late hours, overpowers every one, so that about nine or ten o'clock, every one bids the married couple good night, and they are escorted to their home, accompanied by their respective parents. In the morning the mother of the bridegroom carries two cups of chocolate to the couple, and the bride gives her chemise and the sheets of her bed to her mother-in-law, who shows them to the relatives and friends of the bridegroom, to prove that her daughter-in-law is a 'buona ragazza'. The bride does not issue from her home until the first Sunday or holyday comes, and then she goes forth accompanied by her husband, the compare, and the near relations of the bridal pair. On that day the parents of the bride give a dinner, which is only a repetition of the one already described.

As a rule, the peasant eats every day an almost incredible amount of bread, to this he adds boiled beans with oil and raw onions as condiments, or a salad composed of boiled potatoes, or herbs very often gathered among the wild plants, which are edible and palatable. On Sundays and other holydays he eats macaroni, and in summer, when there are plenty of vegetables, he confines himself to all sorts of boiled and fried dishes of these, and they are very good even to the palate of the foreigner. He eats meat, except in case of a wedding or some other like festive occasion, only four times a year, viz. at Christmas, at Epiphany, at Easter and on the day of San Costanzo, the patron saint of the island. The men have no particular dress, and the old Neapolitan fishing caps are seen only on the heads of very old men, while the others wear hats and caps of all shapes, colours and nationalities. Manchester and its cheap fabrics have triumphed over the old, picturesque costumes of the women, though occasionally a blue bodice and skirt, gathered below the waist, are seen to remind one, in part, of the former costumes described by Hadrava. In Anacapri at the festa of Saint Antonio, their patron saint, old women may still be seen in quaintly cut, old, silk garments of delicately faded tints, but the march of modern ideas induces the Capriotes, both men and women, to ape the modern manner of dress, and on Sundays or holydays, these ambitious peasants can be seen in the piazza, coming out of, and entering the church, or standing about, with their shapely limbs and bodies in such ill fitting garments that any ordinary tailor or milliner would shudder in despair that such crimes against their art should go unpunished.

The hatred between the people of Capri and Anacapri is as strong now as it was centuries ago. A wealthy Capriote, who has occupied the post of town-councillor of the town of Capri, has travelled in many parts of the world, and should have gotten rid of this petty, local hatred, is in the habit of venting his indignation against Anacapri and the Anacapriotes in a manner which compels him to appear in a light somewhat degrading as the son of his father, 'These people of Anacapri,' he is wont to say, 'are born thieves and liars, they are always quarrelling with one another, and going to law. They cannot help it, the very air of Anacapri makes them thieves, whether they wish to be or not. You never see one of them without a sack on his shoulder, to hide in it what he has stolen. Now there is my own father, he was born in Anacapri, and can never go down to my boat-house without stealing a rope, or a bolt, or something which he can sell for a few sous, and then goes off and buys rum with it. He cannot help it, he was born in such an atmosphere as Anacapri, and I cannot blame him. I never let him carry a sack, because I know he will be up to his old tricks, and, who knows? he might be arrested for stealing, and be sent to jail. Every time he goes into my boat house, when I hear of it, I examine his pockets, and always find a bolt, or an iron pin, or something which can be carried off easily. There is no need of his stealing, because we children give him everything he can want. I cannot understand it; these people of Anacapri must steal!' As a matter of course, the people of Anacapri consider the air of Capri woefully deleterious to all moral principle, and wonder how an honest stranger can remain any length of time among such corrupted and evil specimens of humanity. Among these good natured people, it is strange to see this hate, which has come down through so many centuries. It is probably a hate of races. The Anacapriote is almost a pure Greek; blue eyes and fair hair are predominant, and he delights in a broad, sonorous sound of his vowels, which recalls the Greek language; but the Capriote is a mixture of everything, Greek, Latin, Arabic, Turkish, Spanish and French features greet the visitor at every turn, to mark the various conquests of this sun-bathed island, which has been in the track of contending races and civilizations for thousands of years.

Among these descendants of the Sirens, a quarrel or appiccico between two women is an event worth seeing and hearing. A short time ago, a painter employed a boy named Pasquale, to carry his painting impedimenta for him to the various points of the island where he wished to work, and as Pasquale found time hang heavy on his hands while the painter was working, he induced his next door neighbour and ordinary companion, Peppino, to accompany him. These two amused themselves, when Pasquale's services were not required, either by robbing fruit, hunting up birds, catching lizards and pinching off their tails, gambling, lying idly on their backs, and trying to look the sun in the face, with the happy unconsciousness of animals whose bodily organs are all in good order and functioning normally; or watching curiously the painter, and wondering why a man, who was rich enough to wear a gold watch and chain, and who always found pennies in his pocket when he put his hand into it, should bother himself with working. One day, on returning from his painting, the artist, tired of having been in a stooping posture over his easel for a long time, and tempted by the high animal spirits of Pasquale and Peppino, amused himself by throwing stones at Pasquale, who showed a remarkable agility in dodging them. But unfortunately, a stone, intended for Pasquale, struck Peppino, who was grinning at Pasquale's gymnastics, full in the face. The skin was cut slightly, and blood flowed freely. Peppino, a little hurt but more scared at the sight of the blood, cried and yelled like one possessed. The painter, anxious to still his cries, and dry his tears, gave him a franc, whereupon peace was restored immediately. Pasquale accompanied the painter to his hotel, and, when out of hearing, held the following discourse with Peppino.

'Now look here, Peppino, you know the painter threw that stone at me, and if he had not thrown it at me, he would never have hit you, therefore you must give me the half of that franc.'

'No', said Peppino, 'he gave me the money because he hurt me badly, and if I had not cried and yelled so loudly, he would have given me only a penny. I will give you half a penny but no more.'

Peppino changed the franc and gave Pasquale the half-penny, but he had made a mistake in acknowledging that Pasquale had any lien whatever on the franc, and Pasquale, being much stronger than he, helped himself to half a franc. Peppino went home, crying, and related his adventure to his mother, Carmela. Now Carmela was already in a bad humour with Teresina, the mother of Pasquale, because of various little misunderstandings, which are apt to arise between next door neighbours, and the scirocco wind had been blowing for two days, and Carmela's nerves were a little strung by its hot breath. She walked up to the door of Teresina's house, but found it closed, and no one was within; however, with the intention of giving Teresina a bit of her mind and temper, she awaited her arrival. Teresina was in the Piazza, and there met her son, Pasquale, who related the story of the half franc to his mother, and, like a good son, handed her this proof of his diplomatic and military skill. Elated at Pasquale's ability in having gotten his rightful portion from Peppino, she invested the half-franc in chestnuts, and then went home with her son; both of them munching the chestnuts as they went. On seeing Carmela before her door, it may be that she saw there was trouble brewing, and wished to conciliate, or it may be that she was animated with the generosity of a conqueror, and offered a handful of chestnuts to her neighbour. Carmela took them, looked at them for a moment, then at Teresina, then, with a quick, spiteful jerk, threw them at Teresina's door. 'Oh! and you rob my son to buy chestnuts! do you?' This was the challenge thrown in the face of Teresina, who accepted it immediately.

'And you call it robbery, when my Pasquale takes what is his own?'

'Yes, I call it robbery. But what can you expect from the son of such a mother, who has put horns on the head of her husband, and who, before she was married, put horns on her brothers and father?'

'What! and you have the face to tell me this, when everybody in Capri knows that I am an honest woman? By the soul of your mother, who put horns on your father's head before you were born! and you! you have been following in her steps ever since you were old enough! I'll show you who you are talking to!'

Thus both sides opened fire, and, in utter disregard of each other's broadsides, kept on hurling imprecations, ejaculations and vituperations at each other for ten minutes or more. By this time, those living in the neighbourhood had assembled to watch the appiccico, and among the spectators were the husbands of the two women. They said nothing, but lit their pipes and smoked quietly, looking at each other occasionally through their smoke, and seeming rather glad that all this feminine electricity should find vent on other heads than their own. The combatants, meanwhile, had lashed themselves into a rage. Their large, black eyes were dilated, and flashed with insane fury; foam issued from the corners of their mouths; their tresses came down over their shoulders, and writhed, and turned, and twisted like black serpents with every movement; hands and arms were thrown wildly, with quick jerks, in every direction, and finally they commenced swaying their bodies to and fro, screaming out, at the highest pitch of their voices, every ignominious epithet or scandalous story they had ever heard, or could invent, in tones which became fiercer and hoarser as the battle proceeded. Each combatant seemed to take pleasure in unburdening herself, without paying the slightest heed to the abuse of the other.

The mantle of those old Greek and Latin women, who used to celebrate the Dionysian feasts with an orgy of Baccanalian and divine fury, must have fallen on these two, their descendants. Finally Carmela, whose rage had attained such a pitch, that words and screams were no longer a sufficient vent for it, commenced scratching her own cheeks and pulling out her own hair. Teresina followed her example, and as she held a handful of hair in her doubled up fist, impelled by rage and self-inflicted pain, she suddenly approached Carmela, and, giving a vigorous slap with her open hand on Carmela's open mouth, filled it with hair. Carmela spluttered out the hair, and sprang at Teresina with outstretched fingers, but she had not given more than one good scratch, when the two husbands, considering that the appiccico had gone far enough, quickly approached the combatants, and each, placing his arm around his wife, carried her off to his house, pushed her in, closed the door, locked it, and then quietly resumed his smoking. The public, seeing that the spectacle was at an end, quickly dispersed, and left the two husbands alone.

'Well, they have had it out with one another,' said one.

'Yes, and we will have quiet in our houses for a month or two,' said the other.

Thus ended the appiccico. Teresina and Carmela wished to ignore one another's existence, but the parish priest, after wisely letting them sleep for a night, sent for them the next morning and ordered them to make up their quarrel on the spot; thus their old friendship and kindly, neighbourly feelings were renewed, until another appiccico should occur, to break the monotony of their ordinarily amiable existences.

The difference between the type of face and form of the Capriotes, and of the other types around the Bay of Naples has struck nearly every visitor to Capri. Here the women are so handsome, well formed, and tidy, and look so fresh and healthy, whereas at and around Sorrento, Castellamare, Naples and Pozzuoli, there is something very common and vulgar in the faces of the peasant women, and their forms have none of the grace, erectness and springiness, which characterize the Capri women in their walk. There is always something unkempt and slatternly in their dress and persons, and their skins are yellow and wrinkled at an early age; in strong contrast with the neat persons and dresses, and the healthy colour and smooth skins of the Capriotes. Many visitors to the island, interested in ethnological studies, have thought of this question, but have never found a solution to the problem. Fortunately, last winter, the question was solved. As a premise to this solution it should be stated that when Sir Hudson Lowe was in Capri he had only Corsicans and Maltese under his command. Last winter, Colonel Smith, a gallant Irishman who had passed many years in India and had made ethnological studies among the hill tribes, expressed his wonder, at a table d'hôte in Capri, on this difference, and, after eulogizing the beauty of the Capriotes, inquired of his neighbour if she had ever heard any reason which might account for this difference. His neighbour was a countrywoman of the Colonel and a married lady of middle age. She replied, 'Sure, Colonel, and don't you know?' Then with a conscious air, and dropping her voice to a whisper, she added: 'You know we are two old married persons, Colonel, so that you will think nothing of my reminding you that when Sir Hudson Lowe was in possession of Capri, two Irish regiments were stationed here.'

A curious story which had its solution only two years ago, is well worth recounting here, to show the manner of thought of the Capri peasant. Some twenty years ago, a peasant and his wife had born to them a son, with a hare lip. Now the peasants of Capri have a horror of anything ugly, which they have inherited from the old religion of the Beautiful as taught by their Latin and Greek forefathers, and which the Christian religion, after so many centuries, has not been able to eradicate, even when it comes in conflict with the laws of humanity. The father and mother determined to send their ugly offspring to the Foundling hospital in Naples. They dared not expose it to the inclemency of the elements on the shore of the sea, as the old Romans would have done, for the fear of the modern law, which punishes child murder, was before them, so they gave the child to the midwife, who complied with the legal formalities required, and took it to the hospital. There the hare lip was operated, and the operation was so successful that little or no sign was left of the former disfigurement. A shoemaker, who was childless, had made a vow to the Virgin on his sickbed that, in case he got well, he would adopt one of the foundlings, who are called around the Bay of Naples by the poetic name of 'children of the Madonna', and on going to the hospital he chose the child of the Capri peasants. It happened that the peasant's property was near the landing place of the steamers, and gradually his little house was turned into a hotel and by means of the hotel and his land, he waxed rich. One of his daughters married a visitor to the hotel, and, as the marriage raised her above her old level, the other children aspired to the same good fortune.

Time went on, and the passing years made the peasant and his wife forget all about the poor, disfigured child, who had been entrusted to the tender mercies of a large hospital, where a great many of the children meet an untimely death. Their other children either knew nothing about this brother, or had forgotten him, and would never have known anything, had it not been for the conscription law of Italy. The good shoemaker had brought up the boy as his own son, and had never told him the secret of his birth; but when he attained the age of eighteen, he was compelled to

Habits and Customs

appear before the authorities to draw his number, and among the formalities, it is necessary to show a certificate of birth from the Register. But as the Registrar of births in Naples could find no mention of the foundling in the Register of that city, the shoemaker was obliged to divulge his secret, and search was made among the records of the Foundling hospital for information concerning the boy's previous history; there were found the name of the midwife, who had brought him over, and the names of the parents, as the law required. So on a bright spring morning, the shoemaker and his adopted son took the steamer to commence a hunt for the real parents. On landing, the hotel of the father was pointed and the pair presented themselves to the father: 'I am your son,' said the youth.

'What! you are my son? All my sons are here, except one who is in America.'

'Yes, but you forget a son you sent to Madonna eighteen years ago, and here I am to get a certificate of birth from you and the Registrar for the conscription. Look at this paper from the hospital! Do you believe it now?'

The paper was read and the father was compelled to acknowledge all the facts contained therein. Another paper was then given to the astonished father, which demanded a certificate of birth of his son to be signed by him and by the Registrar of births, or by the Sindaco of Capri, to fulfil the formalities exacted by the conscription law. The shoemaker and his adopted son were invited to enter the house, but the long-lost child was not received with open arms. The parents disliked having the evidence of their unnatural cruelty before their eyes, and the other children considered him an interloper, who came to take away from them a portion of the patrimony for which they had laboured for years to augment. The son departed with the shoemaker for Naples, carrying the required certificate, and drew a good number, so that he was not obliged to go into the army. On finding out that his real father was a comparatively rich man, he was no longer content with his modest position as apprentice to a shoemaker; but on his return he was treated with so much contumely by his newly-found relatives that he was glad to kick the dust of Capri from his shoes, and return to his adopted father and his shoemaker's bench in Naples, where, it is hoped, he found the content and peace of mind which he enjoyed before knowing anything of his long-lost and rich relatives in Capri.

Chapter 7
Description

On arriving at Capri, the traveller should take the first opportunity to go around the island in a row boat; this short tour, which lasts from two to three hours, cannot be too highly recommended. The rugged formation of the rocks, their variegated colours, the deep blue or light greenish blue of the water, and the wonderfully beautiful grottoes, with their mysterious sounds, make these few hours seem like time spent in fairyland.

Starting from the pier at the Grande Marina and going west, in a few moments can be seen near the water's edge the cloaca of the old town of Capri; on the shore, and in the water immediately in front, lie broken masses of masonry, which were the continuation of it. Instead of dipping towards the sea, as it did originally, it dips now landwards. From this cloaca to the little church of San Costanzo, and from thence to the military drill ground is a triangular space in which the old town of Capri was situated. In every part of this space are seen old walls and on excavating, cisterns, sewers, streets and the walls of houses have been found. During the last century, a marble tablet was discovered here, on which was chiseled, in finely cut Greek letters, edicts to be observed by the population; tumults were forbidden, and a series of special rules were laid down, not only for the inhabitants of the town but for those inhabiting the public fields outside the town walls.

The church of San Costanzo has the basilica form, and archeologists agree that it was an old temple dedicated to one of the Olympic deities. Some years ago, on excavating inside the church, old Byzantine frescoes were found on the walls, which fact goes to prove that the Basilica was turned into a place for Christian worship at an early period. There is a tradition on the island that this was the first Christian church in Italy. It was formerly adorned with very fine columns of giallo antico, which were transported to Caserta for the Royal Chapel. To the south of the church and midway up the hill are several cisterns, two of them have an enormous length, and though a large part of these two is filled up with earth washed in through the openings above, yet they are used today by the peasants for

Description

collecting and holding water. A little to the north of this church, in 1810, was found a sarcophagus, in which reposed the bones of a female richly dressed in cloths of gold and silver, with heavy bracelets, earrings and a finger-ring with a cameo. A sceptre, about twenty inches long and adorned with three gold rings, was in her hand, and in her mouth was a gold piece bearing the head and inscription of Vespasian. No name was found, nor was there any inscription, nor any clue, which would serve to clear up the mystery attached to the contents of this sarcophagus. The sceptre and rich robes seem to prove that this woman was of Imperial blood, and, as she was buried after the reign of Vespasian, she may have been the wife or sister of the Emperor Commodus.

Going a little farther west, we see the villa of Mr. Haan perched on the summit of the sea-shore. This was formerly a fort, built by the French on the foundations of what was probably a temple of Isis, as Mr. Haan has dug up in his garden many pieces of Egyptian granite, either with hieroglyphics cut on them, or parts of statues made according to the rules of Egyptian art. On the western side of this villa is the military drill ground; it was the largest level space in old Capri which could have been used as a forum, and it is probable that Augustus came here to witness the games of the Epheboi, and, while supping with these youths, took delight in their frolics and scrambles. On the south side of this drill-ground exist antique arches which served to hold in place the earth transported here to make this level space large. In this vicinity have been discovered, at various times, some thirty or more antique cisterns. A little to the west of this probable forum and on the sea-shore, are the remains of the so-called Baths of Tiberius. At the end of the last century Hadrava excavated here and found two beautiful and well-preserved pavements, one of which he sold to an Englishman, and the other to the Russian countess Woronzoff. In addition to these, he found two fine columns of cipollino marble with a base and capital in Corinthian style, which are now in Naples. He found also two fine columns of portasanta marble with a Corinthian base and capital, and about sixteen hundred weight of precious marbles, variously coloured, which had served for making the pavements and probably the wainscotting of the rooms of this villa. Two columns of red African marble, in an unfinished state, lay here for years, and were probably unearthed by Hadrava. They were sold to a marble cutter in Naples by the municipality of Capri, and were taken away by him a year or two ago. The inscriptions on them were:

DCAE   DCAE

and

NXXI   NXXVIII

which probably meant Domus Caesaris No. 21 and No. 28.

The point which comes first, after leaving the Baths of Tiberius, is called Trasele, this word may be a corruption of the name of Thrasyllus, who was a celebrated astrologer and companion of Tiberius, or it may come from a word used in the Capri dialect, which is a corruption of the Latin 'transitus', and was applied to denote the passage of the quails at this point. Shortly after, is seen the entrance to the cave of Lucina, which is accessible only when the sea is very calm. From the prow of a little boat the visitor scrambles up the rock, and, after lighting a candle, crawls on his hands and knees for several yards through a narrow passage until he enters a large cave, which is lighted by a hole from above. In the cave someone has made a dam of the clay, and has thus formed a little basin in which a pool of fresh water, continually renewed by the drippings from the roof, offers a cool drink to the thirsty.

On returning to the boat and proceeding westward, the shadow of the cliff is seen projected on the water, which assumes an indigo blue colour, and is probably unrivalled for the depth aud beauty of its blue. Numerous holes and small caves can be seen at the water's edge, made by the action of the sea, which rushes in and out with deep, hollow mysterious gurgles; and about sixteen feet above these, appears a line of holes made in the same manner by the sea when the island lay deeper in the water. In a short time the Blue Grotto is reached, and the visitor must enter a small boat, to be shot through the narrow entrance into a scene which is so beautiful that its fame has spread over the world. The change from the noise and glare of the outside to the tempered blue, silvery light and weird quiet of the inside is marvellous; and the visitor expects, every moment, that some grave, long-bearded old Triton will come forward from the darker recesses to welcome him to this fairy home of sirens and mermaids. Kopisch, the German poet and painter, named this grotto the Blue Grotto, 'because the

Description

light, coming from the bottom of the sea and passing through water which resembles blue fire, fills and illuminates, in an astonishing manner, the whole of this large, roomy cavern.' As no words can paint the wondrous beauty of the water, which changes everything into silver, it is left to the readers of this, by a visit, to satiate their senses with its fairy-like marvels. The grotto is about 160 feet long, 85 wide and its greatest height is about 50 feet, while the depth of the water is about 65. In the back part is an arch cut out of the solid rock, and under this arch is a pavement made of unhewn stones and masonry; below this pavement and in front is a ledge hewn out of the rock, and on the right of this ledge are the remains of steps, which probably led down to the sea level when the island stood higher out of the water than it does now. This arch and ledge are artificial, because the marks of the chisel can be plainly seen.

The pavement extends a short distance back of the arch into a passage, and then ceases, but the passage, becoming narrower as it proceeds, extends three or four hundred feet into the mountain. There, the passage ends abruptly, and quantities of clay exist on the floor and sides, to show that it was formed naturally by the action of acidified rainwater dripping through a fissure. Many writers have adopted the theory that this passage was a subterranean entrance to the grotto from some palace above, but a close examination of the sides shows no marks of the chisel, nor any other sign to prove that it is artificial. Since the Blue Grotto has been hollowed out to its present size, it has been about sixteen feet lower in the water than at present, and must have remained at that level some hundreds of years, because a line of holes, which in some cases have a depth of several feet, can be seen running around the inside of the grotto, about sixteen feet above the present sea level. When the Grotto was at this lower level, the sea water could run into the passage at the back, and thus destroyed the continuation of the pavement which now exists under the artificial arch with the pavement in the passage; this latter pavement has been cracked, and, in great part, destroyed by the rising and subsidence of the island. This passage opens into the Grotto with three large mouths, which have been enlarged by the action of the seawater when the island was lower in the water.

Many writers, and especially the German, claim that the Grotto was discovered first by Kopisch in 1826. Kopisch had passed some time on the island, and in one of his excursions passed the hole which forms the entrance; he asked the boatmen if any one had ever been inside and they replied: 'No, Signor, because that grotto is haunted.' This excited his curiosity, and he proposed to his travelling companion that they should swim in, which they did. On returning to Hotel Pagano, where he was stopping, he wrote a description of what he had seen, which, any one curious enough may see today as it has been carefully preserved. Kopisch was surprised at, and charmed with, the wondrous beauty of the effects produced by the reflection of light through the blue water, and his glowing description attracted the attention of all strangers who visited the island; until finally, many travellers visited Capri only to see the Grotto, and its fame has become so widespread that now a visit to it is considered almost a necessary part of a visit to Naples.

To Kopisch belongs the credit of having made its beauty known to the world, but he cannot be called the first discoverer, because mention was made of it by two writers who lived many years ago. The first of these was Capaccio in his History of Naples, printed in Naples in 1607. He described the entrance 'as very dark but once inside, the grotto broadens out like a bay, and is full of light; and the dropping of water from above gives a most beautiful appearance to the sea water'. In attempting to give a reason for the effect produced, Capaccio made a mistake, which was corrected by Antonio Parrino, who published a description of the Bay of Naples in 1727. Parrino described the Grotto in the same words used by Capaccio, proving that he must have copied them, but he must have visited the Grotto, for he ascribed, with more truth, the beautiful effect produced, to reflection. From 1727 to 1826 no other writer has made any mention of this Grotto, and it is very curious that so beautiful an object of nature should have escaped the observation of such intelligent men as Hadrava, Conte della Torre Rezonico, Breislak and Romanelli, who spent some time on the island towards the end of the last century and whose observations were printed.

To understand the following explanation, it is necessary to visit the Grotto on a day when the sea is calm. The present entrance to the Grotto is through an arch whose height above the present water-level is three feet and a half, the depth of the water under the arch is three feet, which gives

Description

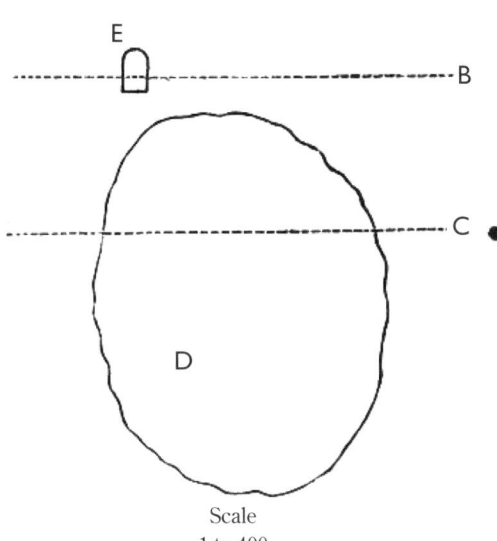

Scale
1 to 400

- A. line of holes inside and outside of the Blue Grotto, formed in the rock by the action of sea-water when the water-level was at that height.
- B. present water-level.
- C. water-level at the time of Tiberius.
- D. large orifice through which day-light, after penetrating the outer water, passes through into the water of the Grotto and produces the illumination peculiar to the Blue Grotto.
- E. present entrance to the Grotto.

MacKowen's schematic illustration of the Blue Grotto.

an arched entrance whose height below and above the water-level amounts to six and a half feet, with a width of three and a half. On close inspection it will be seen that the rock, which forms the floor of this arched entrance, was level, and that this level floor projects several feet into the sea in front of the arch in the shape of a commodious platform. The vertical sides of the entrance meet this level platform at right angles, and it is seen at a glance that this entrance is artificial and has not been formed by the action of the sea water, for under those circumstances the floor would have a round shape. A few feet to the right of the present entrance, and at a depth of seven and a half or eight feet below the water level can be seen the top of a large arch, which widens out until it reaches a profundity of about thirty feet, then the two sides approach each other gradually until they meet, forming thus a large round hole about fifty feet high by forty in width, through which the water of the Bay of Naples flows freely in and out of the Grotto.

To see the shape and size of this hole it is necessary to take a bath in the Grotto, and at a distance of thirty or forty feet from the entrance, by putting the head under water, and keeping the eyes open it can be plainly seen; as the Grotto is illuminated by this hole, and as the water is very clear, it appears like a large silvery-blue blot on the surface of the dark rock. As it is certain that the island of Capri was twenty feet higher out of the water during the time of Tiberius than at present, the Blue Grotto during his reign was not blue, and presented a very different appearance from what it does now. Then, the old entrance, whose top is now seven or eight feet under water, was twelve or thirteen feet above, and a large boat could pass easily in and out. Here Tiberius could come and pass the day agreeably in its cool shade, and take his bath and siesta when the hot scirocco wind was blowing. But, as every one knows who has spent several hours in a cave of this kind, though at first the temperature is very cool and pleasant, yet after an hour or two, on account of the want of ventilation, the air becomes impure and oppressive, therefore an opening, six feet and a half high, was cut through the rock, four feet and a half above the top of the old entrance, and this opening furnishes today the only means of access to the interior of the Grotto.

About eight years ago a flight of steps, which leads down to the water in front of this entrance, was cut out of the solid rock; this was only a renovation of an old flight of steps, which was built in ancient times but had been very much injured and almost totally destroyed by the action of the waves. Remains of the old Roman masonry may still be seen under a modern wall, which has been pierced to make room for the new flight of

Description

steps. To the left of the entrance is a hole, partly cut out of the solid rock and partly formed of ancient Roman masonry; it has the peculiar shape common to the holes made by the Romans for holding a beam of wood; one end of a beam was supported in this hole, while the other end rested on the outer side of the ancient stairway which led from the platform in front of the present entrance to the villa above the Grotto. This beam was most probably the top of a balustrade which served to prevent any one from falling into the sea when going up or down the steps, and formed a loggia of the platform, which, in ancient times, was sixteen or seventeen feet above the level of the sea. The ancient flight of steps led down to this loggia, and from it one could pass into the Grotto dry shod through the opening, which served thus the double purpose of ventilator and as a means of entrance into the Grotto for the inhabitants of the palace above. But as the floor of this opening was sixteen feet above the sea level, some means of descending probably existed. A flight of steps made of wood, or hewn out of the rock, or built of masonry may have furnished a means of descent; at present nothing can be seen which would serve to prove the existence of a stairway, and it may be that the action of the water for centuries, or earthquakes, or the subsidence and upheaval of the island may have destroyed every vestige of what, in ancient times, formed a means of access to the water's edge. From the ledge under the artificial arch inside the Grotto, remains of a descent can be plainly seen, and it is possible that this ledge was in communication with the present entrance, by means of a walk of some material, which was fixed to the side of the Grotto.

During the time of Tiberius the Grotto was illuminated by means of an entrance, which was twelve feet high and thirty or more wide, so that no such beautiful effect of light existed as now. It owes now its exceptional beauty to the fact that through the present entrance very little light can enter, but the sun's rays, passing through the indigo blue water, are refracted, and therefore decomposed; the blue water absorbs the red and yellow rays, and by polarization and reflection the light, which strikes on the snowy white sand of the bottom, passes through the large submerged hole, which puts the waters of the Grotto in communication with those of the Bay of Naples. This light enters the Grotto from the north, and any object floating on or in the water of the Grotto has its northern side silvered by these rays of light coming through the submerged hole, but its southern side retains its original colour.

Immediately above the Grotto are the ruins of a palace, which, from the delicately sculptured marble capitals, and the richly coloured marbles found there, was probably one of the Imperial villas. Last summer excavations were made by Colonel MacKowen, and he found fragments of statues, many bits of valuable, coloured marbles for pavements, capitals of coloured marble, columns and other things, which proved the richness with which this palace was adorned. The building is of a large size, and extends a great length. It is possible that it was destroyed by the same earthquake, mentioned by Suetonius, which threw down the lighthouse of Capri; and later someone rebuilt it, for, from the various kinds of reticulata it is evident that additions and reparations were made to it at a later epoch than that of Tiberius. At the time when it was abandoned, it appears that some one was repairing it, for large pits filled with slaked lime were found during the excavations of last summer. To the right of this palace is a small fort, built by the French to prevent the English from landing here, as there is a well preserved, antique flight of steps leading up from the sea, and on this account the fort and this part of the island are called Gradelle. In ancient times these steps enabled persons to land and mount to the palace above the Grotto, or even to Anacapri. It was the ancient landing place for the Anacapriotes, as it is now for those who arrive by the steamers and wish to go directly to Anacapri. Mangoni says that in his time, about fifty years ago, the traces of a road from the Gradelle to Damecuta were plainly visible, but these traces have been obliterated, probably by earth brought down by the rains, which has completely covered them.

Damecuta possesses important ruins, and the word is probably a corruption from the Latin Domus Augusti. Unfortunately, the owners of the land on which these ruins exist destroy or cover up with earth everything they find, to prevent strangers from visiting this point, as they are afraid lest, in passing through their little vineyards and orchards, visitors may cause damage to their fruits and vegetables; therefore nothing of interest can be seen. Many antique objects have been dug up here, which have been sold to the first buyer, but no serious attempt to excavate has ever been made. The tower of Damecuta, near the ruins, was built as

Description

a watch tower and place of refuge against the Saracens. It was on the level space of Damecuta that the English troops under Major Hamill were camped, and from this place they marched down to meet the French under General Lamarque. Between Damecuta and Anacapri several ruins have been found, the most important of which is a very large and well-preserved cistern, and on this account the place is called Pozzo. This cistern is divided into three parts; each part is 138 feet long by 120 wide, and communicates with one another by means of arches. It was, possibly, the substructure of a large palace. The antique plaster of the walls is so well preserved that the cistern, without having been repaired, still holds a large quantity of water. The antique opening is in a good state of preservation and is still used for the purpose of drawing up water, which is used by the inhabitants in time of drought for drinking, but ordinarily for washing.

On continuing to row westward, Punta Vitareta, the north west corner of the island, is soon reached, and shortly after rounding it the French battery of Orica is seen, near which, at the water's edge, still exists some masonry erected by the French at the place where General Lamarque commenced his successful attack. Between Punta Capocchia and Punta Campetiello an extensive and charming view of the whole western slope of the island appears. Cactus plantations on the rocks, and olive groves on the richer soil give a pleasing foreground, while back of these Monte Solaro stands up with its dark, rugged front in strong contrast to the verdant slopes which go down to the sea. Up the hill stands out prominently a windmill, erected by the French for grinding grain, and farther to the right the well preserved and picturesque tower of Materita, which was erected by the Carthusian monks to protect their goats and afford shelter to their peasants and goatherds against the Saracen Corsairs.

At the Punta di Campetiello and at the Punta di Pino are French batteries. After passing the last mentioned Cape, appears on the hillside the Torre della Guardia built for protection against the Saracens, and a little below it is a line of walls erected by the French, through which passes the road from Anacapri to the first class lighthouse situated on the Punta di Carena; this is the southwest corner of the island. On turning this point, and rowing east, the scenery changes; the rocks are jagged, and jut up out of the water almost perpendicularly to heights varying from three to eighteen hundred feet. Exposed to the south and the hot rays of the sun, the colours of this rocky wall glow with warmth, in striking contrast with the cold greens and blues of the water bathing its feet. The first object of interest is the Red Grotto, the roof and sides of which have a deep red colour in places, which is due to the presence of a red lichen growing on the damp surface of the rock.

The Green Grotto, a few yards only from the Red, is also called the Turk's Grotto, because, according to tradition, one day in the early dawn of the morning, some Capriotes fishing here were surprised by the Saracens. The fishermen ran their boat through this grotto, and plying their oars as best they could when they came out on the other side, succeeded in reaching the Piccola Marina, and gave the alarm before the Saracens could land; for the Corsairs supposed, from the proximity of the Red and Green Grottoes, that the Capriotes had entered the Red, or, not knowing that there was a means of exit on the east side of the Green, thought they were safely entrapped in one or the other Grotto, and thus lost valuable time in hunting for them. The Green Grotto is considered by some to be more beautiful than the Blue; the shape of the roof and of the sides is certainly more picturesque, and the colours are more intense, but the weird impression produced by the Blue is altogether wanting. In a certain angle of the Grotto the smell of sulphur is quite strong, and when the sea is agitated, this smell becomes much stronger. Tradition says that formerly a spring of sulphureous water, which spurted up above the surface of the sea, existed a short distance in front of the cave, but now no signs of it can be found except the smell. The roof and sides of this Grotto have a yellowish tinge, as though derived from the action of sulphureous vapours coming in contact with them, and it is probable that the Green Grotto gets its exceedingly vivid green colour from the mixing of the yellow of the sulphur with the blue of the sea.

From the Green Grotto to the Punta di Mulo is the grandest scenery on the island. Monte Solaro shoots up almost perpendicularly eighteen hundred feet; its rough, ragged sides, many coloured, and seamed by the beating rains and thunderbolts of thousands of years, in contrast with the placid, blue sky above, and the clear greenish blue and violet waters below, form a picture which will always be remembered with delight by every

Description

lover of Nature. The Piccola Marina is called by the islanders Mulo, which is a corruption of the Latin Moles or Italian Molo, for here exist the remains of a pier or mole which dates from ancient times. It probably extended much further into the water, but the convulsions of Nature, and, as it is from its position exposed to the action of the winter storms, the beating of the waves have reduced it to its present size. The term Mulo was applied originally only to the pier, but the peasants and fishermen gradually applied it to the Piccola Marina, using this name alternately with its other name Sirena, which recalls the old tradition of the Sirens.

Immediately beyond the Piccola Marina is the hill called Castiglione with a mediaeval castle on its top, which was built against the Saracens. The outer walls of this castle towards the north are very massive and well preserved, but the parapet on the southern side, and the walls to the west have fallen down. A modern structure inside the castle was erected at the beginning of this century, and was used first as a chapel and hermitage, but was afterwards turned into a powder magazine by the English and French. Under this castle is a very large cave, accessible only from above and from the west by means of a narrow and dangerous path. Within the cave are remains of walls, which date from the times of Tiberius, and, from their massiveness, they probably supported structures of grand proportions. The antique entrance to this cave was from the east, but this old means of access has been destroyed by time, or by the Capriotes of the middle ages, who made a way from the west side, which led from the castle on top of the hill by an extremely narrow path down into the cave, but in such a manner that one or two determined men could hold it against a hundred; and doubtless this cave formed a last place of refuge for the wives and children as well as the men, in case the castle should have fallen into the hands of the Saracens. It is very probable that the Saracens have been here, for the structures and defences of the middle ages have been destroyed, and the cistern, built to collect water for the refugees, has been partially destroyed and filled up. This is the largest cave in Capri, and if properly excavated might furnish something interesting to the archaeologist. An ancient wall of reticulata from the best times and built against the back part of the cave still exists, but the floor is so filled with fallen stones and rubbish that it is impossible to determine the plan of the structures and their probable use. The antique way to the east put this cave in communication with several palaces or villas dating from the Tiberian times.

On the northeast side of the Castiglione Hadrava commenced his first excavations in Capri, in 1786. He found a house of five rooms, the walls of which were beautifully frescoed with colours as fresh as though they had been laid on only a few days. In the first, second and third rooms were found many bits of coloured marbles, tiles and fragments of stucco. The only thing of value exhumed here was a very fine vase of white marble, weighing more than 160 pounds, with figures in bas-relief of exquisite design and finish, which represented a sacrifice. It was sold to Mr. Stevens, an Englishman. In the fourth room was discovered a very fine pavement, probably the most perfect and best preserved of all the antique pavements now known. It was sold to the king of Naples, who placed it in the Favorita palace at Portici, but it was afterwards transferred to the palace of Capodimonte, where it can now be seen. There was also found a fragment of a well-executed bas-relief representing a sacrifice, and among the figures was that of Tiberius; this was sold to Prince Schwartzenberg, the Austrian ambassador at Naples. In the fifth room the workmen found nothing of value. During these excavations were found two heads of boys in marble, the one crying, and the other laughing; these came into the possession of the German sculptor, Trippel. A very fine cameo with the head of Germanicus cut on it, found here, was sent to the Empress Catherine of Russia. Hadrava excavated there also another cameo, bas-reliefs, tiles with the name of the maker stamped on them, lamps, and bits of delicately worked stucco; but they were all of mediocre value and he presented them to the painter Tischbein and to Sir William Hamilton, who was at that time the English ambassador in Naples. Acqueducts led to all these rooms, and in one room were found the conveniences for heating up water; proving that this was a bath, which probably was near some palace situated a little below it towards Valentino. All the peasants in the Valentino have found in their vineyards variously coloured marbles, bronzes, and Greek inscriptions on marble tablets. Above this bath-house were probably large cisterns, because Hadrava found in the acqueducts made of masonry several hundred weight of leaden pipe leading up the hill, but

Description

these cisterns have never been uncovered and rest, probably in a good state of preservation, under the earth. According to the contract made by Hadrava with the owner of the land, he was compelled to cover up his excavations with earth and replant the ground with vines, so that now it is not known where the exact spot is under which these interesting ruins are buried.

Beyond the Castiglione is the Grotto dell'Arsenale, and immediately in front of its entrance is an inclined plane, which is evidently artificial. The entrance is lofty, and the cave itself is of a large size; it has an elliptical shape, and is 130 feet long by 100 wide and 50 high. The antique floor is covered with sand and stones which have been thrown on it by the sea, but on digging down three or four feet this floor comes to light; it is composed of a concrete made by mixing volcanic cinders and broken bits of pottery with lime, and then beaten into a hard mass. On the right of the cave is some ancient masonry, which was a tomb, as human bones were found inside when it was broken open; but this tomb seems to have been built later than the rest of the structures in the cave. On the left and at the back are two small rooms, in each of which at a depth of four or five feet a beautiful, marble pavement was found, and both of them were removed. From this fact it may be inferred that these rooms were inhabited in ancient times, and probably by some officer of the Roman fleet, for from its name, which has most probably come down to us from the times of Tiberius, this cave was the arsenal, or storehouse, for the ships which were anchored near the island for the service of the Emperor. The rooms with the pretty pavements could not be inhabited now, because every strong scirocco wind dashes the waves to the very extremity of the cave, bearing quantities of stones and sand with them. Towards the top and in the sides are holes, either cut out of the rock or formed of masonry with the peculiar form used by the Romans for the insertion of beams. One end of a beam was fixed in each hole, and the other end was placed probably on a large pillar erected in the centre of the floor; the beams thus converged and dipped a little towards the centre; on them was placed a roof, which served to carry off the drippings of water from the roof of the cave. By this means a large, dry space was gained, which served admirably for the preservation of naval stores. A part of an old Roman galley was found here imbedded in the sand; it was of iron, and was bought in 1777 by Doctor Giraldi, who carried it away with him. Immediately to the right of the Grotto dell'Arsenale is another small cave, which contains some old Roman masonry. Farther on is the Albergo dei Pescatori or the Fishermen's Hotel, so called because the fishermen on calm nights run their boats in here, and sleep or wait until the moon goes down, as the moonlight prevents the fish from biting. At the back part is an arched entrance, which looks as though it were artificial, and as though in ancient times it had been hewn out to serve as a means of access from the land to the cave.

The Certosa stands perched on the edge of the cliff above. On the eastern side of it antique Roman walls are seen, which serve as foundations for the monastery wall, and it is very probable that the builders of this religious house used antique foundations in a great measure, for many antique walls can be seen in the vicinity. A Tiberian villa must have stood here, and it was very large, as the remains extend under the Certosa and to the verge of the cliff. When it was destroyed, the greater part was either thrown into the sea by an earthquake, or has been washed down and carried over the cliff into the sea by the rain torrents. Remains of this villa, in the shape of pieces of glass and marble mosaic, or fragments of marble pavements and of statues, are washed up from the bottom of the sea by every storm, and are carried into and deposited on the floor of the Grotto dell'Arsenale, where visitors may amuse themselves by seeking for them among the pebbles and sand. To the Certosa, Count Arcucci, its founder, came like another Cardinal Wolsey, poor and disgraced, to end his days among the monks, who owed this Chapter to his generosity. Here he died, and a marble tomb was erected to his memory in the church attached to the monastery, which will not be uninteresting to the stranger. A little to the east of the Certosa, in a place called the Unghia Marina, was discovered in 1826, by Feola, the Royal Inspector of excavations, the remains of a palace whose walls were beautifully frescoed. Feola found a very fine pavement composed of coloured marbles, which he removed and sent to the Museum of Naples, where it now is. The walls of this palace were built mostly of very large bricks, and on some of them was the inscription,

Description

YACINTHI
JULIAE
AUGUSTAE

From this inscription the antiquarians have concluded that this palace was built by Augustus for Julia. These ruins were covered up with earth again and replanted with vines.

To the north of the Unghia Marina are the so-called Camerelle, which run parallel with the road leading from the village of Capri to the Punta di Tragara. Many laughable theories have been advanced by antiquarians to account for the presence of these small cells, and among these theories the most far-fetched are, first, that which makes these cells the notorious Sellaria of Tiberius, and second, that which considers them the remains of an amphitheatre. The Camerelle were a series of cells formed by arches closed at both ends, which were used as cisterns for catching and preserving rain water, and on top of the arches was a road, which led from the Tragara to Capri and the Castiglione. Back of these cells exist other cisterns much larger, and the quantity of water which could be collected in them must have been enormous. A large sewer passes under the Camerelle near the villa Federico; it seems to come from the hill of San Michele and doubtless served to carry off the sewerage from the antique villa of Tiberius, which was built on top of that hill. The cisterns of the Camerelle were not only built to furnish water for the baths and household of Tiberius, but some years ago a canal was discovered which led down to the Port of Tragara, and in this canal were found large leaden pipes, which could have been used only for conveying drinking water to the Roman fleet, which in all probability was stationed there. Before reaching the Albergo dei Pescatori, may sometimes be seen, on a calm day some ten or twelve feet under water, what appears to be a flight of steps, which seems to have been built of masonry or to have been cut out of the solid rock.

The Faraglioni, three in number, form a prominent feature in the landscape of the southern side of the island. The outer one was climbed for the first time, a few years ago, by an Englishman with the help of Spadaro, a native of the island, and a lazy, good-natured vagabond, who infests the Piccola Marina. Spadaro asserts that on the top they found olive trees, serpents, and a peculiar species of blue lizard. For a few francs he is always willing to risk his neck to procure for any stranger interested in Natural History some specimens of these lizards, which seem to form a species peculiar to this rock. The middle Faraglione has a large hole cut through it by the action of the water, through which boats pass without any difficulty or danger. On the top of the inner Faraglione, tradition has it that a marble sarcophagus was found, which was taken down and carried to Naples. The ancient port of Tragara is formed by the inner Faraglione, and, from the fact that the remains of a landing place still exist, it is very probable that this was the port in which the fleet of Tiberius was stationed. As a complete protection against the scirocco wind there must have been a breakwater, either artificial or natural, between the inner Faraglione and the Monacone, but this has entirely disappeared, either through subsidence, earthquakes, the action of the waves, or all three combined. The landing place is at the north-west corner of the port; a flight of steps still exists, and ancient masonry can be seen in the water to the depth of twenty-two feet. This flight of steps, which still remains, is only a part of the flight which led down to the water's edge; the rest has been destroyed by the waves caused by the southwest wind, which brings more rough seas to Capri than any other wind.

On the western side of the port are massive walls, some of which are ancient, and others which were built during the middle ages to prevent the Saracens from landing here. To the south of these walls is the inner Faraglione, on which, as well as on the rock to the west of it, is plainly visible the old water line hewn out of the stone by the action of the waves, when the island was twenty-two feet lower in the water at this point than it is now. This water line is so well preserved, in spite of the disintegrating power of the elements to which it is exposed, that it cannot be many centuries old. The huge boulders massed against the rock to the west of the inner Faraglione, and which were hurled down from above by some convulsion of Nature, probably took their present position when Capri rose to its present level. As this was almost certainly a port, it is an interesting query whether another port existed on the northern part of the island, and especially at the Grande Marina. Tacitus says: 'Capri pleased Tiberius because it stood alone, and had no ports, and small ships could land only with difficulty.' Suetonius says: 'He retired to Capri, being greatly delighted

Description

with the island, because it was accessible only by a narrow beach, being on all sides surrounded with rugged cliffs of a stupendous height, and by a deep sea.' From these extracts it would seem that there was but one beach at Capri, and this beach was undoubtedly on the south side of the island as an arsenal, a pier and a landing place were here. There are no signs of any port on the northern side, and it is possible that the so-called Baths of Tiberius were high above the level of the water at the time of Tiberius, and were not baths at all; for, from the reversal of dip of the ancient cloaca, it is certain that the part of the island lying between Mounts San Michele and Solaro has dropped down several hundred feet since the time when this cloaca was built, and, from the conformation of the Marina Grande, it is possible that during the times of Tiberius there was no beach here but that a cliff, several hundred feet high, took the place of the present beach, and the foot of this cliff stood in water as deep as we find it along the rest of the northern shore of the island. The masses of masonry in the sea, at the mouth of the ancient cloaca, were in part a continuation of the cloaca, and the others have fallen down from above.

The Punta di Tragara is about five hundred feet above the port, and here a peasant lately discovered the remains of a large Roman palace; he found some fifty rooms on the ground floor, and each room was frescoed with the ordinary Pompeian reds and yellows. This may have been the palace of Augustus, from which he saw the funeral honours paid to Masgabas, and which gave rise to the extempore verses recited on that occasion. It is possible that during the time of Tiberius this palace was enlarged and was used to lodge the officers of the fleet stationed in the port. The island of Monacone, to the east of the port, still has the remains of a tomb, from which however the sarcophagus, if one ever existed, has been removed. To visit it a ladder is necessary to gain a hole, through which the visitor passes over rough rocks until he reaches an ancient flight of steps, which leads to a plateau sloping towards the east. The remains of the tomb, which consists of masonry, are on this plateau, and it is probable that here Masgabas, Augustus' engineer who laid out the island, was buried.

At the Cala di Matromania, on looking up, can be seen the mouth of a cave, which to the antiquary and theologian is probably the most interesting object on the island. It should be entered from the top by means of a long flight of steps, which leads down to it from the road going from Capri to the Natural Arch. This part of the island is called Matromania, and the word is a corruption either of 'Magno Mithrae antro', or 'Mithrae antro'. Here was found a marble bas-relief, now in the museum at Naples, representing a priest of Mithras killing a bull, with a lion, a serpent, and a scorpion grouped at the base, and a dog licking the blood as it flows from a wound in the bull's neck. Also, a few years ago, a terra-cotta figure of a priest of Mithras was dug up in the vicinity of this cave. These prove that the Grotto was a temple dedicated to Mithras, the old Sun-god of the Persians; and like most of these temples its entrance is towards the east, so that the first rays of the Divinity could enter His temple, and gild the altar to be greeted with praise, thank-giving and worship by His priests and disciples. An altar of white marble was dug up in the cave, and is now in the British Museum. The form of the cave is oval, it is about ninety feet long by sixty wide, and is almost sixty high. The walls of the temple were built against the sides of the cave and are sufficiently well-preserved to allow the antiquarian to define the original plan. These walls are faced with well-cut reticulata, showing that they were built during the time of the first Caesars, either Augustus or Tiberius; but, as the religion of Mithras was introduced among the Romans, and more especially among the inhabitants of the Bay of Naples at an earlier date than that of the Caesars, it is possible that this cave was dedicated to the worship of Mithras before Augustus or Tiberius came to Capri. As we know that Tiberius studied the Chaldean mysteries and surrounded himself with astrologers, it is probable that he either introduced the astrological religion of Mithras on the island, or that he amplified and enriched this temple, which he already found in existence.

A semicircular wall runs around the cave. Above this and a few feet back of it runs another wall parallel to the first; in the middle a flight of steps leads from the floor to the tops of these semicircular walls, and then leads farther up into what was probably the 'holy of holies' of the temple. Some antiquarians think that on top of these semicircular walls were laid the offerings to Mithras; in the middle of the floor is a cistern now filled up, which received the blood of the sacrificed animals. The front of the temple was adorned with marble facings and columns of rich colours, as an enormous amount of marble has been found in and around the entrance.

Description

The temple fronted the sea, and its entrance could be seen by sailors on their way to and from the East; it is probable that in going they stopped their vessels for a while, and came up to lay their offerings on the shrine of Mithras with prayers for a safe and prosperous voyage; or on their return came with richer gifts and gave thanks to their beneficent protector. Martorelli gives, among the inscriptions collected by him, a very touching one in Greek, cut on marble, which was found in this temple. The translation is as follows:

> O ye invincible spirits of shadowy Hades, it has pleased you to take me among you on the Stygian shores, me, more miserable than any one else! The Fates had not yet decreed my death, but an unjust and sudden end came to me by force. Caesar had honoured me with many gifts, but what was the hope of my parents is now only a lifeless body! Not twenty summers had passed over my head, nor even fifteen, yet, alas! I will never see the kindly daylight more. Upatos is my name. I implore my parents and unhappy brother to dry their tears.

This plaintive epitaph, written centuries ago, comes to tell us that inside these temple walls poor humanity, with its joys and sufferings, its hopes and fears, shared all its feelings with its God. For the moment the keen, intellectual enjoyment of the antiquarian ceases, and we recall out of these broken walls and ruined shrine the richly adorned temple with its devout and eager worshippers, who came with hopeful and glad hearts to offer rich gifts to the kind Sungod for his love and beneficence, or to pour out the griefs of surcharged hearts, and seek consolation from the mild, compassionate and wise Deity. The priests, elate with pride and joy at the homage paid to Mithras, promised succour to the despairing and gave new hopes to the hopeful. Inspired by the power and glory of their God, who was the author of all life, and who needed only to withdraw His beneficent and life-giving rays to cause gloom and cold and death, they invoked His curse on evil-doers and on those who disregarded His warnings and wishes, which were revealed to the people only by their mouths.

Of all these hopes and fears, of all this richness and power, of all this trust and confidence nothing remains but some broken walls and the dry bones and dust of the worshippers buried near, which are turned by the hoe of the peasant as he toils under the rays of the bye-gone God. Of all the sorrowful things on earth the most sorrowful are these relics of a dead religion and its followers. To the Christian this temple is an object of interest, as the religions of Christ and Mithras were rivals for two or three centuries. When Greek myths had grown stale, and priestly abuses of the Olympic religion had become too transparent, humanity sought another power, which should shield it from misfortune, alleviate its sufferings, give prosperity, and afford peace to the soul. Two religions coming from the mysterious East presented themselves. The one came from Persia with the prestige of age and with myths, which delighted the art-loving Greek and the poetry-loving Roman. Mithras gave warmth, and made the waters sparkle under his glance. He gave grain, and fruits, and flowers. He gave all the good things of life. The other came from Palestine, and represented the self-tortures of a despised and crucified Jew, who sympathized with the poor and made life a series of sacrifices for the good of others. This life was only a preparation for a glorious future existence, which was to be gained by self-denial here. The priests of the two religions waged unceasing war with one another, each accused the other of terrible rites in their meetings, where human sacrifices were offered, and the blood of young children was drunken. For a long time the religion of Mithras prevailed over that of Christ. To the pleasure-loving Greeks and Romans, with their sunny climate and blue, laughing seas where the Sungod was at home, these, the one foremost in art and literature, the other in arms and wealth, could not understand Christ's pity for the poor, his giving up all for them, his socialism, and the self-tortures of his sympathetic heart. Therefore the Christians were persecuted, and pleasure-loving Nero burned them as torches to light the way to his feasts; and even sage, calm philosophers like Antoninus Pius and Marcus Aurelius considered their teachings dangerous to the state, and tried to stamp out the new doctrine with its fanaticism and disregard of worldly things.

But a new element of force was growing up in the Roman empire, which was destined to make the religion of Christ prevail over that of Mithras. The Romans intent on the pleasures of the theatre, the baths and the amphitheatre, and on discussions in their schools of Rhetoric and Philosophy, left the defence of the Empire to foreign soldiers, so that the

Description

army was composed almost exclusively of the strong, hardy men of the North, who brought from their gloomy homes the melancholy and brutal myths of their Celtic and Teutonic religions. To these the doctrines of Christ, who sympathized with the poor, the conquered and the oppressed, who condemned the rich and the powerful, appealed with double force. They were compelled to give their life-blood to support and extend the power of their conquerors, or to butcher one another in the amphitheatre to furnish an hour's amusement to their cruel masters. For them there were no sunny villas, teeming with treasure and works of art; no beautiful slaves and troops of dancing girls; no feasts where millions of sesterces were spent in a single night; but only the hard oar of the galley, the toilsome marches, the scant food and dangers of the soldier, the wild beasts in the arena or the deathful trial of skill as a gladiator. For them the joyous religion of Mithras, which was the religion of their hated masters, had no charms, and they became Christians; so that when the nations of the sunny South had enervated themselves by excesses, and had trained their Northern subjects and slaves to be their soldiers and masters, the day came when Teutons and Celts asserted their supremacy, and with their advent to power the religion of the poor, the ignorant and the oppressed became the dominant religion of the western world. Then followed the dark ages, when ignorance and poverty were considered meritorious, until the Renaissance came; then the South protested against the gloomy dogmas of the Christians and went back to the old Greek and Roman writers, who had worshipped the Sungod, who had analyzed the feelings and sentiments of their times, and had taught humanity that ours is a joyous world, that the bright sun, the sparkling waters, the graceful, laughing woman and the strong, agile man are the true symbols of life, and that the clouded sun, the cold, rainy days with leaden sky and grey sea, sickness, sorrow and suffering are the exceptions, which come only to make us enjoy with greater zest our ordinary life. As we sit at the entrance of this temple of Mithras and look out over the bright, sunny landscape, and see the blue waters of the Bay of Salerno with its beautiful islands, and the coast gradually disappearing as a purple line to where Paestum still furnishes its temples to the old religion of the Beautiful, we are imbued with some of the feelings of an old sun-worshipper, and look up with a reverent and thankful spirit to the sun, stripped now of all god-like attributes but throwing his warm rays over land and sea, colouring everything with magic tints, and shining as bravely and good-humouredly on this deserted shrine as in the bye-gone days when he had his hosts of priests and worshippers.

Dupuis has given a very interesting and ingenious explanation of the myth symbolized by the astronomical figures on the bas-relief found here, but the limits of this book do not permit the insertion of it. He proves that the religion of Mithras was perfected, as symbolized in the bas-relief, some two thousand years before the birth of Christ.

To the north of the temple, in the same little valley, is a large natural arch, which is only one of many on the island, but on account of its grand proportions is called, par excellence the Arco Naturale. After rowing past the Cala di Matromania the next point of interest is the White Grotto; as the boat approaches it, on looking up, can be seen seventy or eighty feet above, stalactites and stalagmites formed by the dripping water laden with particles of stone. The grotto takes its white colour from the lime, and its distance from the surface of the water prevents any reflection from giving it a green or blue tinge.

Farther on, the ancient lighthouse, which rivalled in size and brightness that of Alexandria, looms up above the cliff. Suetonius says that this lighthouse was thrown down by an earthquake a few days before the death of Tiberius, but Statius speaks of it during the reign of Domitian as being 'a rival of the moon' in splendor and it must have been rebuilt by Caligula, or one of his successors. Since its rebuilding another earthquake has thrown it down, and on its southern side, close to its base, is a large fragment which was most probably on top of the present structure. Hadrava excavated here in 1804, and after laying bare the foundations found a subterranean stairway which led to a small chamber beneath, in which were the ashes of burned bodies. He found also a beautifully executed bas-relief in terra-cotta, representing Crispina and Lucilla, the wife and sister of Commodus, who were banished to this island by the Emperor; the two were represented in a suppliant attitude, with faces betokening grief and despair. A bas-relief of a faun and a Doric capital were found here and were sold to Heigelin, who placed them in his villa at

Description

Capodichino. Near these was found a sepulchral inscription on marble, in Greek, which ran: 'Taurilas of Taios, adieu'.

A short distance from the ancient lighthouse is the Salto di Tiberio, down which it is tradition that Tiberius threw those whom he had doomed to death, and when their bodies reached the rocky shore beneath, sailors stood in readiness with clubs to extinguish any spark of life which might still exist.

The little church of Santa Maria is perched on the highest point of the Cape, and under and around it are the most imposing ruins in Capri. This hill is called Tiberio by the peasants, and on account of the strength and magnitude of the ruins of this villa, its high position, and the feasibility with which it could be used as a fortress and defended against an enemy, as well as the fact that it overlooks the hills near Sorrento, Massa and the Punta di Campanella, many antiquarians have given this villa the name of Villa Jove. Suetonius says: 'Tiberius was upon the watch from the top of a lofty cliff for the signals which he had ordered to be made to announce the success or death of Sejanus, lest the messengers should be tardy. Even when he had quite foiled this conspiracy, he was still haunted as much as ever with fears and apprehensions, insomuch that he never stirred once out of the Villa Jove for nine months after.' From these scant details antiquarians have concluded that here was the villa Jove, and from these heights Tiberius must have looked anxiously for the expected signals. But his villa on San Michele was as well adapted for defence and quiet as that on the hill called Tiberio, and from the top of Monte Solaro he could see farther towards Gaeta, in which direction it is most probable the signal fires were built. On account of the beautiful view on all sides of the so-called Villa Jove, it is possible that Augustus first built a palace here, which was afterwards enlarged by Tiberius. Several excavations have been made among these ruins, the first of which during the reign of Carlo III brought to light the pavement which is now behind the altar in the Cathedral of Capri, and a beautiful Greek statue in white marble, which came into the possession of Signor D'Andrea, then governor of the island.

The second by Hadrava in 1806 was not very successful, for though much work was done, yet very little of any value was found; the most valuable find was a marble stairway. Hadrava excavated the cisterns, whose enormous size attracts the attention of the traveller today, and found several bathrooms, but, discouraged at the small amount of treasure found, he gave up his excavations. He prepared for publication an account of his work here, with many illustrations, but his death prevented the book from coming to light, and his manuscript, with the illustrations, was lost.

In 1827 Don Giuseppe Feola, the royal superintendent of excavations on the island, by a special order from King Francesco I commenced excavations here. He uncovered the ruins on the eastern side, and was more lucky than Hadrava, though he found but little of any value. The most precious thing among those found were two marble Puteales, or well-curbs (which the Romans placed at the mouths of their wells or cisterns to prevent any one from falling in), a bas-relief on one represented spring, and on the other represented autumn. He found also a finely executed, marble bas-relief of an old man with a nude young girl seated behind him on horseback; a slave marches before the horse, and leads it towards a pyramid on which is seated a girl, who holds in her left hand a basket filled with branches of oak. These three works of art are in the best Greek style and are preserved in the Museum at Naples.

On the eastern edge of the cliff and to the south of the church of Santa Maria is a semicircular ruin of curious structure, which may have been a theatre or the notorious Sellaria described by Suetonius, as this is the only building hitherto excavated whose form would meet the requirements of such a structure. The immense amount of rubbish accumulated in and around these ruins has deterred all excavators from completing their task; also, from the small amount of valuable things found and from the position of the rubbish, both Hadrava and Feola concluded that excavations had already been made here, and that everything of value had been carried away. It may be that when the lighthouse was thrown down by an earthquake, this palace was also destroyed, and on account of the large amount of art-treasure and rich marbles contained in it, Caligula, or one of his successors, may have sought to rescue some of them from the ruins by excavating. Peasants, at various times, have found here a great many valuable things, such as the large columns of giallo antico, which were placed in the churches of San Costanzo and San Salvatore but which were

Description

carried away to the Royal chapel of Caserta; also the precious stones, which now ornament the silver bust of San Costanzo, which is the pride of every Capriote. A column of lapis-lazuli five feet high and ten inches in diameter was found here, and the finder, not knowing its value, sold it to an Englishman for eight pounds. Bronze candalabras, cameos, Etruscan vases, spintriae, parts of statues, busts, and heads in variously coloured marbles, coins, leaden piping, and an enormous mass of marble of all colours have been dug up here, and were sold by the peasants to any one who would buy them.

There is a tradition on the island that, some years ago, the hermit who lived in the room adjacent to the little church of Santa Maria, found an image of solid gold, which was even more valuable for its workmanship than for the intrinsic worth of the metal; that he took the first opportunity to leave the island with it, and went where he could sell his treasure; and that he lived for the rest of his life at ease on the proceeds of the sale. Another tradition more apocryphal says that, one day, a young Capriote wandering among the subterranean chambers of these ruins came to a grotto where he saw a large bronze horse with a bronze statue of Tiberius sitting on it, and four colossal statues of slaves surrounding it. He made his way, after much difficulty, out of the grotto, but neither he nor any one else has ever been able to find this grotto again.

To the west of the church of Santa Maria exist extensive ruins, and in the terraced vineyards to the southwest, large masses of walls and broken masonry crop out above the earth. This palace, before its destruction, must have been an imposing structure, and to vessels passing through the Strait its marble-faced walls glinting in the sunlight on the edge of the darkly coloured cliff must have produced a wonderful effect. Under these ruins is a grotto, whose mouth is towards the east and which has been the despair of every climber; no one has been able to enter it, and there is a tradition that formerly a subterranean way led down to it from the palace.

The view from Tiberio, as it is commonly called by the Capriotes, is one of the most charming on the island. The sea with its beautifully tinted blues and bluish-greens seems immediately under the feet, but, on trying to throw a stone into the water, the visitor appreciates how far he is from it. After rowing around the Cape, on the north side a battery, a hundred feet above the water's edge, nestles on the side of a steep declivity. It was built by the French to prevent English vessels from passing through the Strait, and on this account was furnished with cannon of heavy calibre. The battery is in a very good state of preservation. Near by is a spring of fresh water, which flows out of the mountain side. A road was built from this battery by the French, which leads up to the top of Tiberio. After passing the battery we come to a many-voiced grotto called the Grotto del Lupo; here some fishermen surprised a large seal and killed it, hence its name. The gurgling of the water, as it passes in and out of the numerous holes in the sides of the cave, resembles at times the growlings and snarls of a hungry menagerie of wild beasts. A little farther to the west is the hill of San Michele, on which exist extensive Roman remains. Mounting the hill from the southern side, the remains of an ancient road which wound around the hill are worthy of attention It was built on a series of arches, and the space under each arch was used as a cistern; this road led from the town of Capri (where remains of it can still be seen behind the old Hotel de France) to the top of San Michele. Here, on the top, is a large quadrangular space surrounded by walls built by the English and French to serve as a fort, having used as a substructure the walls of an old Roman palace. Under the earth lie ruins which have never been excavated. The cistern, now used for holding water, is antique, and near it are several antique chambers, one of which was formerly dedicated as a chapel to Saint Michael, and mass is still celebrated there on Saint Michael's day. On the north side is a very massive, antique wall which was probably built to support the weight of a high structure. Before the English commenced building a fort here, beautifully tesselated pavements existed, which were either destroyed or covered up by the English workmen during the process of building. Two very fine columns of Cipollino marble were still to be seen a few years ago, but they have been carried away and sold. Feola found parts of statues and fragments of columns of giallo and rosso antico, also a large amount of worked, coloured marble. Peasants have found, at various times, many pieces of glass vases and terra-cotta ware.

    About half way up this hill is a grotto of stalactites, which can be visited. The view from San Michele is worth seeing, though not so pretty as that from Tiberio. At the eastern end of the village at the Grande Marina is a

Description

small fort, built by the French to prevent the English from landing here. It was built on the ruins of the old monastery, or hospice of San Francesco. In the middle of the Marina is an old Roman aqueduct, which serves today to carry off the superfluous waters of the fountain. In spite of the many convulsions of Nature which have occurred since it was built, it still retains its shape and dip sufficiently to be of use. This might seem to be a proof that this part of the island had not met with the disasters which have visited the other parts; but the freaks of earthquakes, subsidences and upheavals have furnished many instances equally remarkable. It is only necessary to cite the columns of the temple of Serapis at Pozzuoli which still stand erect in spite of the many convulsions of Nature they have undergone.

In the vicinity of the fountain, during the reign of Francesco I, excavations were made which brought to light the remains of a large palace. It seems to have suffered more from the convulsions of Nature through which it has passed, than any other on the island; all the vaulted roofs were destroyed, and the walls were cracked in every direction. Most of the marble pavements of the rooms were crushed and destroyed by the fall of the vaulted roofs, and only two were sufficiently well preserved to be taken up and sent to Naples. Five marble statues, the heads of which were missing, were dug up here. One of these, of colossal form, was supposed to be a statue of Tiberius, another of good workmanship represented a young warrior, both of these were sent to the Museum at Naples. A third, of small size but of the best epoch, was found and sold by the owner of the vineyard to an Englishman. Two other statues larger than life-size were also found, but in a very bad state of preservation. One of these, with the inscription JULIUS SALIUS FECIT, is now in the possession of Mr. Haan. From the fact that Feola found the pavements of two rooms missing, it may be supposed that either these ruins had already been excavated, and the pavements had been taken away, or that, at the time of the destruction of this palace, these two rooms were undergoing repairs and the old pavements had been taken up to be replaced by new ones. The ruins were re-covered with earth, and the ground was replanted with vines, so that today the exact spot under which they are buried is not known. Along the beach immediately in front of the houses of the Marina, only a few years ago, existed many fragments of finely fluted, ancient, marble columns, which were fixed in the earth and were used for attaching boats. Most of these fragments of columns have been sold, but a few, which have little or no value, still remain.

In the interior of the island the castle of Barbarossa at Anacapri is an interesting specimen of mediaeval skill in the art of fortification. Perched on a lofty cliff, and accessible only from the west, it was easily defended by a small body of men, and must have held out for some time against Barbarossa, who took it in 1535 and destroyed it to such an extent that it has never been restored to its former strength. This fort, in common with many others on the coast of Italy destroyed by the valiant ruler of Algiers, has taken his name and bears it to this day. Inside is the deserted hut of a hermit, who lived here for many years.

The fortress of Monte Solaro is not so large as that of Barbarossa, but is much better preserved, and the view from it is the most extended that can be obtained from any part of the island. This view embraces the Bays of Gaeta, Naples and Salerno, the coast of Calabria, the Ponza group of islands, and the mountains near Rome. Under Monte Solaro and facing the road leading down to the Piccola Marina is the Grotto dell'Arco. This Grotto is called by the English, Fern Grotto, on account of the Maiden's Hair fern growing on its sides; the walk to it is picturesque, and from this Grotto the view of the Faraglioni and Piccola Marina is very fine. Here Doctor Cerio has made partial excavations which have brought to light fragments of pottery of various patterns and nationalities, and among these, many fragments which bear the peculiar ornaments of the Phoenicians. Towards the southern part of this cave are remains of ancient Roman masonry.

From the fact that nearly all the houses in the present town of Capri have been built on antique foundations, and on account of the presence of an ancient Cyclopean wall which runs from the hill of San Michele to that of the Castiglione, and whose remains crop above ground in several places, it is very probable that the present town was built on the site of an old Roman fortified camp. Tiberius always kept a number of soldiers here, and as yet no place has been found where they could have been quartered. A strong wall like this Cyclopean, extending from the Castiglione to San Michele, and garrisoned with troops, with a well-defended port at Tragara would render the eastern end of the island almost impregnable. This

Description

eastern end is now covered with the ruins of palaces, temples, roads and cisterns to such an extent that it is evident that Imperial life centred here during the reigns of Tiberius and Augustus.

A road from Tragara to the Castiglione, another from the present town of Capri to the top of San Michele, and a third leading from the Baths of Tiberius and the old town of Capri in the direction of the present town, or what was probably the old Roman Camp, are the only certain remains of roads to be found on the island. There must have been a road from the palace of Jove to the Camp, and there are probable traces of this way cut out of the rock, but as this road followed the sinuosities of the hill and did not pass over any depression, which would render arches necessary, it is probable that all attempts to trace it from the Villa Jove to the present town of Capri would be futile. This road, which led from the old town of Capri to the old Camp, passing up the valley between San Michele and Solaro, has been almost entirely destroyed by the subsidence of the valley, and only the beginning of it near the Campo Militare can be seen at present. The old steps leading from Anacapri down to Capri are the only remains of a means of communication between the eastern and western parts of the island.

Of the views, the finest is that from Fravicina or Migliara, but that from Monte Solaro, Tiberio or Villa Jove, Tragara and Matromania are well worth seeing. The main road from Capri to Anacapri offers many charming views over the Bays of Naples and Salerno. This road is an admirable specimen of the engineering skill of Italians, and was planned and executed by a Neapolitan engineer, Signor Emilio Mayer. A very pretty walk runs under the cliff of Anacapri from the church of San Costanzo to the Punta di Trasele.

Capri must have been a Paradise under Tiberius, with its many marble-faced palaces filled with works of art, its groves, its gardens, and walks. Here, where Nature had already done so much, the art and wealth of the world were called in to aid in making this island a fit residence for the poetry-loving Augustus and the art-loving Tiberius. Under their reigns art vied with Nature in furnishing delights to every sense, and it was a tradition, false but ben trovata, which made later writers say that the Roman Senate, after the death of Tiberius, sent some thousands of workmen to the island to destroy all the walks, groves, gardens and palaces, for fear that every Roman Emperor might be tempted to forsake Rome and its interests, to pass his time in this Lotus land. An old Greek tradition had hidden under the myth of Sirens the dangerous beauty of Capri, which could induce these worshippers of the Beautiful to forsake and forget wives, children, fatherland, and all the other joys of life, to feed their senses with the intoxicating beauty found here, and this beauty did not pall, but in spite of old age with its waning powers of enjoyment, the Sirens held them fast, until inexorable death came and left only their bones to 'whiten all the ground'.

Chapter 8

An Adventurous Life
Anna Maria Palombi Cataldi

John Clay MacKowen was born in Jackson, East Feliciana Parish, Louisiana on March 26, 1842. His father John McKowen (the family spellings vary) had emigrated there from Castle Dawson, Ireland and established himself as a prosperous landowner and general merchant. He married Mary Ann Langford of Woodville and they had three children: Sarah Elizabeth (1841), John Clay (1842) and Alexander Cooper (1843). After the death of his wife in 1845, he married Jane Shannon of Belfast; they had two children, William Robert (1847) and Thomas Chalmers (1849).[1]

At the outbreak of the Civil War the young MacKowen was in his third year of a medical degree course at Dartmouth College, New Hampshire. He interrupted his studies to enlist in the Confederate Army, in which he served for four years, and was wounded at Shiloh (April 6-7, 1862) during one of the bloodiest episodes in the history of the United States. Both sides were shocked at the carnage of that battle, in which over 13,000 Federal soldiers and over 10,000 Confederate soldiers became casualties. 1,754 Federal and 1,728 Confederate soldiers were killed, with many of those who survived suffering from the physical and mental consequences for the rest of their lives. The battle was fought around the Baptist Church – the church of Herman Melville's poem *Shiloh: A Requiem*:

> Skimming lightly, wheeling still / the swallows fly low / over the field in clouded days, / the forest-field of Shiloh – / over the field where April rain / solaced the parched ones stretched in pain / through the pause of night / that followed the Sunday fight / around the church of Shiloh – / The church so lone, the log-built one, / that echoed to many a parting groan / and natural prayer / of dying foemen mingled there

His brother Alexander Cooper (Aleck) McKowen, who also fought with the Confederate Army, died on July 17, 1863 as a result of wounds sustained two months earlier during the Federal assault on the fortifications at Vicksburg.[2]

MacKowen as a Confederate officer. Courtesy of Mr Michael F. Howell and Col. J.L. Hendrickson.

As a captain later in the war, during the siege of Port Hudson (June 1863), MacKowen achieved distinction by setting out on horseback with five of his men and penetrating the Federal lines to capture General Neal Dow, who was recuperating from wounds in a nearby plantation. The unfortunate general was then used as an exchange prisoner the following year for the Confederate General W.H. Fitzhugh Lee of Virginia. MacKowen ended the war in the rank of Lieutenant-Colonel of Cavalry, receiving two swords in recognition of his valour.

After the war he returned to Dartmouth to complete his degree in 1866 and in the same year entered the School of Medicine in Paris, where he worked at the Charité Hospital and continued with further studies under Drs Wurtz, Velpeau and Fort.[3] Two years later he had a mental breakdown

An Adventurous Life

MacKowen's medical degree certificate. Courtesy of the Cuomo family, Anacapri.

and returned to the United States. He bought a ranch in Los Angeles, became a ranchero, participated in local politics and was elected mayor (alcalde).

In 1870 he sold his ranch and moved to San Francisco, where he became Principal of Public Schools from 1870-73. In a letter to his sister Sarah Pipes dated September 16, 1870 he wrote: '... My life here is a pleasant one; I have eight hours work a day for five days in the week and then a rest of two days. But in addition I have two months vacation during the year when I draw my pay like a man and enjoy myself like a gentleman should in travelling etc, and have the ear entranced with music, and all the senses and the imagination delighted with the chef d'oeuvre of civilization, the opera. Such contact nears off sectional prejudices and opens the mind for impressions which one can get in few places except in so cosmopolitan a city as San Francisco. While there is no danger of growing narrow-minded here yet one feels a want of culture which makes life in Europe so agreeable, where one can see models of beauty in sculpture and paintings. Ah Europe, would that some lucky star might shine over my head in life and light the way soon to that home of all my wishes and hopes!'

His father, who had retired with his third wife to Jersey Island seeking to recover his health, died in 1871. John Clay and his sister Sarah received their share from their mother's estate: lands in East Feliciana, Kansas, Minnesota and Dakota. William Robert and Thomas (his stepbrothers) also received a share from their mother's estate; his widow Christine received money and his four children inherited their father's estate in East Feliciana.

In another letter to Sarah, dated January 26, 1873 he said he had resigned his position and would return home to Louisiana. '... I feel the importance of the step as it will have a great influence over the whole of my future life – and I hope it will be a good one. I will remain with you for three months and probably go on to Europe, as I have a position offered to me as correspondent of The San Francisco Call. But I do not want to leave the United States unless all my affairs are in perfect order, so I may remain longer with you. In fact my whole future is a myth.'

After spending a few months with his sister he accomplished his dream and went to Europe once again. His next move was to complete his advanced training at the medical schools of Vienna and Munich, taking his degree of MD on February 12, 1876 at Munich under the guidance of his great mentor Carl von Voit.[4] He then rented a house in Rome, in the Piazza di Spagna, where he set up in practice.

In 1877, suffering from insomnia and taken with malarial fever, he went to Capri to recuperate. The island clearly pleased him as he soon bought a boat,[5] using it extensively to reach the hidden coves and grottoes, exploring them all to study their geological characteristics and seek out the many remains and signs of their historical past. At the same

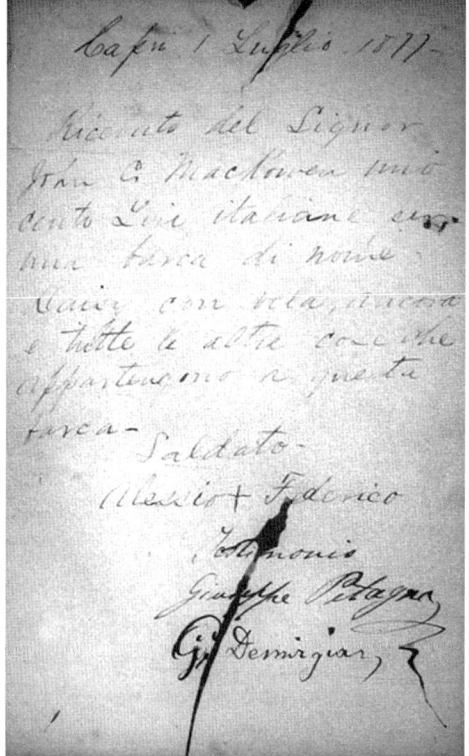

Contract for the purchase of a sailing boat. Special Collections, LSU Libraries, Baton Rouge, Louisiana, by permission.

time he began his long relationship with Mariuccia Cimino, a Capri woman and the daughter of Antonio Cimino, a local fisherman. Numerous other members of Mariuccia's family lived at Marina Grande and were also sailors and fishermen, and through them MacKowen very soon came to buy a boat and a plot of land, where he built a house in the Moorish style. Mariuccia gave birth to his only child, their daughter Giulia Evelina, in March 1879.

Here too he began his friendship with Dr Vincenzo Cuomo, the district doctor. Dr Cuomo had come to Capri for three months to recover from a serious infection and then decided to stay, subsequently describing the island's therapeutic properties in many articles published both in Italy and abroad. He was an accomplished musician, putting his talents to good use in treatments which would now be defined as music therapy.

According to an entry in his diary, MacKowen showed him a zither that he had bought in Munich: '... It was a finely built instrument in superb condition, of which he was very fond. Well aware of my interest in learning to play this instrument, in the end, the colonel very generously gave me this fine specimen as a gift in gratitude for my having worked day and night a few months earlier to save his only daughter, who had come down with a serious form of smallpox. In addition to his much appreciated gesture of giving me the zither, my friend completed his gift with an instruction book. Unfortunately it was in German and I have only been able to translate bits and pieces.'[6] Subsequently the artist Schrelter would teach him how to play the instrument, which he then used in his practice.

In his diary, Cuomo recalled that: '... during the same period my good friend Colonel Dr MacKowen, who, following the war of secession in America in which he was awarded two swords of honour, had been unable in other countries to find the peace and tranquillity necessary to combat his constant insomnia, had come to Capri where he was finally able to sleep.' He went on to describe a scene inside Marina Grande's first hotel 'one of those built in the Gothic style by the well-known American colonel from New Orleans (sic), who had been so cruelly tormented by the most tenacious insomnia following the war that he reached the point of seriously considering suicide. MacKowen was there to supervise the work that was being carried out on his property and was intent upon cleaning two beautiful swords, the very swords of honour that he had so rightly earned in recognition of the courage exhibited in combating the Yankees. It was on that occasion that he spoke in detail about the two battles which had allowed him to attain the rank of colonel and be awarded the swords.' MacKowen told Cuomo that he was grateful to the island, 'the only blessed land where, after such a long time, my mind has found rest. I was tired of life because of my insomnia, which had poisoned my existence, and Capri, with its air, sea and sky, has saved me.'

By the time the two met, MacKowen had already left his private residence at Marina Grande (it was turned into the Hotel Bristol and the ground floor became the Stanford Restaurant du Louvre) and in 1883 had moved to Anacapri. Here he rented a house and began buying plots of land at Gradola, an area rich in archaeological remains. In 1884, based on his years of careful observation and historical enquiry, he published his book *Capri* which, reproduced here in its entirety, forms the first part of this present work.[7]

Between 1887 and 1888 he also bought land and buildings in the centre of the town, including an old Aragonese tower which he began slowly to restore over a long period lasting until 1896.[8] The structure of the tower was similar to a castellated building, with merlons and only a few openings, and the walls were painted Pompeian red. He embellished it with the statues and bas-reliefs and pieces of marble found over the course of his excavations at Gradola and around Damecuta and near the Marina Grande, where his friend the Hungarian painter Antal Haan lived.

In due course MacKowen went to live at the Tower, now known as the Casa Rossa, with Mariuccia and their daughter Giulia. Here, on the top floor, he kept his vast collection of rare books, ancient manuscripts and precious bindings. He also cultivated a passion for old arms which he had collected during the course of his long trips to remote corners of the world. Among his papers there is correspondence with friends in Tunis and shipping documents for arms from North Africa, from where he had also brought back ancient pottery, precious rugs, pipes, armour and Turkish-style furniture. He also collected Capodimonte porcelain figurines and majolica from the workshop of Della Robbia as well as tapestries, paintings and eighteenth-century furniture. Every two years he returned to Louisiana to take care of his American assets, which he had entrusted in part to his brother William and in part to the San Francisco real estate firm of Merrill & Burke.

It was during this same time that he began to buy small plots of land in the Gradola area[9] overlooking the Blue Grotto – he was fascinated by the grotto and conceived a project to build a land route to it with access via steps leading down from his property. He continued to buy more small parcels of land until August 6, 1897, when he bought a plot named Rio (or Zio) Iacolo and another named Vignolella. Although the land was relatively unproductive, with only olive trees and a few vineyards, it was dear to the people of Anacapri because it was an area where quails roosted, and therefore a source of income for hunters.

Indeed, in a letter to the Editor of the Corriere del Mattino, written on February 28, 1887 he referred to the desirability of creating a land entrance to the Grotto, accepting that even though the town authorities were in favour of his project many people were opposed to it. He pointed out that an access route via land would allow foreigners to visit it even

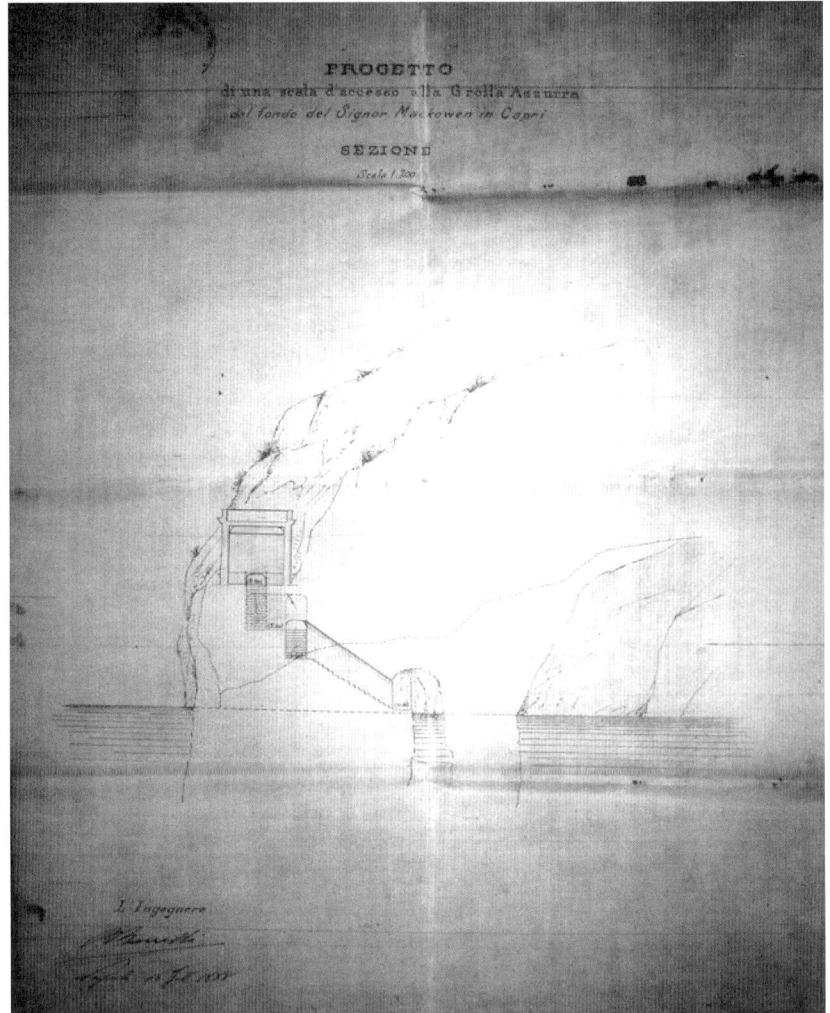

*Engineer's section plan for the land entrance to the Blue Grotto.
Special Collections, LSU Libraries, Baton Rouge, Louisiana, by permission.*

when the sea was rough, and that the town of Anacapri had much to gain because of the hotels and lodging houses for visitors that would certainly be built, thus creating welcome business for the higher part of the island. He realised, however, that the idea was not to the liking of the people of Capri itself, owing to the rivalry that had always existed between the two towns. He warned that failure to proceed with the project would make it likely that tourists would instead be diverted to the island of Busi in Dalmatia, where in 1884 another Blue Grotto had recently been discovered.

A lawsuit immediately followed, prompted by Henry Wreford – the London Times correspondent in Capri – who urged the Prefect and the General Direction of Beaux Arts to oppose MacKowen's project. The lawsuit was immediately reported in the San Francisco Daily Supplement Bulletin of Saturday Evening, March 12, 1887: 'An American, John MacKowen, has become the owner of the soil immediately above the grotto. But the village of Capri, in its corporate capacity, has hitherto regarded itself as the owner of the grotto and as such has levied a small fee from all visitors to it. The village authorities object, both because of their reputed ownership and because the letting in of ordinary light would put an end to the singular appearance now presented by the place. The American undertakes to construct his passage so that no light from above can penetrate below, and promises to put a gate which shall exclude intruders, as well as daylight. The boatmen who now make an income by conveying passengers to the spot (at present the only mode of getting admission to the grotto) object vigorously to the inroad on their vested interests.' (The report concluded with the following tantalising information: 'It is worth recalling that when the Emperor Tiberius appropriated Caprae (sic) for his solitary retreat, he had a passage constructed which led down to the grotto, which he used as a bath. This passage is still in existence, but impassable, being choked up with rubbish.')

Notwithstanding the lawsuit, his dream of creating a land route to the Blue Grotto seemed to becoming true when Pasquale Borrelli, an engineer, completed his drawings and estimated costs for the work 'needed to realize stairs leading to the Blue Grotto from the property of Mr John MacKowen in Capri'. On March 23, 1888 the engineer presented MacKowen with the final plans, with all the necessary stamps affixed, for the project.[10]

From the various testimonies that exist it is clear that MacKowen was on excellent terms with that wide circle of vibrant personalities drawn from all parts of the cultural spectrum who either lived permanently on the island or spent extended periods there. He did not, however, have an easy relationship with the Swedish physician Axel Munthe (1857-1949), who had been captivated by Anacapri as a student on a visit in 1875 and settled there permanently in 1887. His appointment as physician to the royal house of Sweden had led to his acquiring a large and wealthy foreign clientele, which enabled him to purchase numerous plots of land, including some old ruins as well as several small homes which were to constitute the nucleus of the Villa San Michele. He too became interested in archaeological excavations which he began conducting in the areas of Damecuta and the Blue Grotto, thus – inevitably – bringing him into conflict with MacKowen. According to some, there had been a violent argument between the two over a marble fragment found in the Damecuta area. According to others, instead, MacKowen wanted to defend his friend Dr Cuomo from Munthe's offensive accusations of professional impropriety. The two allegedly challenged one another to a duel – which was fortunately never held because they were unable to agree on the choice of weapon.

MacKowen's relationship with the ordinary people of the island was also not idyllic. He walked around Anacapri with his military bearing and sense of command, just as he would have done during the war. He was well known for his brusque manner, his outbursts of rage and his propensity for issuing lawsuits, which not surprisingly led to very many people finding him arrogant and disputatious. At the same time, however, he was unfailingly generous to poor people, above all to those who would not otherwise have had recourse to prompt medical help. The local people knew him as 'ciacca e medica' – strike and heal. A good example of his uncompromising behaviour was his attempt to stop the local coachmen from washing their carriages in the evenings on the road beside his Aragonese tower home. The road was dusty and they would throw the dirty water onto the street, adding to the stench of animal excrement and the other dirt already there. MacKowen turned to the town police force and the mayor, but neither of them showed any interest in trying to improve the situation. There was also a confrontation between him and Bartolomeo Dalmasso, a local innkeeper, who also happened to be a policeman. The next day the man informed the mayor that the Colonel had used abusive and offensive language against him and the mayor, and even against 'our royal sovereign'. Following a report made to the police, MacKowen was accused of slander against the policeman and the mayor and also of insulting the king. Worse, the conciliator, Giovanni Romano, accused him of unlawful behaviour, citing two episodes in which he had practiced his profession in the absence of Dr

Cuomo, the district doctor. An enquiry was held, with much confusing and conflicting evidence offered, following which he was committed to trial for slander, insult, lèse-majesté, the illegal practice of medicine and even the attempted subornation of a witness. After having carefully examined the issues, the judge concluded that much of the testimony was contradictory and unreliable, and together with positive statements in MacKowen's favour by many others, including Dr Cuomo and Giuseppe Orlandi, a member of the Italian Parliament, the case was thrown out (January 28, 1896).

During the summer of that year he travelled widely in the Near East, hoping to 'study the outdoor life of Orientals, which can not be seen in cold weather, when they stay in their houses',[11] but a combination of dysentery, gout, rheumatism and malaria had laid him so low by the time he reached Constantinople that it was only his return to Capri which enabled him to recover. He was nevertheless not inclined to let Giovanni Romano go unpunished, and on his return cited him for attempted subornation of a witness. Thus another series of witnesses, both for and against him, testified before the court. Despite the many depositions once again in his favour, it was clear from the testimony of many people of Anacapri that the Colonel was not well liked.

Several months afterwards, during the Spring of 1897, he began to experience stomach symptoms, '... great nervous prostration and nervousness ... during which time I lost eighty pounds ... After a week in bed I dragged myself into the open air where I sat the whole day on my loggia wrapped up in rags ... Death was staring me in the face under the form of gradual decay ... my disease had to do with stomach, intestines, liver and nerves ...'[12] It was probably at this time that he began to think about returning to Louisiana in order to be near to his sister and brothers.

His intentions became clear in a letter concerning his book collection dated May 9, 1897 to his friend Dr J. M. Pike: 'I have a choice collection of rare, old and costly books including a remarkably fine old missal of the fourteenth century, a hundred years before the invention of printing, then I have copies of all or nearly all the celebrated printers' work from the first century of printing (from 1454 to 1554) from 1554 to 1645 including the celebrated Elzevire and Aldines, from 1654 to 1754 and from 1754 to 1854. Many of these volumes belonged to emperors, kings, princes, cardinals, bishops, nobles of all ranks and to rich men who liked costly and quaint bindings. Many of them are very profusely illustrated with steel, copper or wood engravings, and taking my collection all together I doubt if there be many libraries in the world, if any, which would furnish a more comprehensive objective lesson in the art of printing and illustrating books from the first century of printing and illustrating down to the present day. Certainly there is nothing of this kind in America and I have been making the collection for thirty years, because I had the intention of founding a library in New Orleans out of my own pocket. The Howard family forestalled me in this worthy work, but I am sure that not one of them has made such a collection as I possess. It requires means, education, leisure and travel among the capitals and out of way places in the world to pick up the treasures which I possess, from the standpoint of a bibliophile.

This collection has cost me about twenty thousand dollars and I propose to donate the cream of it, let us say books to the value of twelve thousand dollars or more, to the Howard Library, so that our good people of New Orleans and Louisiana and the South generally (for New Orleans is the capital of the South) may educate their eyes and their aesthetic notions about books by seeing and studying these precious specimens of the printer's and bookbinder's art.' He was asking Pike to introduce him to his brother-in-law (Frank T. Howard from the Howard Library) in order to explore the possibility of donating part of his valuable collection. He must have already resolved to leave Capri and move back to Louisiana.

In the meantime, a series of witnesses testified before the judges in Naples regarding MacKowen's action against Giovanni Romano for slander. The testimony of many of them was vague, because Romano was a powerful man who was feared in the community; it was said that he was called the King of Anacapri or the Saint Januarius of Anacapri. Owing to contradictory testimony, the Court acquitted Romano (May 8, 1897). The sentence embittered MacKowen, who believed he was a victim of persecution by the man. Furthermore, new obstacles continued to arise relating to the building of the stairs leading down to the Blue Grotto. Although he was acknowledged as being the owner of the land in Gradola, the possibility of boring a hole into the land and opening a passage was contested because the Grotto was not his property. The colonel, instead, had planned to proceed in the conviction that his ownership extended to the grotto based upon the principle of *usque ad*

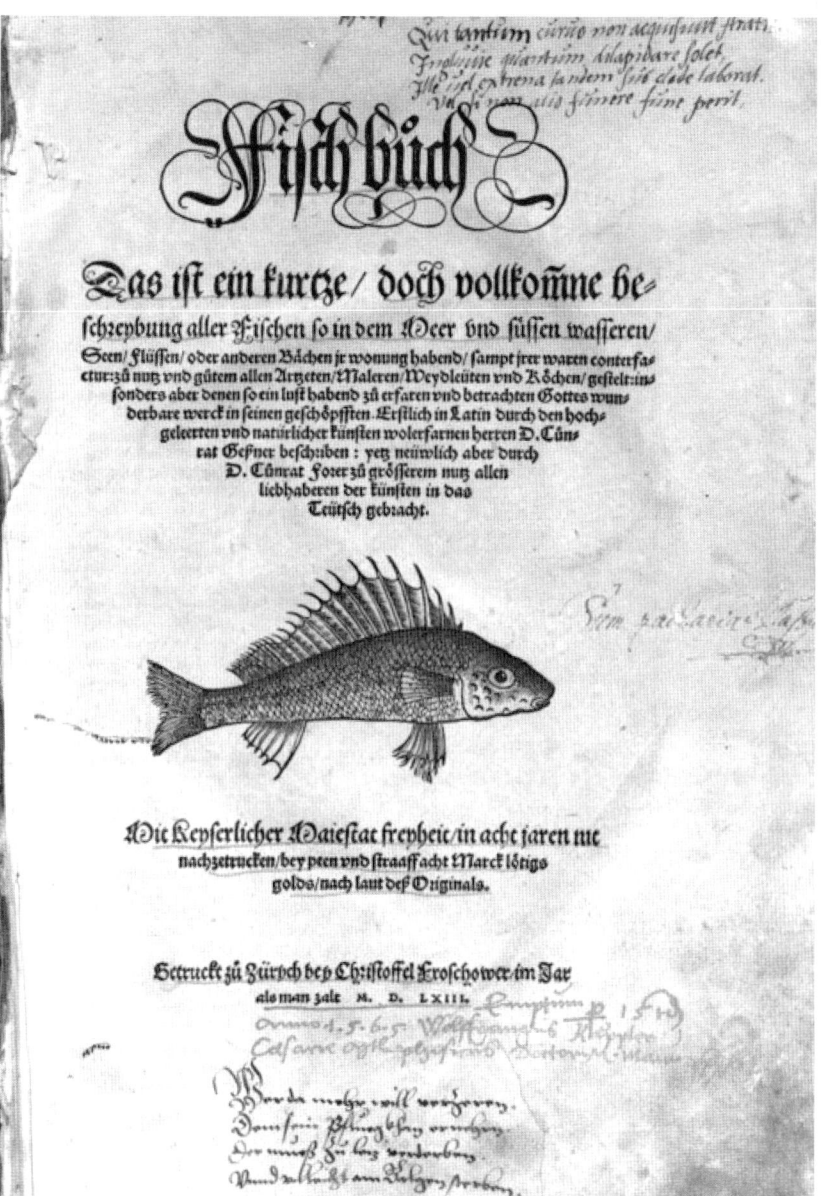

Frontispiece of Gessner Fischbuch, *1563. Courtesy of the Rare Books Collection, Special Collections Division, Howard-Tilton Memorial Library, Tulane University, New Orleans.*

inferos. In the light of such protracted and determined resistance, he must at that point have decided to abandon his cherished project and leave the island for good.

In a subsequent letter to Dr Pike dated December 9, 1897, in reference to his intentions of making a donation to a museum in New Orleans, MacKowen wrote: '... I have four collections, one of rare books, another of rare arms, a third of majolica and porcelain and a fourth of antique Greek and Roman statues, bas-reliefs, inscriptions etc. ... I start for home in a week or so, having delayed my departure on account of yellow fever.' Thus, after postponing his journey owing to his health and a yellow fever epidemic that was raging in Louisiana, he finally left Capri at the end of December 1897, taking with him two trunks containing his collection of books.[13]

His daughter Giulia wrote to him from Anacapri thanking him for the lovely, elegant shoulder cape he had sent her and inquired about a bronze ring and some pieces of marble he had asked her to send him. She informed him that the antique ring would be given to his friend Arthur King, who would then have it sent to him in Louisiana from London. She also informed him that she would personally see to having the antique pieces of marble that decorated his home in Anacapri detached from the walls and sent on to him.

He now pursued his enquiries as to which library should receive his book collection. Dr Pike had contacted the Howard Library, but also recommended the Fisk Library in New Orleans, and Frank T. Howard offered to put up a building for his collection. On February 27, 1898, MacKowen received a letter from Brandt V.B. Dixon, President of H. Sophie Newcomb Memorial College, who informed him that he was prepared to have some cases built for the exhibit of his books. He wrote: '... Mrs. Newcomb [the founder of the college] expresses to you her sincere appreciation of your generous offer to donate to the Newcomb College your collection of arms, armours etc. where they may form a permanent exhibit for the use of the college and of the public. She is willing to provide for them a suitable fireproof building in which they may be properly cared for, and to open this to the public on stated days ... She is willing to deposit the sum of twenty thousand dollars for the purpose.'

In September 1898 he published his paper *Aromatic Toxins* in the New Orleans Medical and Surgical Journal, dedicating it 'To my Master in physiological-chemical-laboratory work, Voit'.[14] He received the compliments of W.F. Engman, the Director of the St Louis Medical Gazette and of his friend Vincenzo Cuomo, who wrote: 'Your reasoning about the action of aromatic toxins and the role they play in the pathogenesis of various ailments is, beyond doubt, logical and convincing.'

During the years to come he received innumerable letters from his friend Arthur King, whom he had met in Munich where they were both working in the same research laboratory. MacKowen had convinced King to purchase half of the land he owned in the area of Gradola and helped him to purchase a large vineyard and building in the Caprile area, as well as the Materita Tower once owned by the San Giacomo Monastery. King kept his friend informed of the problems relating to their Blue Grotto property and the possibility of still being able to build the land entrance to it. He also wrote to him about his property at Caprile and about Giulia, who missed her father very much.

In a letter addressed to a Dr W. B. Herduran, MacKowen complained about a Chicago Herald interview, published the year before on May 15, 1897, in which a Colonel Candler claimed for himself the glory of having captured General Dow, denying that MacKowen had at all participated in the action. MacKowen was furious and demanded a rebuttal in the papers, not to exult over his accomplishments because he had no need to do so, but rather in the interest of the truth. He wrote. 'I do not cling lovingly to having captured Dow. I hoped eagerly during his capture that he would have resisted or attempted to escape so I could have a decent excuse for killing him, as I was heartily ashamed of being seen by my friends in his company. ... I have practiced medicine with honor and profit for twenty-two years. I have gained the respect of poor and rich with as serious outlay of time and money as most physicians must do, and you as one ought to know this. I have travelled around the world three times and to all parts that interested me. I speak fluently six languages and read another six. I have written several books ... historical, archaeological and scientific, and a book on Capri which has been cited and criticized by the London *Atheneum* as the best of its kind.' After describing his activity as a doctor in Rome he added: 'I exchanged the tempestuous life in Rome for boating into the coves and grottoes of Capri with its blue clear waters and views over its picturesque cliffs.'

By December 1899 MacKowen's health had evidently worsened, as can be inferred in a letter from King who wrote that he had not

*MacKowen in later life, after his return to Louisiana.
In The National Cyclopaedia of American Biography, 1897.*

understood that he had health problems, even though, prior to his departure from Capri, 'You had fits of passion, your nerves have been in very bad conditions ever since your importunate trip to the Caucasus and you have been irritable in proportion.' He [King] was of the opinion that the climate in New Orleans was not good for his health, even though he could well understand his desire to be close to his brothers and sister.

In February 1900 MacKowen signed a one-year rental contract for The Old Clifford House – a home with a garden – in Clinton. He ate too much, drank and smoked and had gained a great deal of weight. He was tormented by his gout and suffered from serious depression. Later that month his brother William, who administered his estate in East Feliciana, wrote: 'If you need some money for your current expense let me know

& and I will send you what you need. I am always willing to assist you, but won't be a party to your law-suits ... law-suits are a nuisance at best.'

A little later on William reprehended him for his excessive expenses and his entanglement in expensive lawsuits. He added '... I am glad to know the buggy came at last and that you like it.' The buggy must have been a good substitute for his horse, because his health was declining further and he continued to travel frequently from Clinton to Wilson, Jackson, New Orleans and Baton Rouge.

In April, 1901 MacKowen sold his property on Capri to his half-brother William in the presence of Cavaliere Carlo Magenta, the Italian Consul in New Orleans,[15] and on May 2 he wrote to his agents Merrill & Baker about his books and the donation of his valuable collection: '... I brought my collection to America and placed it in the Library of Sophie Newcomb with the elated feeling of a contented bibliophilic victor.'[16]

The final phase of his life was dominated by his involvement in a dispute over a boundary between land belonging to his sister Sarah Pipes and that of her neighbour Robert Emerson Thompson, a Senator of the State of Louisiana.[17]

In a letter dated May 21, 1901 from the Wall & Laycock Clinton Law Office, the firm mandated by Thompson to verify the documentation regarding the boundary between the two properties, the attorney informed MacKowen that he was willing to receive him and provide him with all the necessary explanations. Thompson wrote from Wilson to Sarah Pipes on May 27, 1901: 'Dear Mrs Pipes, referring to the dividing line between our lands where there seems to be a dispute, I think as we are the interested parties we now settle the matter without any trouble or hard feelings in any way. Mrs Pipes, I do not want one inch of land that is not mine nor do I think otherwise of you. Now to make an amicable settlement I propose to have the case in the hands of two or more arbitrators & to select the first two ... I will select W.R. Mckowen & J.C. Mckowen. They are business men and will administer justice ... and I will be perfectly willing to abide to their decision.'

MacKowen's health continued to decline. He suffered from headaches, bad digestion and pains in his back and was depressed and easily excited. He corresponded with doctors in New York who advertised 'miracles', maintaining that they could treat him through magnetism and hypnotism. In May and June he received many letters from a Dr J.M. Peebles based in Battle Creek, Michigan, whose practice was limited to chronic disease. Dr Peebles wrote that he was certain he could treat him with psychic and magnetic medicines. As far as we know, MacKowen did not choose to be treated by him, although among his papers there are many newspaper cuttings advertising the doctor's successfully treated cases.

He continued with investigations that he had started on his return to Louisiana into the prevailing yellow fever epidemic and wrote a pamphlet entitled 'Murder as Money Making', published in Baton Rouge. He maintained that 'a part of the doctors in New Orleans combine with the traders to keep the truth from coming out.' He was subsequently sued for libel, but won the case.

On June 12, 1901 his nephew David Pipes wrote to him about the dividing line between the Pipes and Thompson plantations: 'I have never given Emerson Thompson permission to remove any part of the partition fence dividing the Bellevue place from his … place. I only learned that he had moved part of it. I wrote to him about it & after considerable correspondence on the subject between us he agreed to furnish me with sufficient wire to replace what he had removed as soon as the negroes have laid by their crops. I will have the fence put up and will then call on him for the wire. So this matter will not need your attention. Many thanks for your interest.' His nephew could not possibly have imagined that in reality the matter was far from settled.

Arthur King's last letter from Capri was dated August 29, 1901. Over the course of the previous years he had written about his own health, his shares and what was happening in the world. He sent his friend newspaper cuttings about the riots in Milan (May 1898) and the American war against Spain in Cuba, remarking that because of the early end of that war he was relieved his friend would no longer run the risk of enlisting for combat, and commented on the Transvaal war in South Africa; he wrote about Giulia and about their joint enterprise at the Blue Grotto.

September 18, 1901. A local newspaper, published in Wilson, Louisiana reported: 'Dr. John Clay Mckowen (sic) of Clinton, was shot and killed by State Senator R. E. Thompson, on the Wilson and Clinton road, about four miles from Wilson, to-day. Mr Thompson was on horseback going to Clinton and passed a buggy going in the same direction, with top and curtains drawn. As he passed he asked if the occupant was Dr John

Mckowen. Without responding, Mckowen opened fire on him. Thompson immediately drew his revolver, which was in his saddle pocket, and returned the fire, one ball striking Dr Mckowen on the right knuckle, which disabled him, the second bullet striking below the chin, which afterwards proved fatal. The pistol used by Mckowen was a 44-caliber, one chamber discharged, and a couple of cartridges failing to fire. Thompson's pistol was a 38-caliber, which was discharged six times. The trouble which brought about the shooting, as near as can be learned, emanated from charges instigated by Dr Mckowen against Mr Thompson at the behalf of his sister, Mrs Pipes, which were thrown out by the grand jury. Mr Thompson will have a preliminary trial in Clinton on Thursday.'[18]

The following day, September 19, testimony in a preliminary hearing took place in Clinton. Dr Irwin, the Court medical officer, testified as to MacKowen's cause of death. Next, the witness Robert Y. Mills, a Negro who had heard his last words, took the stand. He told the Court that MacKowen could only speak very indistinctly in a whisper, but was able to say that Mr Emerson Thompson had shot him. He had then also given Mills a written statement. The statement, written with his left hand and barely legible, and stained with his own blood, read: 'Emerson Thompson crept up behind me + murdered me like the cowardly assassin he is. John C MacKowen' (statement and part of testimony overleaf)

R.E Thompson's testimony was as follows: 'Yesterday morning I was travelling along the public road, near the Comite River, and passed a buggy, and after getting a little piece ahead, I turned in my saddle and looked around and saw a man that I took to be John Mckowen. I asked him the question if that was John Mckowen, he made some remark to me that I did not understand. And immediately after making this remark reached around behind him and in an instant he had me covered with a large pistol. I at once reached for my pistol which was in my left-hand saddle pocket ... From the time I spoke to him and he to me he had his pistol sticking right at me and I think I hit him in the hand the first shot. I fired just as rapidly as I could. I was horseback. My horse was very fractious, stood on his feet and tried to get away and I just held him in. I was shooting and the horse was floundering around and I thought that Dr Mckowen fired a number of times but I could not state that positively. I shot six times. After I shot six times he drove off very fast. I did not know whether I had hit him or not. The top of the buggy was up and the

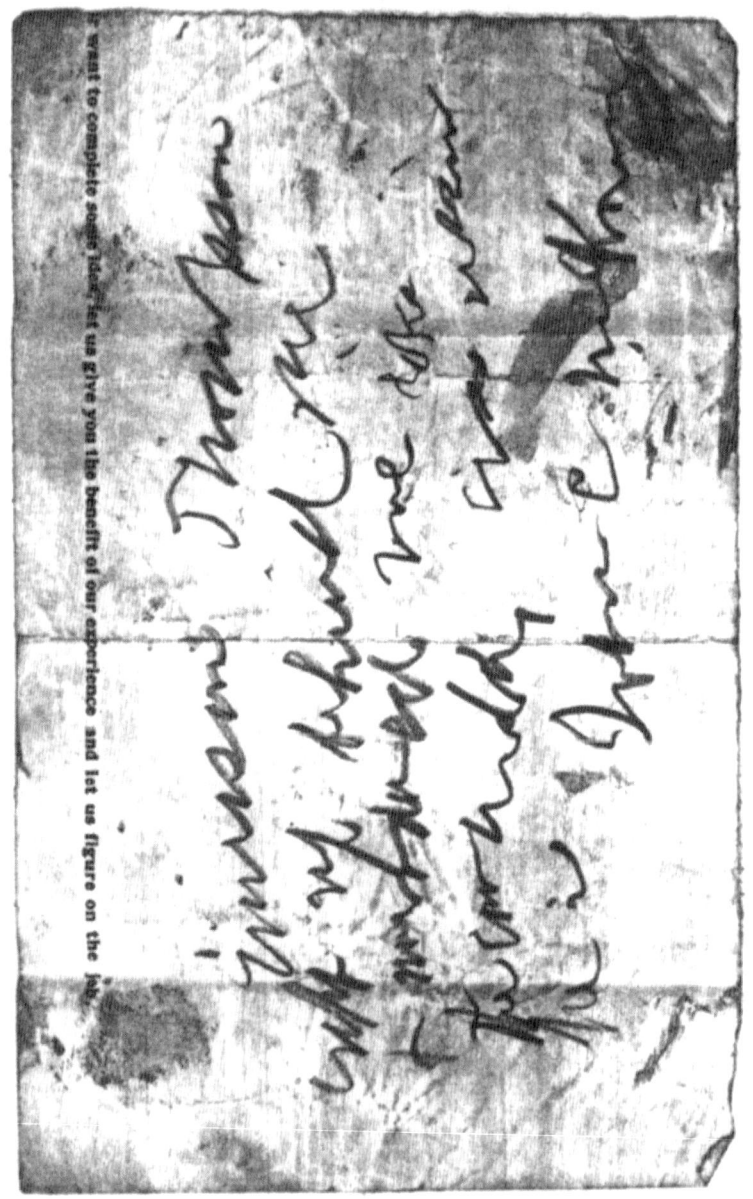

MacKowen's bloodstained note, scrawled in the moments before he died. Courtesy of Mr Michael F. Howell and Col. J.L. Hendrickson.

9

I was ahead of Dr McKuens
horse when I fired the first shot.
I think the first shot hit him in
the hand. I can't say positively
about that but that is my opinion.
I formed this opinion because I
am informed that he did not
shoot but once, but made several
attempts. I cannot say whether
he shot at me before I fired
at him or not, but that was
my impression. I was shooting
a 38 caliber pistol. The last
shot that I fired I aimed to
shoot through the buggy curtain.
To the best of my judgment I
was firing him + in sight of him
until the last shot:::
It has been about two years ago
to the best of my recollection when
I saw Dr McKuen at his
table. I don't remember of
ever seeing him before or
after that.

Redirect:-
My opinion that I disabled him at the
first shot is based on what I have since
heard, because I did not know then I had hit

Part of State Senator Thompson's testimony. Courtesy of Mr Michael F. Howell and Col. J.L. Hendrickson.

curtains drawn when I rode up. I did not know Dr Mckowen at all, I never seed him but once before in my life. This was on the road between the little bridge and Nettlewood gate. I have a place on the other side of the Comite and part of it this side. I did not know Dr Mckowen was in that neighbourhood or on that road. I was over there looking at my crop ... The reason why I spoke to Dr Mckowen was that I had been informed that Dr Mckowen was having my land enclosed with a wire fence ... After I had shot the six shots I broke the pistol down, threw the shells out and reloaded the pistol and I called to Dr Mckowen to come back and if he wanted a settlement I would give it to him ...'

In the cross-examination, R.E. Thompson stated: '... My object in addressing him was that I wanted to ask him about the fence he had had put up on my land ... I cannot say whether he shot at me before I fired at him or not, but that was my impression ... To the best of my judgment I was facing him and in face of him until the last shot. It has been about two years ago to the best of my recollection when I saw Dr Mckowen at Mrs Auel's. I don't remember of ever seeing him before or after that.'

Sherriff J.B. Bennett's testimony followed: 'As soon as I heard of this I went to the place. I saw the tracks of a shod horse which I supposed was the tracks of Mr Thompson's horse. I saw the same tracks coming out of Mr Thompson's field on the other side of Comite River. I picked up a lap robe and six empty shells 38-caliber. I picked them all up in the same place.' Shown pistol says it is the pistol handed to me as Dr Mckowen's. Offers the pistol. 'There was one empty shell that had been fired.'

Testimony closed, Sept. 19, 1901, J.L. Cravens, Clerk of the Distr. Court

It is ordered that the accused be released on giving bond in the sum of Five Thousand Dollars.[19]

In commenting on these proceedings it can be said that R. E. Thompson's testimony is rife with contradiction. ... As he was shooting, the horse became fractious and was floundering about so he was obliged to restrain him and therefore could not see where he was shooting. At the same time, however, he also claimed that Dr MacKowen had him in his sights the entire time. Even after having shot his adversary in the hand he continued to shoot – six shots – and the shells were found by the Sheriff at the site. Then, when MacKowen drove away, he reloaded his pistol and called to him to come back to find a solution (sic!). He also claimed that he had met MacKowen 'once before in my life. This was between the little bridge and Nettlewood gate.' Later in his testimony, however, he declared: 'It has been about two years ago to the best of my recollection when I saw Dr Mckowen at Mrs Auel's. I don't remember of ever seeing him before or after that.'

A Grand Jury investigated the incident but failed to indict Thompson. He was found not guilty – there were no witnesses and MacKowen was armed. The Grand Jury concluded it was a matter of self-defence and that there was insufficient evidence to proceed to trial.

John Clay MacKowen now lies in the Old Jackson Cemetery in East Feliciana, close to his brother Alexander's tomb, back home, resting in his Old South.[20]

MacKowen's grave, Old Jackson Cemetery, Jackson, Louisiana. Courtesy of Col. J.L. Hendrickson.

Epilogue

This story would be incomplete if fuller mention were not made of MacKowen's much-loved daughter Giulia, who in May 1900 had married Giovanni Maresca. The Maresca family produced dairy products brought to Capri from Massa Lubrense by Giovanni, which was how they had come to meet. When on the island he would stay at the home of a local priest living along the via Filietto in Anacapri. This narrow street led out on to the main road directly across from the Casa Rossa, where Giovanni could see Giulia on the balcony. The two fell in love, though their relationship did not at first meet with the approval of her father. As Giulia would relate years later, he once even turned her suitor out and threatened him with a pistol. A few years later, however, he evidently changed his mind. She was a tall, attractive young woman who played the piano and painted, and spoke English fluently. She had travelled with her father on one of his trips to America, and in later correspondence his American friends frequently referred to her as 'your beautiful daughter', expressing the hope of seeing her again in Louisiana.

Following her father's final departure, as is clear from her letters to him, she took an active part in managing the Marina Grande and Anacapri properties, and continued to hope for his return to Capri. In a letter of March 1898 she wrote: 'Foreigners are arriving in large numbers and the lovely season of spring has begun. The trees are in bloom, the peach and plum trees are laden with lovely pink and white blossoms, my two little birds are constantly chirping and everything here is very cheerful.' She never failed to send the warmest regards from Dr Cuomo and her father's other friends, and a kiss from her and her mother. MacKowen's papers contain the card shown here with her sketch of the Caffè Bitter, now the Hotel Caesar Augustus, where she sends him their greetings for Christmas 1899. She continued to write affectionate letters telling him about events in Anacapri – births, deaths, quarrels, tenants who weren't paying, the killing of a pig – 'they have killed the son of mamma (the pig), who was greatly grieved, he weighed 100 *rotoli.*'

Giulia and Giovanni Maresca lived in Sorrento for some years and then moved into the Casa Rossa. They had four sons, Armando, Guido, Mario and Silvio and two daughters, Clelia and Flora. Following the death of her husband, Giulia went to Argentina for a period to stay with Flora, but then returned to Capri. She is still remembered by elderly people as 'Donna Giulia', dignified in her behaviour, elegant in her

An Adventurous Life

Giulia's Christmas greetings from Caffè Bitter, 1899. Special Collections, LSU Libraries, Baton Rouge, Louisiana, by permission.

manner of dress, and as a person who unfailingly had tea at five in the afternoon. She wrote, read, painted, and received old friends to whom she frequently spoke of her father with pride, and she felt a part of the old Southern aristocracy. She died in Capri on May 20, 1964.

As long as she lived in her Anacapri home she kept things exactly the way her father had left them. The entire ground floor was furnished with Turkish antiques, azure-coloured, wooden furniture encrusted with mother-of-pearl and small mirrors. On the first floor there was a hall where the weapons were kept, just as in a museum, including the armour, daggers, pistols, arquebuses and finely inlaid rifles which her father had brought back from his trips to North Africa and the Orient. A library on the same floor housed maps and books that he had not taken with him when he returned to Louisiana. The walls were lined with paintings and old prints, and antique pieces of ceramics and porcelain were displayed on the furniture. In the courtyard there were some archaeological finds, as well as the large marble statue which can still be seen there today. At the time, the Casa Rossa attracted more visitors than Axel Munthe's villa.

When Giulia moved to Marina Grande, where her son Mario successfully managed the Pensione Maresca, the building began to decline.

The Casa Rossa. Reproduction in black and white of a colour painting by Mr Sergio Rubino, Anacapri. Courtesy of the artist.

Many of the most valuable furnishings were sold at auction in Venice, and following a series of unrelated ventures it was purchased by the Naples Superintendency for Architectural and Landscape Heritage and granted for use as a museum to the town of Anacapri.

MacKowen would surely be satisfied to see the Casa Rossa in its present role, serving the best possible purposes of a museum, staffed by a dedicated and knowledgeable team of curators and with much of its statuary and other artefacts still in place. It now also houses a number of statues of sea divinities that were found on the seabed inside the Blue Grotto between 1964 and 1974, a very fine collection of nineteenth-century paintings on the landscape and life of the island, and a display of photographs and documents relating to the archaeological findings and historical studies undertaken since MacKowen's time. This remarkable red-painted building in the centre of Anacapri, witness to so much of the long history of the island, is once again open for all to visit.

Notes

1. All the quotations, unless otherwise quoted, are taken from the McKowen-Lilley-Stirling Family Papers, Special Collections, LSU Libraries, New Orleans, Louisiana. These consist of correspondence, legal documents, financial papers, professional and personal papers, printed items, and photographs. For the most part the documents bear witness to the activities of John C. MacKowen but they also include papers of John McKowen, William Robert McKowen, David M. Pipes and other Louisiana figures. The correspondence is essentially related to the activities of John C. MacKowen and general correspondence to and from his family. There are letters regarding the possible donation of MacKowen's book collection to a New Orleans Library; letters in Italian, French and German which are for the most part personal and include correspondence with MacKowen's daughter Giulia and her husband, Giovanni Maresca; and MacKowen's medical correspondence and letters from publishers and editors concerning the publication of his works and articles. Included are plans and drawings of Mackowen's Blue Grotto property in Anacapri and many newspapers cuttings.
2. A.W. Bergeron, Jr., *Guide to Louisiana Confederate Military Units 1861-1865*, LSU Press, 1989.
3. Alfred Armand Louis Marie Velpeau (1795-1867) was a surgeon who provided the first accurate description of leukaemia. Charles Adolphe Wurtz (1817-1884) was a chemist for whom the Wurtz reaction was named.
4. The original university degree is currently in possession of the Cuomo family. MacKowen, upon his departure from the island, entrusted his degree to his close friend Dr Vincenzo Cuomo. Carl von Voit (1831-1908) had been a professor of physiology at the University of Munich since 1860 and is considered to be the 'father' of modern dietetics. As a chemist and a physiologist he found that the amount of nitrogen in excreted urea is a measure of protein turnover. He was also a successful teacher, attracting international students to the University of Munich and thus also significantly influencing US nutritionists.
5. 'Have received the amount of 100 Italian Lire from Mr. John C. Mackowen for a boat with sail named Luisa as well as all the equipment belonging to this boat. Payment settled Alessio Federico. Witnessed by Giuseppe Petagna and G. Demirgiar.' Alessio Federico (who signed with a cross) and his brother were the owners of a piece of land adjacent to the property MacKowen was to purchase in Marina Grande. Giuseppe Petagna, the son of Don Salvatore Petagna (1800–1875), the owner of the Hotel Villa di Londra, the first true hotel in Marina Grande, signed as a witness.

6. From the unpublished diary of Vincenzo Cuomo (1858-1935) which was generously made available by the Cuomo family.
7. Horace Stuart Cummings, *Dartmouth College, Sketches of the Class of 1862* (15 June, 1884) wrote: 'He has a fine villa, a vineyard and an olive orchard, and occupies his time in writing, painting, making oil and wine, for a portion of the year, and travels the rest, spending his winters in Egypt, Greece, Tunis, Southern Spain, and other localities. A Southerner in political faith, and seems to think that his religious tendencies are Buddhism mixed with the maxims and precepts of our old college friend Horace.'
8. On June 16, 1887 he purchased a three-storey property in the district of Torre, with balcony ... wash-house, court yard, cistern ... in mediocre state adjacent to the carriageable road and on the other sides with a building belonging to Francescantonio and Luigi Farace. April 10, 1888 he purchased other property, cistern and courtyard and the freehold of a plot of land at the foot of the tower from Francescantonio Farace. On May 13, 1896 he bought a small room and entrance for use as a cattle shed from Salvatore Savastano. The property was adjacent to the public road to the north, with the MacKowen property to the east, the property of Salvatore Savastano to the west, and to the south with a fountain and mill used for making olive oil, owned by Luigi Farace.
9. I conti delle quaglie / 'O buono trassito', a specific area where migratory quails roosted, as recorded in certain deeds of purchase.
10. In his essay of 1846, Chevalley de Rivaz wrote that it would have been desirable to dig a passage through the upper part of the grotto as 'it would be a great advantage for the inhabitants of Capri and for the tourists to get a comfortable access to visit the grotto.'
11. Quoted in *Aromatic Toxins* (1898).
12. *Aromatic Toxins*.
13. In New Orleans he rented an apartment on the ninth floor of the Hennen Building (now named the Maritime Building) for use as an office and an apartment to live in. In his archives there are numerous letters from his patients thanking him for his advice.
14. John C. McKowen M.D., New Orleans. 'Aromatic Toxins'. Reprinted from *New Orleans Medical and Surgical Journal*, June–September 1898. 'TO MY MASTER in Physiological-Chemical-Laboratory Work, VOIT, Professor of Physiology at the University of Munich, Germany. This description of a new disease, of its remedies, of its relations to and complications with other diseases, and of its diagnostical worth in throwing light on morbid processes not understood until now, is dedicated as a tribute of respect by one of the workers in the laboratory of this sharp observer, deep thinker, and indefatigable searcher after scientific truth.'

An Adventurous Life

15. Deed of sale dated March, 1899 signed in New Orleans and registered in Sorrento on 14 April, 1901.
16. The receipt of the munificent donation of his priceless books and ancient bindings, together with a collection of engravings illustrating the history of printing and bookbinding, was acknowledged on behalf of Mrs Josephine Louise Newcomb, the College founder, by the College President Brandt V. B. Dixon in the Tulane Bulletin of 1897-1898. The collection was the subject of a major display in February 1916 and again in October 1935, receiving in both cases wide coverage in the local and regional press. MacKowen's valuable manuscripts and rare books were kept there until 1941, when the Howard Memorial Library, the F.W. Tilton Memorial Library and the Newcomb Memorial Library were merged into the Howard-Tilton Memorial of Tulane University. During the course of the merger the collections were joined together into a combined Rare Books section and MacKowen's donation can no longer be identified as such. It is still possible, however, to consult a record of the books from his donation. In *A Brief History of H. Sophie Newcomb Memorial College 1887–1919* (1928, p.106) Brandt V.B. Dixon, by then President Emeritus of the Newcomb Memorial, wrote: 'For the display of these (books), carved oak tables were specially made, upon which were placed large glass cases'. In *The History of the Boston Club* (New Orleans, 1938, p.314) there is a short biography of Colonel MacKowen which mentions his donation to the Newcomb College Library. In the footnote we can read: 'The memory of impetuous John MacKowen will be kept alive by these 500-year old books as long as they shall last, and this will probably be for another five hundred years, because they were printed on handmade paper with loving care by craftsmen who were thorough. In a word, these books were, like their donor, stoutly made.' The display cases are now in the Art Department building – one of them still with a little silver plaque on it, two inches in length: 'Donated to H. Sophie Newcomb Memorial College by Dr. John C. MacKowen'.
17. Robert Emerson Thompson (1857–1932) was the owner of 'Glencoe', a beautiful house built in 1870 which was destroyed by a fire in 1898 and then rebuilt. In order to avoid another devastating fire, it was shingled in galvanized aluminium.
18. Newspaper cutting, Wilson, Louisiana.
19. MacKowen's last words and preliminary hearing (courtesy of Mr M.F. Howell and Colonel J.L. Hendrickson).
20. In his will, MacKowen left his property in America to his nieces and nephews and his property on the island of Capri to his daughter Giulia Cimino. On 31 May, 1902 William Robert McKowen, represented by Maria Cimino, the daughter of the late Antonio, sold the following assets in the district of Marina Grande to Giulia Cimino, the wife of Giovanni Maresca: a building

composed of several storeys known as the Louvre, together with lots of land located to the rear of the building; in the town of Anacapri in the area known as Torre, another building composed of several rooms, a ground storey and first storey; in the area of Gradola, several lots of adjacent land overlooking the Blue Grotto for an extension of 116 ares (1.16 hectares, or just under three acres) to be destined as a resting place for migratory quails. The agreed sale price was 30,000 Lire. On June 6, 1902 Arthur King, son of the late Carlo Guglielmo King, sold to Axel Munthe the Materita Tower and plots of land located in the Pino or Perillo area; another plot, with a well named Materita, Marisotto or Pistello, and a large expanse of property which had once belonged to the Certosa. On May 18, 1911 he sold to Giulia Evelina Cimino uncultivated land with a limekiln and an adjacent storage area, as well as two other small lots of uncultivated land used for accommodating nets to capture the quails on either side of the Blue Grotto.

Chapter 9
The Geology of Capri: a noble endeavour
Filippo Barattolo

To the geologically well-informed reader MacKowen's work appears dated, and viewed from a modern perspective some of his interpretations would not now be acceptable. Nevertheless, his thinking was in keeping with what was held to be valid in the scientific circles of his time and although he had not studied geology, the precision of his efforts to reconstruct certain geological events is commendable. In principle, it is fair to say that the methodology he adopted in reconstructing past events was essentially correct, even though it was based upon assumptions now considered to be erroneous.

It would also have been difficult for him to deal simply with his subject matter, because the period in which he was writing was a very particular moment in the course of the geological knowledge of Capri. In fact, certain significant geological concepts proposed by the naturalist Scipione Breislak,[1] who visited the island between 1787 and 1794, did not give rise to any subsequent in-depth research by nineteenth-century geologists. Further information had been published in 1840 by Pasquale La Cava,[2] yet to all intents and purposes the geological framework remained essentially unaltered for nearly a century, and was to remain so until the arrival of a group of eminent German scholars[3] who conducted innovative geological studies between 1886 and 1898.[4] Therefore, without access to the wealth of material in these studies, the geological theories proposed by MacKowen were essentially the fruit of his own knowledge of the available geological literature and his own original interpretations as they applied to the context of Capri.

The re-issue of his book *Capri* allows us to look carefully at the merits of his contributions. Before doing so, however, it is necessary to present a modern geological outline of the geology of the island, so as to provide a sufficient commentary and contextualisation of certain obsolete hypotheses and thus avoid their being re-circulated.

From a geological perspective, Capri is a natural continuation of the Sorrento peninsula. These two elements represent a raised mass (horst) of a carbonate nature (limestone and dolomite), laterally bordered by

Capri and the Sorrento peninsula, circa 1905. Centro Caprense Ignazio Cerio Archive, Capri.

depressed blocks of land (graben) by means of normal faults which run in a predominantly NE-SW direction; these depressed areas now constitute the substrate of the sea bed. Capri is therefore to be considered an integral part, and the westernmost offshoot, of the Southern Apennines and it has been involved in all the geological events which have led to the current state of the Apennine mountain range.[5] This mountain range is a complex system of nappes (that is, on a regional scale, sheet-like bodies of rock) formed during the Neogene period; these underwent horizontal translation, over-thrusting, interlocking and verging towards the Adriatic between 15 to 2-3 million years ago.[6]

The sediments deposited prior to that period of Apennine mountain-building currently constitute the backbone of this mountain range and they can be roughly categorised into two types of marine successions dating back to between the Triassic and the early Miocene periods. The former, composed of carbonates (limestone and dolomite) from a shallow water environment of at least a few thousand metres in thickness, corresponds to a carbonate platform similar to that of the modern-day Bahamas, whereas the latter varies in nature (carbonate, siliceous and

The Geology of Capri: a noble endeavour

terrigenous sediment), thus indicating a deep-sea deposition. The white, massive calcareous bulk of the island of Capri can be regarded as the result of a deposition of mud and the remains of marine organisms along the western edge of a vast carbonate platform[7] known as the Apennine Platform, which outcrops from the Lepini Mountains (Latium) to the Coastal Chain in Calabria.[8]

In an interval ranging from the late Pliocene to the mid-Pleistocene (circa 3 million to 120,000 years ago), following the emplacement of nappes which comprise the Apennine range, the Tyrrhenian coastal strip underwent appreciable subsidence, i.e. it tended to shift downward, a typical example of which is Piana Campana. This sinking followed a stepwise pattern towards the Tyrrhenian Sea and, along the coastal strip, left structurally elevated areas arranged at right angles to the direction of the mountain range, that is with a NE-SW way (known as anti-Apennine direction), one of which is, precisely, the Sorrento Peninsula/ island of Capri horst. On the contrary, however, the westernmost Apennine sector was subject to gradual uplift.

The particular position of Capri, facing the Tyrrhenian Sea, is such that owing to the distribution of marine and continental deposits and the old shore terraces that are present at varying altitudes, this island landscape conserves in a spectacular manner the erosive processes that have taken place since the late Pliocene (circa 2-3 million years ago). These landscape-modelling events have led to the current conformation of the island by means of a series of transformations which can be classified in four successive phases.[9]

Initially (Phase I: 2-3 million to1.6 million years ago), the area of Capri had substantially emerged and was characterised by relatively uneven elevations; the island's extension, conformation and connection with other emerged areas in the Campania area are not easily assessable. During this phase, erosion sculpted and softened the slopes. The Mount Solaro and Cetrella sectors in Anacapri and the Tiberio / Mount San Michele sectors in Capri were situated at the same altitude. At the end of this first phase a general uplift of some one hundred metres took place, followed by a collapse involving only the eastern part of Capri island, which underwent submersion.

During an interval between the early Pleistocene and part of the mid-Pleistocene (Phase II: some 1.6 million to 400,000 years ago), level ground was created by the sea on the slopes of this profoundly modified landscape at an elevation of 300–320m (for example, the Migliara terrace). At that time, other elevations must have existed which have since disappeared, including at least one located south of the area of Mount Solaro / Migliara and another which rose in the valley between Capri and Anacapri. Subsequently, there was a progressive uplift which led to a gradual emergence of the island. Terraces created by marine abrasion during this uplift are visible at an elevation of 260–250m as well as at an elevation of 150–130m (of which one example is the Damecuta terrace). This uplift triggered the dismantling of the relief dominating the valley between Capri and Anacapri, which had rested upon a clay complex.

In the Mid-Pleistocene (Phase III: some 400–200,000 years ago), the island underwent further uplift, resulting in the formation of the terraces currently situated between 100m–30m (for example, along the eastern versant (Materita / Punta Campetiello). The terrace situated at 100m is the site of an ancient coastal lake or lagoon once located near what is now the Hotel Quisisana, where the remains of large mammals were discovered in 1905, clearly indicating that Capri had once been part of the Sorrento Peninsula. Moreover, the island's calcareous slopes had been profoundly sculpted; the valley between Capri and Anacapri was completely dismantled, as were the elevations located to the south of Mount Solaro / Migliara and those which linked Capri to the Sorrento Peninsula. By the end of phase III, Capri had assumed the form of an island.

During the Late Pleistocene (Phase IV: 124,000–10,000 years ago), the island's configuration was almost definitive and the phenomenon of uplift came to a halt. The island appears to have reached tectonic stability some 124,000 ago.[10] Only some limited slope modelling caused by sea level oscillation took place after the last glacial phases. At this point Capri was separated from the mainland, but the lowering of the sea level, coinciding with the coldest phases of the last glacial period (i.e. Last Glacial Maximum or Würm), assessable in lowering down to –120m, temporarily created peninsular conditions. These brief periods allowed for the settlement of various fauna that would gradually assume insular characteristics. Over the past 10,000 years, only minor oscillations of the sea have occurred.[11]

MacKowen's chapter on geology begins with a description of the oldest rocks composing the bulk of the island,[12] which he dated to the Tertiary period without however providing any proof.[13] Although Cenozoic sediments are present,[14] to all intents most of the calcareous mass dates back to the Mesozoic era (Jurassic and Cretaceous).[15] He then described the disposition of the strata and deserves credit for having provided the first measurements of immersion and inclination of these dislocated strata.[16] Next he considered the process of calcareous dissolution and the formation of the grottoes – a process which, in modern times, is known as karstification.[17] In general, the process is accurately described. In his time, however, knowledge was fragmentary and a reconstruction of the process, although available in scientific articles,[18] was not to be found in geology manuals or summarised treatises. Using his knowledge of limestone dissolution to 'read' the island's rugged landscape, his precise observations led him to reach scientifically-based conclusions.[19]

He hypothesised that repeated events of subsidence and uplift of the ground, together with earthquakes, would have had their repercussions on the formation of Capri's rocky mass.[20] The shorelines modelled by the sea, the traces of which are visible at various heights, are indeed proof of these alternating vertical movements. In his book (pages 2–3, 5–6) he states that the 'Temple of Serapis in Pozzuoli' was the key to understanding the historical time-frame of these movements. Furthermore, the abundance of Roman ruins which cropped out here and there on the island seemed to allow for a precise correlation with those found in Pozzuoli,[21] and thus for the uplift and subsidence of the ground as well as for the westward tilting of the island mass.[22] According to him these events – as in Pozzuoli – were tightly intertwined with the chronology of human history; hence his impassioned search for archaeological remains of the Roman period, especially those close to the sea-level and natural emergences which could bear witness to such ancient movements.[23]

In Capri the most evident sea level indentation (notch) indicator of relative sea-level change is situated at a little less than eight metres above sea level.[24] Credit should be given to MacKowen, notwithstanding the limitations of his chronology, for having identified and correctly interpreted Capri's Tyrrhenian notch, from which he drew his conclusions in reconstructing the island's movements. In confirmation of movements which took place in ancient times, he cited the uplift in the area of Torre del Greco following the 1861 eruption,[25] although his reconstruction of the presumed, significant movements of the island's central sector (pages 6–7) seems a little far-fetched. For example, he estimated a subsidence of the Marina Grande sector with a vertical displacement of some 150m, a figure based exclusively on the southward inclination of a sewage line, which he believed was a *cloaca* or ancient sewer and assumed had initially inclined northward.

His chapter on geology concludes with an extremely interesting description of vegetation carbonised into volcanic ash, and an evocative though somewhat disquieting image of the eruption of the Gulf of Naples, the 'Crater of the Greeks'.[26] Aspects partially related to geology can be in fact be found throughout his entire book,[27] whereas it is noticeable that the rich botanical diversity and the zoological peculiarities, such as the blue lizard found on the Faraglioni,[28] only marginally attracted his interest. On the whole, it was the island's rugged, craggy landscape and its wealth of ancient history that captured MacKowen's imagination and which, according to him, constituted 'the dangerous beauty of Capri'.

Notes
1. S. Breislak, *Topografia fisica della Campania*, Florence 1798. Capri is described on pp. 37–42 as well as in 'Mineralogia dell'isola di Capri. Lettera del sig. Breislak professore di Mineralogia in Napoli del Real Corpo degli Artiglieri diretta al sig. Hadrava' in D. Romanelli, *Isola di Capri. Manoscritti inediti del Conte della Torre Rezzonico, del professore Breislak, e del Generale Pommereul*. Naples 1816, pp. 111–22.
2. P. La Cava, 'I. Geologia', *Statistica fisica ed economica dell'isola di Capri. Esercitazioni accademiche degli Aspiranti Naturalisti*, 2, I. Naples 1840, pp. 1–22.
3. Among the numerous works on the subject, the following are cited: J. Walther, 'Über die Geologie von Capri', *Zeitschrift der Deutschen Geologischen Gesellschaft*, 41, 1888, pp. 771–6; G. Steinmann, 'Über das Alter des Apenninkalkes von Capri', *Bericht Naturforschenden Gesellschaft Freiburg*, 4, 1889, pp. 48–52; P. Oppenheim, 'Beiträge zur Geologie der Insel Capri und der Halbinsel Sorrent', *Zeitschrift der Deutschen Geologischen Gesellschaft*, 42, 1889, pp. 758–64; H. Karsten, 'Zur Geologie der Insel Capri 1', *Neues Jahrbuch für Mineralogie, Geologie und Paläontologie*, 1895, pp. 139–161.
4. Paul Oppenheim was also the author of a book on the geology of Capri for the German-speaking public: P. Oppenheim, *Die Insel der Sirenen von ihrer Entstehung bis zur Gegenwart. Eine populäre Darstellung der physischen und politischen Geschichte der Insel Capri. Mit einer geologischen Karte der Insel Capri*. Berlin 1890.

The Geology of Capri: a noble endeavour

5. A. Bosellini, *Storia geologica d'Italia. Gli ultimi 200 milioni di anni*. Zanichelli, Bologna 2005; A. Schettino, E. Turco: 'Tectonic history of the western Tethys since the Late Triassic', *Geological Society of America Bulletin*, 123, 1/2, 2011, pp. 89–105.

6. As regards the Apennines, the first evidence of such movements was only presented in the early eighteenth century (M. Anelli, 'Sulla presenza di falde di ricoprimento nell'Italia meridionale', *Atti della Società dei naturalisti e matematici di Modena*, 70, 1939, pp. 1–13). With reference to Capri, the nappe theory was advanced by Gaetano Rovereto in 1907 (G. Rovereto, 'L'ile de Capri est un lambeau de recouvrement?', *Bulletin de la société géologique de France*, 7, 1907, pp. 162–3), but was harshly criticized by Giuseppe De Lorenzo (G. De Lorenzo, 'L'isola di Capri', *Rendiconti dell'Accademia dei Lincei, Classe di Scienze Fisiche*, Series 5, 14, 1907, pp. 853–7). For a summary of the interpretive models, reference is made to: F. M. Guadagno, 'L'isola di Capri: geologia, morfologia e rischio da frana tra salvaguardia dell'ambiente e turismo', *Conoscere Capri*, 3, 2005, pp. 11–29.

7. F. Barattolo and A. Pugliese, 'Il Mesozoico dell'Isola di Capri', *Quaderni dell'Accademia Pontaniana*, 8, 1987, p. 172; F. Barattolo, 'Capri nel Cenozoico', *Conoscere Capri*, 2, 2004, pp. 15–29; B. D'Argenio, C. Violante, M. Sacchi, F. Badillon, G. Pappone, E. Casciello and M. Cesarano, 'Capri, Bocca Piccola and Punta Campanella Marine. Marine and on-land geology compared', *Mapping Geology in Italy*, ed. G. Pasquare, C. Venturini and G. Groppelli, Florence 2004, pp. 36-42.

8. MacKowen makes reference to this limestone (p. 1, lines 2–3).

9. F. Barattolo, A. Cinque, E. D'Alessandro, M. Guida, P. Romano and E. Russo Ermolli, 'Geomorfologia ed evoluzione tettonica quaternaria dell'Isola di Capri', *Studi geologici camerti*, Special edition, 1993, pp. 221–9.

10. MacKowen's attempt to utilise archaeological remains dating back to the Roman era to extrapolate a chronology of significant movements of uplift and subsidence in the order of tens, if not hundreds, of meters is dated. During the past 124,000 years, only minimum deviations of a few decimetres have taken place: L. Ferranti and F. Antonioli, 'Misure del solco tirreniano (mis 5.5) nell'isola di Capri: valutazione di attività tettonica durante il Pleistocene Superiore', *Il Quaternario, Italian Journal of Quaternary Sciences*, 20(2), 2007, pp. 125–36.

11. K. Lambeck, F. Antonioli, M. Anzidei, L. Ferranti, G. Leoni, G. Scicchitano and S. Silenzi, 'Sea level change along the Italian coast during the Holocene and projections for the future', *Quaternary International*, 232(1–2), 2011, pp. 250–7.

12. 'The island of Capri is composed of limestone from the Tertiary period, with a small deposit, here and there, of sandstone'. MacKowen, p. 1, Breislak (*op.*

Capri – The Island Revisited

    cit., p. 114) is much more precise in his description of siliciclastic sediment (the 'sandstone' referred to by MacKowen).
13. Neither Breislak (*op. cit.*), nor La Cava (*op. cit.*) attempted geological dating attribution. The use of fossils in attributing sedimentary rock to geological ages only began to take form in the first half of the 20th century, and was subsequently developed.
14. Barattolo, *op. cit.*
15. The remark made by Ignazio Cerio is more well-founded. He wrote: 'Geologically incorrect. The main rock of the isle is calcareous (limestone) and Lower Cretaceous in age. The Tertiary covers the valley between Mount St. Michele and the relief of Anacapri as well as from the road called Due Golfi (Two Gulfs) leading to Marina Piccola and Marina Grande.' However, it is not known whether it was written before the work of the German geologists (see Note 4) in which attribution of Capri limestone to the Late Jurassic or the Early Cretaceous was thoroughly and, at times, heatedly debated.
16. MacKowen, p. 1. The first report of stratified limestone is attributed to La Cava (*op. cit.*, p. 12).
17. P. E. LaMoreaux, 'History of karst hydrogeological studies', *Proceedings of the International Conference on Environmental Changes in Karst Areas –* I.G.U. – U.I.S. – Italy 15–27 Sept. 1991, *Quaderni del Dipartimento di Geografia dell'Università di Padova*, 13, 1991, pp. 215–29; W. B. White, 'A brief history of karst hydrogeology: contributions of the NSS', *Journal of Cave and Karst Studies*, 69, 1, pp. 13–26.
18. Studies on karstic modelling process would only be developed in the following decades; for example, see S. T. Trudgill, 'Chapter 4. Limestone Landforms, 1890–1965', *The history of the Study of Landforms on the Development of Geomorphology*, ed. T.P. Burt, R.J. Chorley, D. Brunsen, N.J. Cox and A.S. Goudie, Bath 2008, pp. 107–25.
19. J. C. MacKowen, pp. 1–2.
20. J. C. MacKowen, p. 2.
21. The Serapis in Pozzuoli served as a classic reference for geologists of the late 19th and most of the 20th centuries owing to the clearly evident traces of past sea levels. MacKowen's writings were in keeping with the scientific theories of the time. As regards the Serapis, see the fine work of L. Ciancio, *Le colonne del tempo. Il tempio di Serapide a Pozzuoli nella storia della geologia, dell'archeologia e dell'arte (1750–1900)*, Florence 2009, in addition to S. J. Gould, 'Lyell's Pillars of Wisdom' in *The Lying Stones of Marrakech: Penultimate Reflections in Natural History*, New York 2000. Italian translation 'Le colonne della saggezza di Lyell', in *Le pietre false di Marrakech, appunti di storia naturale*. Milan 2007, pp. 187-213.

The Geology of Capri: a noble endeavour

22. According to MacKowen (p. 6), the western part of the island is 10 feet (3 metres) less uplifted than the eastern portion.
23. For example, the Blue Grotto is viewed as proof that at the time of Tiberius the island was uplifted some 6 meters higher than today (p. 96). Ironically, a few months prior to the publication of *Capri*, the Italian geologist Arturo Issel published a momentous work on the gradual land movements (bradyseism): A. Issel, 'Le oscillazioni lente del suolo o bradisismi', *Atti R. Università di Genova*, 5, 1883, p. 422, summarised by the same author in: 'Le oscillazioni lente del suolo', *Nuova Antologia*, 71, 20, 1883, pp. 646–66. Issel attributed the sea level fluctuations recorded on the columns at Serapeo to local phenomena related to the volcanic activity in the area and thus not 'exportable' to adjacent areas. In relation to the Blue Grotto, see also Rossella Zaccagnini's chapter in this present volume, pp. 173–5.
24. The notch reasonably corresponds to the one located near the Sorrento Peninsula which can be radiometrically dated to circa 129,000 years ago: L. Brancaccio, G. Capaldi, A. Cinque, R. Pece and I. Sgrosso, '230Th-238U dating of coral from Tyrrhenian beach in Sorrentine Peninsula (Southern Italy)', *Quaternaria*, 20, 1978, pp. 175–83. In geological literature, a notch refers to the Tyrrhenian geological stage (also known as the Tyrrhenian notch). MacKowen utilises the Tyrrhenian notch which at Punta Masullo (site of the modern day Villa Malaparte) he calculates at 22 feet (circa 6.6m), and circa 3.6m at Punta Carena (where the displacement is 3 meters). Recent measurements (L. Ferranti, 'Movimenti "lenti" nell'isola di Capri negli ultimi 124.000 anni', *Conoscere Capri*, 6, 2007, pp. 11–37), have confirmed that a gradual differential subsidence towards NW has occurred since 124,000 ago and it cannot be excluded that a slight movement may have taken place in the past. Instead, the notches indicated by MacKowen are, respectively, located at quota 7.1m and 6.3m (L. Ferranti, *op. cit.*, fig. 6). Further on in the text, MacKowen returns to the question of the Tyrrhenian notch in reference to the Grotta Azzurra and the Faraglioni (pp. 92, 106).
25. J. C. MacKowen, pp. 6–7. This passage, written by the illustrious Neapolitan geophysicist Luigi Palmieri, was presumably taken from a letter, perhaps written to MacKowen. The eruption and uplift to which reference is made in the text were described in: L. Palmieri, 'Intorno all'incendio del Vesuvio cominciato il dì 8 dicembre 1861', *Rendiconti dell'Accademia Pontaniana*, 10, 1862, pp. 40–61, 72–83.
26. See also p. 9.
27. J. C. MacKowen, pp. 8–9. Actually, the Gulf of Naples is a tectonic depression (graben), the pyroclastic material which was deposited on the island came, for the most part, from the Campi Flegrei (Campanian Ignimbrite Eruption) although a coeval small eruptive centre in Capri Marina Grande is not excluded (personal communication of Prof. Giuseppe Rolandi).

28. For example, in 'Topography and Climate', pp. 10–11, it was observed that following a rainfall, even one that was intense, the land remained dry and the water did not stagnate, nor was it absorbed by limestone. Indeed, limestone is impermeable; however this is true only in terms of matrix porosity, but not in terms of fracture and conduit porosity. These last two factors determine the rapid infiltration of water into the subsoil and the characteristic dryness following a rain shower. The lack of water does not depend so much on scarce rainfall as on the island's geological nature and conformation: there are aquifers, but they flow into the sea and the few utilisable springs were insufficient even in Roman times. On the other hand, rainfall in Capri is not scarce: the recorded 900mm of annual rainfall falls well within the average for the region (the Campania Region, 'Piano Regionale per la Programmazione delle Attività di Previsione Prevenzione e Lotta Attiva contro gli Incendi Boschivi – Anno 2007', *Bollettino Ufficiale della Regione Campania*, special issue dated 12.07.2007, p. 154, and especially pp. 7–8).
29. A few years earlier, this interesting chromatic phenomenon had attracted German biologists and triggered bitter scientific dispute. For a summary, see: V. Caputo, 'Le lucertole azzurre di Capri', *Almanacco Caprese*, 7, 1994, pp. 39–51. In reference to the evolutionary phenomenon, see: P. Raia, F. M. Guarino, M. Turano, G. Polese, D. Rippa, F. Carotenuto, D. M. Monti, M. Cardi and D. Fulgione, 'The blue lizard spandrel and the island syndrome', *BioMed Central Evolutionary Biology*, 10, 2010, pp. 289–305.

Chapter 10
It All Began with Cave-dwellers: MacKowen and the ancient history of Capri
Eduardo Federico

In his book *Capri*, MacKowen traces the ancient history of the island in keeping with the customary eighteenth- and nineteenth-century scheme, according to which it had been inhabited first by the Phoenicians, followed by the Greeks and then by the Romans.[1]

However, encouraged by the scientific researches of Ignazio Cerio – and particularly by Cerio's archaeological collection – MacKowen chose to introduce a new player to the island's ancient history. He stated that after having viewed the utensils and pottery found by Cerio in the Grotta dell'Arco, he was convinced that the first inhabitants of Capri had been cave-dwellers.[2] The abundance of such finds in the grottoes, many of which, as in the case of the Grotta dell'Arco, had been at sea level in ancient times, led him to believe that the island's first inhabitants had belonged to a community which enjoyed well-established relations with many other peoples, linked either by sea routes or else during times when the island was still joined to the mainland. In addition, the utensils were made from a kind of stone not found on Capri and the pottery even displayed 'exotic' characteristics.[3]

Convinced also that historical facts could in some cases be inferred from the poems of Homer, he held that the myth of Ulysses visiting the island of the Sirens was in fact a historic vestige of relations between the island's prehistoric inhabitants and other seafaring peoples. For him, *Sirena*, the name of the rock located on the same side of the island as the Grotta dell'Arco, was sufficient proof. And again, the presence of human bones – which in the episode related by Homer covered the island – may well have reinforced his support for Cerio's idea that the story of the Sirens referred to the existence on Capri of a very ancient population of cannibals.[4] Even so, MacKowen's otherwise idyllic and rather puritanical view of the island's history doubtless persuaded him against openly proposing the likelihood of such a 'scandalous' practice.

*Grotta delle Felci (a small grotto situated within the Grotta dell'Arco).
Ink sketch by Edwin Cerio, circa 1920. Centro Caprense Ignazio Cerio Archive, Capri.*

He also continued to support an idea, based on a theory starting in the eighteenth century and in his time still much in vogue, that because Phoenician characteristics could be recognised among the 'exotic' pottery from the Grotta dell'Arco, the Phoenicians had therefore been present on the island. From this he concluded that the Phoenicians had supplanted the cave-dwellers, paving the way for the arrival of the Greeks. He felt that it was improbable, although not to be completely

It All Began with Cave-dwellers

discounted, that the name 'Capri' had originated from the Semitic word 'Capraim' (two towns). Whatever the case, the presence of the Phoenicians was thought to have been unobtrusive and sporadic, with no lasting influence on the island. Interestingly, he makes no mention of the 'Phoenician Steps'.[5]

On the other hand, he attributed a significant role to the Greeks. According to Virgil, the Teleboi, a mythical people from Acarnania, had lived on the island and MacKowen took this to imply that the first Greeks to settle on Capri would have come from Arcarnania.[6] He also maintained that the name 'Capri' had been given to the island by the Greeks, that it originated from the Greek word *kapros* (boar), and that it could not have come from the Latin *capra* (goat) because the Romans had only arrived much later. It was known that there had been an abundance of wild boar on the island and he surmised that the Greeks could reasonably have given it a name associated with that animal.[7] He referred to the island's dependence on the Greek town of Cuma when he conjectured that the Cumans had built the 'Cyclopean wall' on Capri (which was used as a prison for common lawbreakers or prisoners of war).[8] And he was of the opinion that their presence on the island was deeply rooted and long-lasting, as evidenced by the Greek cemetery discovered in the area of Castiglione,[9] the Greek inscriptions found on the island,[10] and the information provided by Suetonius that Greek traditions and institutions were still thriving when Augustus arrived on Capri.[11]

Recalling that Augustus, according to Suetonius, used to amuse himself playing with the youths of Capri, MacKowen regarded the emperor's stay on the island as a respite from the excessively busy life he led in Rome.[12] His arrival in about 30 B.C. had brought large sums of money to the island, with the result that the inhabitants were no longer obliged to live the hard life of fishermen and sailors and were employed instead in the construction and maintenance of villas.[13] Our author however was more concerned with the emperor Tiberius, devoting an entire chapter to the reasons that had led him to withdraw to Capri and remain for a whole decade (27–37 A.D.).[14] In contrast to his description of Augustus' time in Capri, he drew from a large body of ancient sources describing the decade that Tiberius spent there as one of the darkest in Roman history, scarred by cruelty and licentiousness. MacKowen followed the tradition of certain scholars who defended his behaviour from a psychological point of view, even to the extent of analysing the most important effigies of him, particularly those that displayed any hint of sadness. This led him to conclude that family problems, especially his dreadful relationship with his mother Livia, had had a terrible effect on him. Capri, in MacKowen's view, was an island of refuge for an old man whose character had been damaged from his earliest infancy.[15]

He retraces rapidly the history of Roman Capri after Tiberius in the first part of his chapter on the island's mediaeval and modern history:[16] Caligula received his *toga virilis* in Capri[17] (a sort of coming-of-age in which the transition from boyhood to manhood included starting to wear the toga) and Vitellius spent his childhood there.[18] Reference is made to the verses in which the poet Statius celebrated the lighthouse on Capri[19] as well as to the testimony of the historian Dio Cassius, who described Capri as a place of exile for Crispina and Lucilla during the rule of Emperor Commodus.[20] MacKowen believed that in all probability the island was considered as the personal property of the imperial family until the fall of the Western Roman Empire.

The pages in *Capri* dedicated to the island's ancient history are not innovative. MacKowen does not appear to have had a background in philological studies nor any direct knowledge of the ancient sources he cited[21] – his information was largely taken from reference books.[22] Important issues such as the etymology of the name of the island, its mythical past, its change in status from being a dependance of the Greek Neapolis to an imperial estate, or the period spent by Tiberius on the island, are for the most part discussed in a somewhat uncritical manner. Nonetheless, his treatment of these topics reveals a comprehensive knowledge of eighteenth- and nineteenth-century archaeological excavations, great familiarity with the terrain and a special appreciation for ancient inscriptions[23], as well as a serious interest in prehistoric Capri. In this respect MacKowen deserves full recognition as being one of the first to have widely circulated Ignazio Cerio's research into the island's prehistoric period. In addition, his book is of much documentary value with regard to local place names.[24]

The underlying motif of MacKowen's pages dedicated to the ancient history of Capri is in keeping with other amateur literature of that time, interpreting the island's history according to an evolutionary plan in which Roman Capri was considered to have been a golden age and the apex of its historical, economic and social progress, making the Capri of the Emperors a precursor of the wealthy, touristic, industrious and

It All Began with Cave-dwellers

modern Capri of today.[25] And in both these cases we see that it was the presence of the *forestiero* (the outsider) that provided, and continues to provide, the essential dynamic for the island community's civil and economic progress.

Notes
1. J.C. MacKowen, *Capri*, pp. 14–16.
2. *Ibidem*, pp. 15–16. MacKowen was evidently referring to the Grotta delle Felci, a small grotto famous for being the site where Ignazio Cerio had excavated prehistoric finds. This grotto is located within a large cavern known as the Grotta dell'Arco. In reference to the alternate use of the names Grotta delle Felci and Grotta dell'Arco see E. Federico, 'Felci e toponomastica caprese (Grotta delle Felci, Filietto, Follicara, Fuorlovado). Per una storia linguistica di Capri antica' in *Conoscere Capri 3. Studi e materiali per la storia di Capri*, ed. M. Amitrano, E. Federico and C. Fiorentino, Capri 2005, pp. 90–94. For information regarding the materials found in the Grotta dell'Arco and the Grotta delle Felci, see C. Giardino, 'L'isola di Capri dal Neolitico alla prima Età del Ferro', in *Capri antica. Dalla preistoria alla fine dell'età romana*, ed. E. Federico and E. Miranda, Capri 1998, pp. 67–105.
3. MacKowen, *Capri*, pp. 15–16.
4. *Ibidem*, p. 15. With regard to Cerio's theory, see Ignazio Cerio, *Scritti inediti e materiali di lavoro*, Giulianova 2001, pp. 88–9. To place the myth of the Sirens on Capri, see C. Simeone, 'Il 'mito' delle Sirene a Capri', in *Conoscere Capri 2*. Atti del 2° ciclo di conferenze sulla storia e la natura dell'isola di Capri (Capri-Anacapri, novembre 2003–febbraio 2004), ed. M. Amitrano, A. Cafiero and C. Fiorentino, Capri 2004, pp. 43–55; E. Federico, 'Le Sirene, la morte e il destino di pietra. Impressioni mitiche nel paesaggio naturale', in *Illusione e seduzione*, ed. R. Aragona, Naples 2010, pp. 97–101.
5. MacKowen, *Capri*, pp. 14–16. For information regarding the Phoenicians in Capri, see E. Federico, 'I Fenici e Capri: messa a punto e prospettiva', in *Almanacco Caprese* 5, 1992, pp. 39–54.
6. Virgil, *Aeneid* VII, 733–5. MacKowen, *Capri*, p. 16 (which erroneously cites Livy as the source). For information regarding the Teleboi on Capri, see E. Federico, 'Capri dall'espansione cumana nel Golfo (VII a.C.) al *foedus Neapolitanum* (326 a.C.)', in *Capri antica ...*, pp. 383–8.
7. MacKowen, *Capri*, p. 14. The author naively thought of the Romans without considering the serious possibility that the name 'Capri' might have originated from an Italic language: see D. Silvestri, 'Il nome di Capri e la toponomastica insulare dell'Italia antica', in *Capri antica ...*, pp. 115–16.

8. MacKowen, *Capri*, p. 16. The interpretation is naive, however his interest for this little known monument in the history of Capri is significant. See A. Pelosi, 'Mura di fortificazione', in *Capri antica* ..., pp. 133–6. Elsewhere (MacKowen, *Capri*, p. 118) the 'Cyclopean wall' is mentioned as a fortification dating back to the age of Tiberius. As regards the relations between Cuma and Capri, see Federico, 'Capri dall'espansione cumana nel Golfo ...', pp. 390–4. For general information regarding the Campania region in ancient times, see M. V. Frederiksen, *Campania*, ed. N. Purcell, London 1984.
9. MacKowen, *Capri*, p. 8.
10. MacKowen, *Capri*, pp. 109, 113. See P. Lombardi, 'Le iscrizioni greche', in *Capri antica* ..., pp. 299–342.
11. Suetonius, *Life of Augustus*, 98, 3; MacKowen, *Capri*, p. 16.
12. MacKowen, *Capri*, p. 16.
13. MacKowen, *Capri*, p. 18. As regards Augustus in Capri, see E. Savino, 'Capri dal *foedus Neapolitanum* (326 a.C.) al VI secolo d.C.', in *Capri antica* ..., pp. 420–6. For information regarding the presence of villas and the Roman aristocracy in the Gulf of Naples, see J.H. D'Arms, *Romans on the Bay of Naples and other essays on Roman Campania*, ed. F. Zevi, Bari 2003.
14. MacKowen, *Capri*, pp. 24–40.
15. For an historical analysis of the period Tiberius spent in Capri see Savino, 'Capri dal *foedus Neapolitanum* ...', pp. 426–37.
16. MacKowen, *Capri*, p. 41. As regards the period subsequent to Tiberius, see Savino, 'Capri dal *foedus Neapolitanum* ...', pp. 437–9.
17. Suetonius, *Life of Caligula*, 10, 1–2.
18. Suetonius, *Life of Vitellius*, 3, 2.
19. Statius, *Silvae* III, 5, 100–101.
20. Dio Cassius, *Roman History* LXIII, 4, 6.
21. The passages from Homer were taken from the English translation by Alexander Pope (Edinburgh 1773), while the numerous passages from the *The Lives of the Twelve Caesars*, by Suetonius were taken from the English translation by Alexander Thomson (London 1876).
22. For example, the works of Domenico Antonio Parrino (*Nuova guida de' forestieri*, Naples 1751) and Rosario Mangoni (*Ricerche storiche sull'Isola di Capri*, Naples 1834) are cited yet MacKowen was apparently unaware of the considerations on Capri expressed by Julius Beloch in *Campanien*, Berlin 1879.
23. MacKowen edited a collection of epigraphs at the Casa Rossa in Anacapri: see E. Miranda, 'Le collezioni epigrafiche', in *Capri antica* ..., p. 295.
24. MacKowen made an effort to indicate the local pronunciation of the island's name (*Crapi*) (*Capri*, p. 14). In addition to reporting place names which have since fallen into disuse (*Trasele*: *Capri*, p. 92), he also referred to the local

It All Began with Cave-dwellers

custom of using the name *Sirena* for the rock at Marina Piccola (MacKowen, *Capri*, p. 15); furthermore, he provided documentation that the local custom of inverting the words (*Piccola Marina*), still present today, dated back to as early as the nineteenth century (*Capri*, p. 101).

25. See E. Federico, 'Capri antica: uno schizzo storiografico', in *Capri antica* ..., p. 21.

Chapter 11
John Clay MacKowen: an archaeologist in Capri
Rossella Zaccagnini

Even today, John Clay MacKowen's classic text on Capri remains a fascinating and captivating narrative, immediately transporting the reader back to the atmosphere of an island poised between the rediscovery of its glorious past and its involvement in the cultural life of late nineteenth-century Europe. The reason for the island's sudden fame was above all due to the 'discovery' of the Blue Grotto,[1] which placed it firmly on the list of sites to the visited on the Grand Tour (the island fishermen had always known of the grotto's existence, but avoided it as a place of evil spirits).

MacKowen swings easily between accurate archaeological, historical, philosophical, naturalistic and geological disquisitions, supported by scholarly citations, and light-hearted anecdotal accounts that take us back to a period when romantic idealism was rapidly giving way to a desire to apply the scientific method to every sphere of knowledge and human life.

What emerges is the personality of an erudite, inquisitive and impassioned man who sought an explanation for all that he observed and who tried, not always completely successfully, to rise beyond the status of a mere 'connoisseur', with the dual label of archaeologist and antiquarian, to that of a true scientist. Nonetheless, his work deserves to be included in the list of books that are fundamental to an understanding of the archaeology of Capri. He had the privilege of witnessing at first hand some of the important discoveries of the day and was able to gather direct information about excavations that had been conducted only a few years before he first arrived on the island in 1876.

The book is of major interest throughout, but his Chapter 7 with its topographic description of the island is the most significant one from an archaeological perspective, even though some of his preconceived geological notions occasionally led him to mistaken conclusions.[2] His advice that the best way to get to know the island was to go out in a rowing boat is still valid; he gave as an example a trip setting off from the Marina Grande in a westerly direction and described each of the

John Clay MacKowen: an archaeologist in Capri

Map of the island from MacKowen's Capri.

stages in detail. His account is clearly the result of an in-depth visual study of the sites, while his digressions about the inland topography appear to have been added later, in keeping with a logical progression based on a map of the island.

Thus his description starts from the northern part of the island and chronicles information by previous authors including Hadrava, Romanelli and Mangoni, such as the discovery near the Church of San Costanzo in 1810 of a sarcophagus containing the remains of a woman who was identified as Crispina, the wife of the Emperor Commodus, who was exiled to the island in 182 A.D., and numerous cisterns. Only a few years before, Mangoni had defined the entire small valley as being 'cluttered with ruins; and even the smallest excavation made in this cultivated area, brings new finds to light.'

His report on the presence of a *cloaca* (an ancient sewer) in the vicinity of the Church of San Costanzo[3] which was part of a more extensive system of canals and conduits is of interest; he believed it to be archaeological proof of the existence of the ancient town of Capri, not far from the sea and mentioned by Strabo, the historian who lived during the reign of Augustus, in Book V of his work ('in ancient times, Capri had two small settlements, which then became one').[4] There is still discussion as to whether the area of Marina Grande, where some artefacts datable to pre-Roman times were found and which unfortunately have been since lost, was the location of the island's first Greek nucleus, or, whether the more important centre was located higher up in the area where the medieval town would later be located, with Marina Grande serving as a small hamlet (the two settlements mentioned by Strabo). What is certain, however, is that during the Roman Age, the centre and its infrastructure extended towards the area of Marina Grande, as related by MacKowen.

Unlike other nineteenth and early twentieth century authors,[5] who sought to bring some order to the information coming out of excavations that were being carried out in a confusing and increasingly frantic manner in the hope of unearthing works of art, MacKowen's work is noteworthy in its attempt to provide an overview or – in more modern terms – to 'map' the known ruins based upon a proper scientific interpretation of the sources. During his time, archaeology in Capri referred almost exclusively to the search for the remains of the twelve so-called 'Augustan-Tiberian' villas, each one dedicated to a different divinity, resulting from a combined reading of the texts by Tacitus and Suetonius.[6] MacKowen distanced himself from this approach, pointing out on several occasions that there were many more than twelve sites with ruins and that in addition to the emperor an entire court had been quartered on the island.[7] He was not however immune to the temptation of considering all the particularly luxurious buildings to have been the personal property of the emperor, including the villas at Palazzo a Mare, Damecuta, Tragara, Unghia Marina, Castiglione and Monte San Michele, all of them with exceptionally beautiful views. In addition, like the majority of archaeologists, he identified the villa on Mount Tiberio as the Villa Jovis – the site from which Tiberius, whom he admired greatly both as a statesman and as a soldier, scanned the horizon for signals announcing the death of Sejanus.[8]

The first imperial villa described by MacKowen was that of Bagni di Tiberio, better known as Palazzo a Mare, stretching between Punta Vivara and Marinella di Torre. Like other villas on the island, this one, too, was not so much excavated as subjected to continuous pillaging on the part of individuals who considered the ruins to be the sum of single finds rather than an architecturally unified whole. The villa had an 'open' design and was closely incorporated into the surrounding environment, stretching out in an asymmetrical, informal manner in the form of several blocks, with a well-developed *pars maritima* (coastal area).[9] Even he did not grasp the unitary nature of the construction, believing that only the part of the complex facing the sea was the residence, and that the vast open space, now occupied by the old playing field, was the forum of the ancient town, whereas in fact it was actually the *xystus*, or garden, of the villa.[10] Based on the texts of previous authors (and/or diggers), he writes of the other villas but provides no substantially new information. His report, however, is especially useful for anyone seeking information about the dispersion of movable artefacts which had been disposed of separately, finding their way on to the antiques market and into private collections.[11]

It is very interesting to note the modern slant of his thinking when he emphasised the essential function of view as a factor in selecting the locations of the villas, a selection which was to some extent limiting but which also enhanced the architectural qualities of the buildings and reflected their owners' personalities and social positions. In particular with regard to Villa Jovis, which according to him was commissioned by Augustus and enlarged by Tiberius, he provided a detailed description; to all intents and purposes it seemed, and still does seem, to be very much at odds with the traditional concept of the Roman villa. It was an original structure which eluded any form of classification, more similar to a glittering marble fortress than a dwelling.[12] Although he reported that both Norbert Hadrava[13] and Giuseppe Feola[14] – the first official diggers of the villa – had not found any great treasures because they were hampered by the presence of enormous amounts of debris, he was unable to escape the powerful fascination of the site. Even stripped of its precious furnishings the building continued to exert a powerful attraction, resulting in innumerable accounts that there was still an immense amount of hidden treasure to be found. He also succumbed to the temptation of placing Suetonius's *sellariae*,[15] a place set aside for sexual encounters, inside the semicircular structure situated along the eastern side of the building.[16]

In fact, Villa Jovis is an entirely original Roman structure, albeit with evident Graeco-Hellenistic influences. It is a compact building, without a basement and developed on at least seven (or more probably eight) levels, with four wings arranged around a peristyle built on top of the four enormous central cisterns. It combines in one single structure the functions of a private residence as well as those of a representative and administrative facility, thus constituting the Western prototype of a 'palace', that is, the architectural embodiment of the idea of a principality. This was a daring endeavour which would reach its pinnacle after the end of the first century A.D. in the imperial buildings of the Palatine in Rome and which culminated in the construction of Diocletian's fortified palace in Split two centuries later.

In addition to his descriptions of the imperial villas, MacKowen's work is also useful to anyone interested in archaeology on Capri, especially with regard to some apparently minor items of information relating to the remains of those buildings that were still visible in twentieth century Capri[17] and which could not be associated directly with the imperial villas. He witnessed for example the excavation of the necropolis at the Parate,[18] had first-hand information regarding Ignazio Cerio's earliest excavations in the Grotta delle Felci (generally attributed to non-indigenous peoples or to the 'Phoenicians')[19] and, above all, focused his attention on the ancient 'Cyclopean' wall, that is to say, made of square blocks of calcareous stone. According to him, the wall ran between the hills of San Michele and Castiglione, and although crumbling was still visible in his time.[20] The exact chronology of the structure is still uncertain, but there is little doubt as to its 'Greek' origins, although recently the term 'pre-Roman' has come to be preferred, and it is believed to date back to circa 250 B.C., the period of the First Punic War.[21]

Although many authors[22] have suggested that the true site of the Graeco-Italic settlement was behind the Marina Grande in the vicinity of the Church of San Costanzo (as previously noted, he too believed this to be the site of the citadel described by Strabo), the best strategic position remains the centre of Capri, allowing for better visual control over the landing sites as well as a better view of the sea to the north-west and the south-east. This consideration did not escape MacKowen, who envisaged the ancient Roman military camp to have been positioned just behind the fortification where Tiberius had garrisoned his soldiers, thus effectively making the island impregnable with only a few men. Indeed, many passages of the book are influenced by his military 'eye', which clearly gave him the advantage over other scholars of perceiving some of the strategic aspects of the remains present on the island. Augustus, and especially Tiberius, were first and foremost the heads of their armies, and it was precisely this role which appealed to the author, as is evident throughout his work.

Lastly, consideration should be given to the descriptions of the Capri grottoes, which fascinated MacKowen enormously. He explored them all, both those accessible by land and those which could only be entered from the sea, and he recommended that all visitors should undertake the same venture. He provides a valuable description of the excavations being conducted in that period in the Grotta dell'Arsenale which, in agreement with Hadrawa and Mangoni, he believed had been a storage area for the ships of the Roman fleet, with adjacent areas set aside for use by officers.[23] His disquisition on the Matromania grotto is lengthy and detailed; in all probability this natural but artificially remodelled cavity, reinforced by walls in opus reticulatum style and datable back to the early imperial age, would also have served as a monumental *nymphaeum*, or sanctuary of the nymphs.[24] The interpretation that these structures were the remains of an ancient temple dedicated to the god Mithra (thus Matromania from *magno Mithrae antro* or from *Mithrae antro*), based upon the previously recorded theories of Mangoni,[25] provided him with the opportunity for a philosophical digression on Christianity and Mithraism, thus shedding light upon his own thoughts.

Without question the grotto which fascinated MacKowen most was the Blue Grotto, which he visited on numerous occasions and described

LA GROTTA AZZURA A CAPRI

Blue Grotto, circa 1850. Centro Caprense Ignazio Cerio Archive, Capri.

Entrance to Casa Rossa with Greek frieze. Courtesy of Mr Antonio Federico.

in painstaking detail, marred only by his erroneous belief with regard to the subsidence of the island.[26] In the summer of 1883 he conducted excavations on land owned by him in the area above the grotto (a place known as 'Gradola' or 'Gradelle'), which, in view of the opulence of the decorative features and the marble adornments he salvaged, he identified as the site of one of the imperial villas.[27] The excavated structures had been built in at least two different periods – one dating back to the early imperial age and the other, perhaps, dating back to the late 1st century A.D. – and extended over at least three terraced levels of land.

Some statues of sea divinities[28] were found on the seabed inside the grotto between 1964 and 1974. The discovery of these statues, sculpted from the knees upwards and resting upon bases that jutted out from niches created in the rocky walls some 1.20 metres below sea level, made it possible for the Blue Grotto to be identified with certainty as a *nymphaeum*. In view of the presence of what would appear to be a landing-site dating back to before the Roman period, the statues were designed to appear as if emerging from the sea bottom to receive the visiting emperor. The Gradola *grotto-nymphaeum* and structures must therefore be considered to be the maritime base and a part of the imperial villa of Damecuta, located 150 metres above sea level. MacKowen reported that until about 1830 traces of a road leading from Gradola to Damecuta were still visible, but that they had disappeared following a landslide.

The fate of the statues found inside the grotto was fortunate; they are now in the Casa Rossa, the building that MacKowen created in about 1877 around a 16th-century Aragonese tower in Anacapri, designing this eclectic structure as a museum-home according to a model that was very fashionable at the time. The entrance bears the inscription in Greek, 'Greetings, citizen of the country of idleness.'[29]

Notes

1. The grotto, previously known as Gradola or Gradelle (V.M. Coronelli, 'Isolario', in *Atlante Veneto*, II, Venice 1696, p. 113), became world-famous thanks to the Polish poet and painter August Kopish who entered it for the first time in 1826 (A. Kopisch, 'Entdeckung der blauen Grotte auf der Insel Capri', in *Annuario Italia*, ed. A. Reumont, Berlin 1838, pp. 155–210). The entire episode is reported in G. Cantone, B. Fiorentino, G. Sarnella, *Capri: la città e la terra*, Naples 1982, pp. 262–5.
2. MacKowen believed there were traces of subsidence on the island, similar to those in nearby Pozzuoli. In relation to the 'subsidence', see also pp. 155–6.
3. The conduit might be the 1.80m high and 0.80m wide tunnel reported in the early twentieth century, four metres below sea level under the road near the former Hotel Metropole, now the J.K. Palace Capri Hotel. Cf. P. Mingazzini, *Vico Equense (Penisola Sorrentina ed isola di Capri)*, Edizione Archeologica della Carta d'Italia al 100.000, foglio 196, Florence 1931, p. 48.
4. Strabo, V, 4, 9; regarding problems related to the comment from Strabo's text, see E. Federico, 'Capri dall'espansione cumana nel Golfo (VII a.C.) al *foedus Neapolitanum* (326 a.C.)', in *Capri antica. Dalla preistoria all'età romana*, ed. E. Federico and E. Miranda, Naples 1998, in particular pp. 390–2.
5. Just to mention the most important sources: G.M. Secondo, *Relazione storica dell'antichità, rovine e residui di Capri umiliata al Re*, Naples 1750; N. Hadrava, *Ragguagli di vari scavi, e scoperte di antichità fatte nell'Isola di Capri*, Naples 1793; D. Romanelli, *Isola di Capri. Manoscritti inediti del*

Conte della Torre Rezzonico, del Professor Breislak e del Generale Pommereul, Naples 1816; G. Feola, *Rapporto sullo stato attuale dei ruderi Augusto-Tiberiani nell'Isola di Capri*, previously unpublished manuscript dated 1830, published and annotated by his great-nephew Dr Ignazio Cerio of Capri, Naples 1894; R. Mangoni, *Ricerche topografiche ed archeologiche sull'isola di Capri da servire da guida ai viaggiatori*, Naples, 1834 (long held to be the 'canonical' list); A. Canale, *Storia dell'isola di Capri dall'età remotissima sino ai tempi presenti*, Naples 1887. An idea of the level of plundering can be gleaned from M. Ruggiero, *Degli scavi di antichità nelle provincie di Terraferma dell'antico Regno di Napoli, dal 1734 al 1876*, Naples 1888.

6. Tacitus, *Annals*, IV, 67: '*Sed tum Tiberius duodecim villarum nominibus et molibus insederat*'; Suetonius, *Life of Tiberius* 65, 2: '*...(Tiberius) pro novem proximos menses non egressus est villa, quae vocatur Io(v)is*'; it should be noted that MacKowen confused the two passages, mistakenly attributing the report that Tiberius possessed twelve villas on Capri to Suetonius.

7. Cf. pp. 52–3.

8. Cf. p. 113; Suetonius, *Life of Tiberius* 65, 2. There is a vast bibliography concerning the imperial villas on Capri, however, see *Capri antica...cit.*, in part. pp. 179–223, (see previously cited bibliography); with reference to Villa Jovis, see C. Krause, *Villa Jovis: l'edificio residenziale*, Naples 2005.

9. As regards the Roman concept of villas, see J. S. Ackerman, *La villa. Forma ed ideologia*, Turin 1992; with reference to the seaside villa typology, see X. Lafon, 'À propos des villas de la zone de Sperlonga. Les origines et le développement de la "villa maritima" sur le littoral tyrrhénien à l'époque répubblicaine', in *Mélanges d'archéologie et d'histoire de l'école française de Rome* 93, 1981, pp. 297–353.

10. In a fundamental study, Maiuri noted that the cadastral divisions existing between properties in the area in his day and age still roughly corresponded to those of ancient times; A. Maiuri, 'La villa augustea di Palazzo a Mare a Capri, in *Campania Romana*', 1, 1938, pp. 115–41. The fact that the complex was imperial property was confirmed by the presence, reported precisely even by MacKowen, of a quarry marking on the two red marble columns attesting the fact that they belonged to a building of the Caesars. It is possible that a tondo conserved in the Naples National Archaeological Museum is part of one of these two columns; see E. Miranda, 'Le iscrizioni latine, in Capri antica...cit', pp. 345–6, E20.

11. All that remains of this wealth, most of which has been lost, has been rightly defined as 'disiecta membra'; S. Adamo Muscettola, 'L'arredo delle ville imperiali: tra storia e mito', in *Capri antica...cit.*, pp. 241–74; V. Sampaolo, *Le collezioni private*, in *Capri antica... cit.*, pp. 275–90.

John Clay MacKowen: an archaeologist in Capri

12. J. C. MacKowen, too, was of the opinion that this was the *Tiberis principis arx* mentioned by Pliny the Elder (Pliny, *Naturalis historia* III, 6, 82, ed. H. Rackham, Cambridge, Mass. 1947).
13. Norbert Hadrava, secretary to the Austrian ambassador at the Bourbon Court, had arrived on the island in 1786 in the entourage of King Ferdinand IV. He excavated at Villa Jovis between 1800 and 1804.
14. Giuseppe Feola was mayor of Capri for many years as well as Inspector of the Excavations of Ancient Ruins on the island. His excavations at Villa Jovis took place 1826–7.
15. Suetonius, *Life of Tiberius* 43, 1–2.
16. With reference to this structure, see A. Moneti, 'Le ville di Tiberio a Capri e la villa sotto la Farnesina', in *Rivista d'Archeologia* 15, 1991, pp. 89–96.
17. In this regard, the author repeatedly reports how, in order to avoid the continous coming and going of 'tourists' through their vineyards and olive groves, the inhabitants of Capri systematically destroyed anything unearthed that could not be sold. This occurred to such an extent that even MacKowen noted a significant loss of archaeological finds as compared to the drawings by Alvino (F. Alvino, *Due giorni a Capri*, Naples 1838), which had been drawn only some forty years earlier.
18. Excavations of the necropolis began in 1830; based upon bibliographical information, it is possible to envisage a vast burial ground which had been in use from the fourth century B.C. to the mid-imperial age; A. Pelosi, 'La necropoli', in *Capri antica...cit.*, p. 152.
19. On the subject of research on the island into the prehistoric age, see C. Santagata, *La preistoria a Capri. Cronaca delle ricerche all'epoca di Ignazio Cerio*, Naples 1994.
20. Only two stretches of this defensive wall which once barred access to the site where the ancient residential area must have been are still visible. The wall was incorporated into the Angevin fortification on top of which the modern homes still standing along Via Longano were built. With reference to the fortifications of Capri, see A. Pelosi, 'Mura di fortificazione', in *Capri antica... cit.*, pp. 133–6.
21. In the battle between Rome and Carthage, the Roman navy depended heavily upon the collaboration of *socii navales* in southern Italy to defend the coasts and keep watch over the African route; during this time, *Neapolis* provided *ex foedere* ships and logistic support to the Roman fleet.
22. It is sufficient to cite J. Beloch, *Campanien. Geschichte und Topographie des antiken Neapel und seiner Umgebung*, Breslau 1890, p. 284, followed also by A. Maiuri, *Capri. Storia e monumenti*, Rome 1957, p. 15.
23. Definitive recognition of the grotto as a rich *nymphaeum* dating back to the Tiberian age can be attributed to Maiuri and Mingazzini; A. Maiuri, 'Grotteninfei imperiali dell'isola di Capri', in *Bollettino d'Archeologia* XXV, 1931,

pp. 149–160 e in part. p. 158; P. Mingazzini, 'Le grotte di Matermania e dell'Arsenale a Capri', in *Archeologia Classica* VII, 1955, pp. 139–63 and in particular p. 155.
24. Maiuri, *Grotte-ninfei...cit.*, pp. 149–60; M.V. De Crescenzo, 'Grotta di Matermania', in *Capri antica...op. cit.*, pp. 145–8.
25. Mangoni, *op. cit.*, pp. 103–32. Feola is of a different opinion based upon the finding by Hadrava of an altar to Cybele, thought to be the *Magna Mater*, and thus believed the site to be *magnae matris antrum*, from which the toponym is derived (Feola, *op. cit.*, pp. 18–22).
26. While there has never been any doubt that the Romans used the grotto, especially in the light of the evidence consisting of the structures present there, another theory that attracted many followers held that the original entrance used by the Romans was the one now below the water and that, in the interim, the island has sunk by 6 or 7 metres. See R. Belli, 'Grotta Azzurra', in *Capri antica...op. cit.*, pp. 215–16, see previously cited bibliography.
27. The Swedish physician Axel Munthe also appropriated two coloured marble columns from this site; one of them fell into the sea when being transported, while the other is still at Villa San Michele in Anacapri (A. Andrén, *Capri from the Stone Age to the Tourist Age*, Gothenburg 1980, pp. 79–80).
28. In 1964, a statue of Poseidon hurling a trident and one statue of Triton were found; in 1974, another two parts of the statue of Triton, a bust, a headless *peplophoros*, an altar, two tufa bases as well as other fragments were also found; A. De Franciscis, *Le statue della Grotta Azzurra nell'isola di Capri*, Naples 1964; R. Neudecker, *Die Skulpturen-Ausstattung Römischer Villen in Italien*, Mainz am Rhein 1988, p. 137.
29. T. Fiorani, *Le dimore del mito. Residenze letterarie a Capri tra Ottocento e primo Novecento*, Naples 1996, pp. 199–201. The house was purchased by the Naples Superintendence for Architectural and Landscape Heritage; following careful refurbishment it is now used as an exhibition site by the Anacapri town council.

Chapter 12
From Capri to the Mainland: an island on the fringes of a capital
Anna Maria Palombi Cataldi

A land of myths and sirens, Capri has always had an uncanny ability to cast a spell upon those travellers who landed on her inhospitable shores. Many of them were educated and articulate people, with the result that the island possesses an abundant bibliography, amongst which John Clay MacKowen's book *Capri* stands out as one of the very best.

Once the Roman period of the imperial residences had come to a close, and despite its position at the centre of the Gulf of Naples, Capri slid progressively into obscurity, away from the important trading and cultural routes of the Mediterranean. There is therefore a void in large parts of the island's story, and the author concentrates on those episodes for which the historical record was better described by contemporary sources.[1] Reduced to little more than a lighthouse for seafarers and its occasional use as a place of imprisonment or exile, the island's scarcity of resources and the poverty of its inhabitants led to its complete dependence on the mainland.[2]

After the fall of the Roman Empire the island fell into vassalage under the Byzantine Duchy of Naples[3] and in the ninth century passed into the control of the duchy of Amalfi,[4] eventually becoming state property during the Norman reign. Granted as a fief in 1230 to Admiral Eliseo Arcucci by Frederick II of Swabia, the island enjoyed the favour of its new lords until they too were deprived of their dominions under the Anjou dynasty.[5]

The Anjous were the first to grant Capri the exemptions and privileges that would contribute towards making life more attractive in such a begrudging land. They established two *universitates*, each representing a part of the island, the one characterised mainly by agriculture and sheep rearing, with the other clearly dependent on the sea. They formed two municipal entities which obtained independence from one another in 1496 when the 'land' of Anacapri, which until then had been under the administrative management of the 'land' of Capri, was granted the right to have its own independent Royal 'Capitan' and mastrodatti (curial notary). As MacKowen expressed it, the Anacapri inhabitants 'had petitioned the monarch (Frederick, the last of the Aragon kings) for redress against the many wrongs inflicted on them by the people of Capri. This was the official commencement of a quarrel between the two communes, which had probably already existed for a long time, and has not abated to the day.' (p. 45) The intense rivalry between the two communities is a recurring theme in the documentation of the scant historical record of Capri. There were also, however, moments of staunch collaboration, during which representatives of the two communities united in a common front in order to obtain, for example, tax relief or exemptions from military service.[6] In actual fact, the organisation of the Capri *universitates* was to all intents and purposes the same as that of the other municipal communities of the Kingdom of Naples.

When describing this phase of the island's history, MacKowen's cultural background leads him to depict a backward society, at the mercy of social circumstances determined by privileges imported from the nearby capital. This prejudice is attributable to his lack of familiarity with the intricate working relationships within the government of the day. It explains his assumption that the cultural backwardness of Capri society was the reason why military officers were sent from Naples to govern the island, men whom he refers to as 'favourites of the viceroys'. (p. 48)

He does not fail to mention religious issues – an aspect of southern Italy that had already fascinated foreigners, though true to style he limited himself to a perfunctory listing of passages that he felt might be of interest, without showing the least interest in the deeply religious tradition of the island. This stance led him to judge certain devious actions on the part of the clergy rather more harshly than would have seemed reasonable to the historically more tolerant island community

After outlining the old story of Saint Costanzo, the patron saint to whom the medieval church of Marina Grande is dedicated and who, according to legend, ordered 'the flames to become extinct … [and to have] also caused a panic among the Saracens, who retreated immediately to their ships' (p. 46), he recalls another aspect which, more than any other, served to reinforce the identity of the people of Capri.[7] In 987 the local religious community had been elevated to a diocese no longer under the authority of the Bishop of Sorrento (to which the island was to return in 1818 when the seat was suppressed and eliminated from the ecclesiastical map of the kingdom). Even though Capri's poverty made it unappealing as an Episcopal appointment, the ecclesiastical status was attractive and the clergy, especially during the sixteenth and seventeenth centuries, remained the predominant influence within society.

The bishops did their utmost to piece together the income necessary for a dignified lifestyle but, as MacKowen learned from Antonio Parrino,[8] they had to make do with the proceeds from the capture of quails, so much so that for a long period one of them was known as the 'Bishop of the Quails'. (p. 49) Almost all of the scanty wealth was the perquisite of the powerful San Giacomo Charterhouse, founded in the second half of the fourteenth century by Giacomo Arcucci, a descendant of Count Eliseo and an influential figure at the court of Joan I of Anjou. The construction of this monastery was to prove the main opportunity for local economic growth during those years, fostering the development of trade and the transfer of crafts and professional skills between Capri and the mainland. However, the monastic rule of the institution prevented the monks from maintaining any proper communication with the local populace, who regarded them as alien to their social fabric. Suppression of the monastery – the transfer of all its property to the state – was decreed by Joachim Murat on November 2, 1808.[9]

There are numerous examples of the gap between MacKowen's Anglo-Saxon background and the Catholic customs of the island.[10] His apocalyptic tone in describing the disastrous outbreak of plague in 1656 which had halved the population of the two local communities is a case in point. The epidemic had actually struck Capri with the same virulence with which it had affected the other towns along the coast of the Gulf, and the speed of the contagion merely reflected the close ties between the people of Capri and those of the coast.[11] In addition to repeating the legendary tales about the arrival of the infection on the island, our author appeared to have been particularly struck by the practice of devolving to religious institutions the assets of any person dying without a known heir. 'Many families became extinct, and no relatives, however distant, survived to inherit their property. The Carthusian monks appropriated these possessions, and thus acquired a large portion of the island.' (p. 48) His description of the monks' rapacity contributed towards intensifying the accusations recorded in the sources of the time that they had ignored the plight of the population in order to safeguard their own interests. 'On the first outbreak of the disease, they shut the doors of the monastery, and refused to have any contact or communication with the outer world.' (p. 47)

With his minimal knowledge of the consolidating function of religion in southern Italian society, MacKowen also failed to mention an important figure in the history of Capri. Mother Serafina di Dio (1621–1699), known more widely as Prudenza Pia, was a member of one of the island's few prominent families and her unswerving determination to found a female monastic tradition inevitably caused a great social stir in both the island's towns. Her commitment to this ambition resulted in a project being initiated in both Capri and Anacapri, from where her religious institutions spread, giving rise within a thirty-year period to the vigorous establishment of female monastic communities throughout the whole area between Naples and Salerno.[12]

In the normal course of life in the two communities during the middle centuries of the modern age the most significant aspect was undoubtedly the constant menace of the Saracen forays with which the people of Capri had to live.[13] Attacked in 1534 by Kahir-el-Din, known as Barbarossa and then a few years later by the terrible corsair Dragut, they continued to be subjected to violence and looting even after the Ottoman expansion in the Mediterranean had been checked by the efforts of the Catholic powers. For this reason, defence was the top priority for all the Spanish captains sent by the viceroys to Capri to represent the Crown. MacKowen had read about the terrible condition of affairs in Parrino's 1727 description, 'Every day many unhappy fishermen are carried away into captivity by the Mahometan corsairs.' He described how in 1786 many of the local men were scraping together a livelihood in which they 'passed the summer fishing coral near the coast of Sardinia ... [but some of them] fall victims to the Saracens, and are carried off to Africa into slavery.' (p. 48)

The pirates, however, were not alone in marking the island's destiny with war and violence. By the end of the eighteenth century, transformations in European political geography were also to overwhelm Capri. The island's strategic position for the protection of the Gulf made it a battlefield upon which the French, having in 1806 ousted Ferdinando IV from the throne of Naples, were to confront the English allied with the sovereigns who had repaired to Sicily. After conquering Capri, the English General Sir Hudson Lowe took command of the garrison, which thus became an outpost for the cause of Bourbon legitimists.

From Capri to the Mainland

Fortifications with cannons of heavy calibre were erected and the island was considered impregnable, like 'a little Gibraltar'. However, Pietro Colletta, a Neapolitan engineer officer in the service of the French, sailed around the island disguised as a fisherman and spotted a suitable place for the French troops to disembark, and on October 4, 1808 duped the English in a brilliantly executed landing at Orrico. It is recorded that Joachim Murat himself watched the closing stages of the battle from Andrea Rossi's mansion (Villa Murat) at Santa Maria dell'Annunziata near Massa Lubrense on the Sorrento coast. Sir Hudson Lowe was unable to receive help from the English fleet, which had been compelled by bad weather that day to seek safety in Sicily, and was obliged to surrender on October 16. 'Sir Hudson and his command embarked at the Piccola Marina on English vessels, which set sail immediately for Sicily.' (p. 62) The record of the French conquest of the island is inscribed as 'Prise de Capri' on the Arc de Triomphe in Paris.

MacKowen had had the opportunity of reading complete accounts taken from both English and Bourbon sources as well as letters written by Hudson Lowe and General Lamarque,[14] though he remarks that the two accounts are somewhat different. It was also recorded by Pietro Colletta in his *Storia del Reame di Napoli dal 1734 sino al 1825*, published in 1834. Colletta is not entirely reliable, according to modern historians. MacKowen himself comments: '… the bitterness of exile and the persecutions of the Bourbons may have tempted him to exaggerate the gallantry of his friends.' (p. 65) At the end of the Napoleonic Wars in 1815 the Bourbons returned to Naples and the old order of affairs was restored in Capri. According to him, the Bourbon kings 'who thought more of stamping out liberalism, and establishing their divine rights [were] not encouraging commerce or manufactures [and] Capri suffered.' (p. 67)[15]

MacKowen published his book in 1884 and had already been living in Italy since 1876, but surprisingly enough scarcely mentions the annexation of the Kingdom of Naples to that of Italy, and does so only in passing to draw attention to the 'political astuteness of the Capriotes … when a vote was taken for the annexation of Naples to Italy [October 21, 1860] and it turned out to be favourable, the worthy councillors ordered that the shield should be plastered over to hide the fleur de lys.' (p. 7) Should His Majesty Francesco return, the plaster could easily be removed and the Capriotes could boast that … they had remained true

Capri – The Island Revisited

Bourbon coat of arms. Courtesy of Mr Antonio Federico.

to their rightful king.' (p. 70) However, the end of the vice-regal period and the ascent of the Bourbon dynasty to the throne of Naples gave the people of Capri a glimpse of growth and prosperity.

It also marked the arrival of the Austrian diplomat Norbert Hadrawa, a cultivated man with a wide knowledge of classical antiquity.[16] His interest provided the decisive impetus that led to the rediscovery of Capri's classical period and the organisation of excavations similar to those underway at that time in other parts of Southern Italy. It was his recognition of the island's heritage that taught its inhabitants to look at their heritage with respect, and to realise just what great wealth past

From Capri to the Mainland

centuries had placed into their hands.

Notes
1. A classic reference work is F. Braudel, *La Méditerranée et le Monde Mèditerranéen à l'Epoque de Philippe II*, Paris 1949.
2. In this regard, see G. Galasso, *Una periferia insulare*, now in Id., *Capri insula e dintorni*, Capri 2004, pp. 26-45.
3. With regard to the importance of Naples in the general setup of the Kingdom, see G. Galasso, *Napoli capitale. Identità politica e identità cittadina. Studi e ricerche 1266–1860*, Naples 1998. For all the historical events of the medieval and modern periods, reference may be made to the five volumes by the same author *Il Regno di Napoli*, Turin 1999–2007.
4. Cession to Amalfi, decreed by Ludovico II, took place in 866. In addition to the unequalled M. Del Treppo and A. Leone, *Amalfi medioevale*, Naples 1977, for a more up-to-date perspective see the series of treatises collected in *Medioevo Mezzogiorno Mediterraneo. Studi in onore di Mario Del Treppo*, ed. G. Rossetti and G. Vitolo, Pisa–Naples 2000.
5. With reference to this issue, see G.L. Borghese, *Carlo I d'Angiò e il Mediterraneo. Politica, diplomazia e commercio internazionale prima dei Vespri*, Rome 2008.
6. As at the time of the pleas submitted to the King on June 29, 1782 aimed at obtaining exemption from military service mentioned by Galasso, in *Anacapri nei suoi capitoli, privilegi e suppliche*, in Id. *Capri insula ...* op. cit., p. 71.
7. L. Fatica, 'San Costanzo di Capri: patriarca di Costantinopoli?', *Campania sacra* 23, 1992, pp. 155-162. With reference to the Church of Capri, see the chapter entitled *La diocesi e i vescovi* in E. Cerio, *Capri nel Seicento. Documenti e note*, Naples 1934, pp. 193-211 and, as regards the late 18th century, M. Miele, *La Chiesa del Mezzogiorno nel Decennio francese*, Naples 2007, passim.
8. Dom. Antonio Parrino, *Nuova Guida De' Forastieri*, Naples 1727 [1709].
9. In 1815 the complex was to become first a barracks and then a home for the disabled. Following the unification of Italy and until 1898, it was the V Compagnia di Disciplina, a company of the army to which anarchists and members of the military accused of improper conduct were assigned. See R. di Stefano, *La Certosa di San Giacomo a Capri*, Naples 1982.
10. In reference to this aspect of Anglo-Saxon culture, S. Patriarca, *Italianità. La costruzione del carattere nazionale*, Rome–Bari, 2010.
11. For further information, see V. Fiorelli, *Capri al tempo della peste. Prospettiva sulla vita religiosa del Seicento, in Conoscere Capri*, Proceedings of the 1st cycle of Conferences on the History and Nature of the Island of Capri, Naples 2003, pp. 143-63.

12. See, on this subject: V. Fiorelli, *Una esperienza religiosa periferica. I monasteri di madre Serafina di Dio da Capri alla terraferma*, Naples 2003.
13. See *Capri e l'Islam. Studi su Capri, il Mediterraneo, l'Oriente*, ed. E. Serrao and G. Lacerenza, Capri 1998; M. Mafrici, *I mari del Mezzogiorno d'Italia tra cristiani e musulmani, in Storia d'Italia*, Annals 18, *Guerra e pace*, ed. W. Barberis, Turin 2002, pp. 73-121.
    For further information, see the treatises collected in *Mediterraneo in armi (secc. XV-XVIII)*, ed. R. Cancila, Palermo 2007.
14. See Mariano d'Ayala, *Memorie storico-militari dal 1784 al 1815*, Naples 1835 and J. E. Chevalley de Rivaz, *Voyage de Naples à Capri et à Paestum*, Naples–Paris 1846. For a more up-to-date perspective see G. Amirante, *Capri francese, inglese, napoleonica (1806–1816)*, Naples 2011.
15. See R. Mangoni, *Ricerche storiche sull'isola di Capri colle notizie più rilevanti sulla vicina regione del cratere ...*, Naples 1834 and F. Alvino, *Le antiche ruine di Capri disegnate e restaurate*, Naples 1837.
16. His *Ragguagli di varii scavi e scoverte di antichità fatte nell'isola di Capri*, originally published in 1793, was reprinted in Naples in 1984.

Chapter 13
Looking Beyond:MacKowen and the habits and customs of the island
Carmelina Fiorentino

From the eighteenth century onwards the inhabitants of Capri and the culture and economy of the island have been comprehensively described, criticised and eulogised by foreign writers. The process started with visitors on the Grand Tour and was followed by professional travellers, and after them by the artists and writers who began to arrive in steadily increasing numbers.

Few of these visitors made any real effort to delve into the reasons that lay behind the occasionally confusing, frequently irritating and often congenial customs of the islanders, who were observed and described with the condescending attitude of a supposedly superior culture examining a tribe of savages. The prevailing idea in the minds of contemporary travellers, so succinctly summarised by Atanasio Mozzillo,[1] was that Southern Italy was a luxuriant and bountiful garden infested with lazy, baleful savages.

The onset of the Napoleonic Wars brought an end to the era of the Grand Tour. Travel resumed once peace had been established, but by now it had undergone a significant change: the discovery of the Blue Grotto and the ensuing increase in tourism brought a category of visitors to the island whose vast culture constitute a story in itself. Those who arrived in the nineteenth century now endeavoured to look beyond appearances and capture the realities that lay beneath ordinary life.

John Clay MacKowen was not merely just one of this enlightened group. He was an established member of the foreign colony on the island whose houses had been built or adapted into museum-homes in the style of the period, and who – in many cases – married local women. During his years on Capri he came to acquire a profound knowledge of the territory, and from his cultivated background was able to comment with perspicacity on the habits and customs of the local people amongst whom he lived.

At the start of his chapter entitled 'Habits and Customs' he would certainly have had good reason to state: 'The Capriote of today is as avaricious as his ancestor of a hundred years ago.' He strongly recommended establishing a price before making arrangements for the hire of a boat or the transport of baggage, and not to be moved – as many foreigners were – by the fanciful tales that he would almost certainly be told. The islanders' propensity to harass visitors in offering various services and goods was already well documented by the early nineteenth century (and to some extent and with less reason has continued to be the case up to the present).[2] In truth, as MacKowen later explained, it was poverty that distorted the responses of these good-natured and hardworking people.

Those Italian and foreign writers who, like him, were able to look beyond appearances made no mystery of the indigence of so many of the islanders, and gave them justice. Among those few was Mary Shelley, who in 1844 befriended a young girl leading her donkey on the walk up to Tiberius' villa. She wrote: 'The wretched lot of these poor people is very sad ... here where the sun kisses the heart, the sea is abundant in fish; fish and meat they never touch – all that is caught of the former is taken to Naples. The heart rebels yet more vehemently against the hungry poverty of the hard working peasants; English tourists get very angry at the perpetual demands made on their purses ... but, poor people, who can wonder!'[3] In an essay published in 1876 the English historian John Richard Green, well known for his tireless efforts to apply his learning to life and social problems, wrote that in the light of the widespread poverty on the island coral fishing provided the only means of survival for many families.

Many other descriptions of island life followed MacKowen's book, including one in 1888 by Mary E. Vandyne in which she concluded: 'The Caprians lead a life of which want and privation make up a large share.'[4] One inevitable consequence was that the men had no choice but to leave the island in search of more lucrative work: 'Most of the men are away from the island ... at sea ... and for this reason almost all labour is made by women; so that ... all the houses in Capri have been carried ... on the heads of women.'[5] The fact that the hard daily labour on the island was exclusively the domain of women was reported in all of the contemporary sources, and until the 1970s women with various sorts of burdens on their heads could still be seen. Now, fortunately, the only traces of this remain in literature and old photographs and drawings.

Among those foreigners who praised the hard work performed by women – which, they noted, went hand in hand with their beauty – there

Teresa Esposito, Capri 1970. Private collection.

were people who attempted, as early as in 1835 but without effect, to dissuade some of them from carrying the excavated debris from the Villa Jovis on their heads.[6] Mary Shelley, however, seeing such poverty and brutalising work, found relief in the fact that 'their religion is a great, a real comfort, to them despite it being hung round with falsehood.'[7] Even the mere act of quenching one's thirst required physical work. In an article dated 1868 the journalist Henry Wreford, another foreigner who had come to live on the island and did his utmost in every way to help the local people, wrote of the terrible lack of water, which obliged the poor 'to toil a mile for the precious liquid, which is doled out in quantities just sufficient to keep body and soul together, but not a drop to spare for bodily cleanliness.' He was firmly convinced that 'an abundant supply might be provided with one tenth of the money expended on festas and other mysterious matters.'[8]

In his *Fünf Jahre auf Capri*, August Weber, a German who had landed on the island and decided like many other foreigners to remain for ever, described the sacrifices women were obliged to undergo to be able to earn a living. 'In Capri, a large part of the work is performed by women and young girls who can be seen everywhere gathering lime and stones, earth and water which they then carry in baskets or jugs along silent footways with their pleasant postures, so reminiscent of the ancients, which serve as inspiration for artists and sculptors.'[9]

Other women expressed their solidarity with those on Capri in the late nineteenth century. In *Harper's Monthly Magazine*, Mary E. Vandyne wrote that everything was transported by the women on their heads, concluding: 'The Caprians seem to have no idea that anything can be carried any distance in the hand.'[10]

Their poverty continued unchanged well into the early twentieth century. By 1924 it had been some thirty years since the men had last gone coral fishing, because the industry had been monopolised by the men of Torre del Greco. '...When the elderly Capriotes speak of the loss of this industry they do so with great nostalgia, for since then they have been reduced to working the coral into necklaces which are sold for a few lire.'[11] Emigration, however, was flourishing. Many residents were obliged – as Friedlaender noted in 1938 – to emigrate to the mainland or further away, many of them to the United States or Argentina, and their departure was a source of relief to the island's economy.[12]

The artist and illustrator Frank Davis Millet, who was later to die on the Titanic, reflected on the island's landscape and women in an interesting article in 1898 entitled 'Home of the Indolent'. He wrote: 'The healthy, robust peasant girls still perform the larger part of the manual labour, and are the hod-carriers, the navvies and the burden-bearers.'[13] Nor did the new century bring any changes in the poverty level or in the hard work of the island women, as the French writer Adolphe Ribaux wrote in 1912: 'The cultivations are entrusted to the women ... who work, hoe, plant and harvest. Without complaint, they carry enormous burdens, defying wind, rain and sun, and from this rocky terrain they manage to extract an abundant production of vegetables and

J.S. Sargent, 'The epitome of a young Capriote girl', 1878. Private collection. Courtesy of Adelson Galleries, New York.

fruit. The instinctive elegance of these young women gives them a willowy appearance.'[14]

In 1946, Edwin Cerio, whose writings were always characterised by his ironic wit, concluded a chapter on the means of transport thus: 'The young girls of Capri still carry anything which is lovely or useful on their heads, harmoniously and gracefully balancing the weight with their torsos swaying over their well-rounded hips ... and not only all of the homes in Capri ... but even the wood, herbs, hay, must, milk, manure for the lands and the produce from the fields. But now this primitive form of transport is falling into disuse and lorries occupy the place of honour; if someone prefers a lorry, perhaps an American jeep, to a girl from Capri, well ... too bad for them.'[15]

These young women frequently dreamed of marrying a *forestiero* (an outsider – someone not from the island) to enable them to escape a life of sacrifice and poverty. They often managed to do so, as it happened that artists fell in love with their models and married them, sometimes remaining on the island and sometimes taking them away with them. Mariuccia Cimino was one of such women who had the good fortune to meet and become the partner of a *forestiero* – in her case, John Clay MacKowen.[16]

One of the events that captured MacKowen's attention was childbirth. He described the strange habits of the midwives, their invocation of various saints, the rush to baptise the newborn child and the celebrations that followed. He failed to comment, however, on the difficulties that the women faced just after giving birth. In 1879 Dr Ferdinand Bergamo, the island's district doctor, wrote of the many types of ailments that these poor women and their babies had to endure. In part, the problems were related to the hard physical work they had performed: 'In the absence of the men, and in order to feed their families, the women often subject themselves to taxing work which they also oblige their young daughters to carry out, many of whom succumb.'[17] And so, if we look beyond the fine portraits and the romantic attention paid to these lovely young girls with their proud carriage, we see a life of unremitting hard work that frequently brought in its train an array of health problems.

Another tradition MacKowen focused on was matrimony. He wrote in detail of the life of young couples from the day of their engagement to the second day of their marriage. Once again, if we look beyond appearances, various aspects are of interest. He tells of a young man who, though perhaps able to write, was not confident enough of his rhetorical skill to put his sentiments onto paper and therefore turned to a hunchback who acted both as scribe and postman. His account illustrates the level of education in the second half of the nineteenth century – as in most parts of southern Italy, access to education was severely limited, both with regard to the available structures as well as the professional training of the teachers. This was also confirmed by Dr Bergamo, who stated that there were two teachers in Capri, one in town and the other down at the Marina Grande, and in a newspaper article of December 1, 1889 reporting on the dire situation of the boys' school, went on to say that the girls' school was even worse, being reached through a cattle shed. The school, surrounded by rainwater wells and therefore very humid, lacked the necessary basic supplies such as school furniture, registers and notebooks.[18]

The precarious state of education was also confirmed in a report by two honorary school inspectors. One of these was Henry Wreford, appointed in 1861, who did much to rectify such inadequacies, setting up boys', girls' and nursery schools, providing much of the necessary funds out of his own pocket. The other honorary inspector was Ignazio Cerio, who in a report in 1884 complained that the island was full of unauthorised schools run by ignorant semi-literate women and 'poor-spirited' priests. Attendance was low: 'Nearly half the children of compulsory school age wander about the streets or work in the fields.'[19]

Interesting information regarding the island's economic and social life can be found between the lines written by MacKowen about marriage. Nowadays we are confronted on a daily basis with the difficulties encountered by young islanders in starting a family, but these problems involve housing and are of a social nature whereas in his time they were essentially economic. He used such statements as 'Pasquale has been coral fishing … Carmela has been carrying stones … for the last two or three years' to explain how young engaged couples saved enough money to get married, and further, that upon the death of their parents, they would inherit 'their little vineyards and olive orchards so that the future will be provided for.'[20]

He describes a custom which continues to this day, although with some variation: 'Friends await the procession and throw grain mixed with flowers on the head of bride and groom.'[21] It is an old Latin custom[22] whose origins have been lost in time, but Francesco de Bourcard, a painting by E.A. Sain and a tale by Charlotte Hamilton all provide some insight.[23] The event is described by de Bourcard: 'as the bride leaves her father's home, her parents sprinkle copious amounts of grain over her hair to wish her abundance.' Sain, a contemporary of MacKowen, immortalised the father of a bride in the act of strewing grain on his daughter's hair, while, as narrated by Charlotte Hamilton in 1924, she [the bride] 'would kiss the hands of her father and mother, asking them in turn to forgive her for all the unfortunate things that she had ever done.'[24] The parents would then be joined by friends who would 'throw' all sorts of good wishes at the couple. 'Flowers betoken wishes for happiness, and grain augurs a fruitful union', explained MacKowen. The festive atmosphere was also described by Hamilton: 'A crowd of children … collided with the procession … Most of the dogs of the place have considered it their duty to take part', jostling together in the attempt to secure the sugared almonds being thrown into the air – which over the course of time had become part of the tradition, symbolising joy and serenity. Still today, friends and relatives assembled along the route taken by the newlyweds hold a *guantiera*,[25] in which more easily available rice has replaced the grain, and coins have been added to represent prosperity. The custom of throwing beans at the bride whose condition did not match 'the virgin white of the orange-blossom on her head'[26] no longer exists. Even now, elderly women, who perhaps have no recollection of having thrown beans, still identify the gesture as one which bodes ill.

According to MacKowen, both the form and the menu of the nuptial lunch were rigorously based upon tradition. It took place at the home of the groom and the seating arrangements were rigidly established by custom. Guests were extremely severe in their judgments regarding the portions, which were generally gargantuan in size. Still in 1924, 'the festa lasts the entire afternoon and evening'[27], and it is interesting to note that the presence of an outsider was considered auspicious, bearing witness to the fact that the arrival of *forestieri* had always been synonymous with economic wellbeing.

He referred repeatedly to the small amount of food the Capresi ate as opposed to the amount of work they were obliged to perform. In an 1898 medical paper entitled 'Aromatic Toxins' he commented on the typical Italian farmer's diet (now called the Mediterranean diet): 'He eats enormous quantities of rough food, like unbolted cereals and dried or

Looking Beyond

E.A. Sain, *Wedding on Capri, 1881. Parents blessing the bride. Casa Rossa, Anacapri.*
Courtesy of the Municipality of Anacapri.

green fruits, cooked herbs or raw herbs as salads ... which furnish large quantities of cellulose, woody fibres and starch grains.' Prior to him, numerous authors had reported that all that was fished from the sea as well as the fruit of the land was sent to Naples to be sold; thus very little remained for local consumption with the exception, perhaps, of low-quality produce and catches which were not worth the trouble of sending to the mainland. He noted that pasta was only served on Sundays and that meat was consumed four times a year – at Christmas, the Epiphany, Easter and the Feast Day of San Costanzo, as Mary E. Vandyne was to confirm a few years later.[28] In 1927, the situation was not very different: '[The Capresi] are not rich. There is little cultivable land, which is not sufficient to nourish the local population, also owing to the fact that the farmers do not own, but lease the land they work.'[29]

Ernesto Mazzetti defined farming on the island as a life of 'hardship and sacrifice which has allowed for a meagre means of sustenance for a small population: for centuries only fishing and the capture of migratory

QUAIL-CATCHING IN NETS AT DOMECUTA.

C.C. Coleman, *Quail-catching in nets at Damecuta*, circa 1898, in F.D. Millet, 'Home of the Indolent. The Island of Capri', *The Century Magazine*, Oct. 1898. Centro Caprense Ignazio Cerio Archive, Capri.

birds with nets have provided precious nutritional integration to the islanders' very poor diets.'[30] It has only been since the end of World War II, and most markedly since the Sixties, that social change has resulted in widespread economic well-being and better nourishment. This, however, has not been the result of more efficient land exploitation (between 1960 and 1990, the cultivated hectares of land fell from 696 to 109), but rather an affluent condition marked by occasional peaks of opulence as the island's economy progressively shifted from agriculture and fishing to tourism.

MacKowen's numerous references to the clothing worn by the islanders culminated in open, perhaps excessive, criticism of the way that on the feast of the patron saint and other holidays, ambitious farmers adapted 'to the modern manner of dress ... that any ordinary tailor or milliner would shudder in despair that such crimes against their art should go unpunished.'[31] In actual fact, their costumes had always been praised for their simplicity and beauty: two centuries of artists deemed their clothing worthy of being portrayed down to the smallest detail of the embroidery.

Looking Beyond

One of the last reflections in MacKowen's interesting chapter on habits and customs concerns the physical features of the island women. He compares their beauty, proud bearing, neatness and cleanliness with those of the mainland women who, according to him, were unkempt and vulgar. As early as the eighteenth century, visitors to the island, each in their own way and according to his or her literary or artistic abilities, took note of and praised the island girls, and indeed this may be one of the features which most served to spread the legend of Capri.[32] MacKowen, as usual, looked further: in pondering upon the reasons for such beauty and such contrast, he attributed it – through the words of a mysterious Colonel Smith, an expert Irish ethnologist – to the presence of English soldiers on the island in the early nineteenth century. While these men undoubtedly left their descendants on the island, MacKowen may simply have been reflecting his Anglo-Saxon certainties, thus proving Mozzillo correct in his statement that the foreigners who observed our country either overstated or understated what they found, distorting the facts on the basis of the perspectives by which each of them had been conditioned.[33]

None of this detracts from MacKowen's achievement in having been one of the first to put together so valuable a body of information on the island. It proved to be of great use to the tourists of his day and in our own time remains a very important historical document, to such an extent that Norman Douglas, in his *Footnote on Capri* wrote: '[the book] is so scarce and so informative that it deserves to be reprinted – this time, let us hope, with an index.' A tribute to the merits of both these men.

Notes
1. A. Mozzillo, *Il giardino dell'iperbole. La scoperta del Mezzogiorno da Swinburne a Stendhal,* Naples 1985, Foreword. The history of the Grand Tour is skilfully illustrated by C. de Seta in 'L'Italia nello specchio del 'Grand Tour' in *Storia d'Italia, Annali,* V, *Il paesaggio,* Turin 1982 and in C. de Seta, *L'Italia del Grand Tour da Montaigne a Goethe,* Naples 1992. For information regarding the Grand Tour in Capri, see C. de Seta, *Capri,* Turin 1983, F. Durante, *Prima e dopo la Grotta Azzurra,* in *Capri nell'Ottocento da meta dell'anima a mito turistico,* ed. G. Alisio, Naples 1994; C. Fiorentino, 'Viaggiatori anglosassoni a Capri', in *Conoscere Capri 1.* Atti del 1° ciclo di conferenze sulla storia e la natura del isola di Capri (Capri-Anacapri), novembre 2002–aprile 2003), Capri 2003.
2. See C.D. de La Chavanne, D.D. Farjasse, A.C.H. Haudebourt Lescot,

Capri – The Island Revisited

L'Italie, la Sicile, les iles Eoliennes, l'ile d'Elbe, la Sardaigne, Malte, l'ile De Calypso, etc ..., Paris, 1835; M. Shelley, *Rambles in Germany and Italy in 1840, 1842 and 1843*, London 1844; J. R.Green, S*tray Studies from England and Italy*, London 1876; F. Bergamo, *Statistica medica-topografica-igienica di Capri ...*, Naples 1879. As regards modern times, numerous articles in the press have reported the practice of harassment: including, for example, 'Guerra alla petulanza: controlli ...', in www. caprinews.it dated 22 April, 2010 and G. Catuogno, *'Caos petulanza...'* in the *Giornale di Napoli* dated 28 April, 2010.
3. M. Shelley, *Rambles ...*, p. 273.
4. M. E. Vandyne, 'Sketches of Capri', in *Harper's Monthly Magazine*, Vol. LXXVII, 457, June 1888, pp. 27–34.
5. J. C. MacKowen, *Capri*, p. 77.
6. C.D. de La Chavanne, D.D. Farjasse, A.C.H. Haudebourt Lescot, *L'Italie* ... p. 25.
7. M. Shelley, *Rambles ...*, p. 272.
8. H. Wreford, 'The small communes of South Italy', in *Naples and Florence Observer*, 14 November, 1868. Henry Wreford was born in Bristol in 1806 and died in Capri in 1892.
9. A. Weber, *Fünf Jahre auf Capri ...*, Munich 1888.
10. M.E. Vandyne, *Sketches ...*
11. G. Narni Mancinelli, 'L'isola di Capri nel sole di luglio' in *Roma della Domenica*, 28 July, 1924.
12. I. Friedlaender, *Capri*, Rome 1938, p. 95.
13. F. D. Millet, 'Home of the Indolent. The Island of Capri', in *The Century Magazine*, Oct. 1898, p.857. Francis Davis Millet (Mattapoisett 1846–(on the Titanic 1912) was in Capri in 1873 and from 1892 to 1893. The article was illustrated by Charles Caryl Coleman (Buffalo 1840–Capri 1928), an American artist who lived in Capri at Villa Narcissus from 1886.
14. A. Ribaux, *Capri (Impressions et souvenirs)*, Paris-Naples 1912, p. 57. Ribaux (1864–1915) was a traveller and a journalist.
15. E. Cerio, *Guida inutile di Capri*, Rome 1946, pp. 192–3.
16. See the extensive and innovative biography by Prof. Cataldi Palombi in this book.
17. F. Bergamo, *Statistica ...*, final table.
18. F. Bergamo, *Statistica ...*, p. 8; G. Perrone Consiglio, 'Libro nero', in *Il Risveglio Educativo*, Milano, 1 Dec, 1889.
19. I. Cerio, *Relazione sulle condizioni delle scuole a Capri*, Capri 10 December, 1884. As regards education on Capri, see also: CENSIS, *Alla ricerca di una nuova identità: realtà e problemi dell'isola di Capri ...*, Rome 1982; E. Mazzetti, *Capri Ischia e Procida. Dal mito alla metropoli*, Naples 1999; S. D'Angiola, *Ignazio Cerio delegato scolastico*, currently in press.

20. J.C. MacKowen, *Capri*, p. 79.
21. J.C. MacKowen, *Capri*, p. 80.
22. It is superfluous to recall how, since antiquity, hair has always strongly symbolised fertility.
23. F. de Bourcard, *Usi e costumi di Napoli e contorni*, 1977 [1853]; E.A. Sain (Cluny 1830–Paris 1910). *Matrimonio a Capri*, a painting dated 1881 to be seen in MacKowen's home, the *Casa Rossa*, now a museum; Ch. Hamilton, 'Peasant wedding in Capri', in *The Cornhill Magazine*, London 1924.
24. Ch. Hamilton, *Peasant ...*, p. 74.
25. A tray for sweets which, for the occasion, is filled with sugared almonds, rice, flowers and coins.
26. J.C. MacKowen, p. 81.
27. Ch. Hamilton, *Peasant ...*, p. 76.
28. M.E. Vandyne, *Sketches ...*
29. H. Aubert, *L'Ile de Capri*, Capri 1927, p. 13.
30. E. Mazzetti, *Capri Ischia e Procida ...*, p. 60.
31. J.C. MacKowen, p. 83.
32. The numerous artists include R. Ormond and E. Kilmurray, *John Singer Sargent, Figures and Landscapes, 1874–1882*, New Haven, London 2006; A. Basilico and G. Aprea, *Omaggio alla venere caprese ...*, Capri 2007. In recalling authors and artists who praised (in writing or in paint) the beauty of the island women, it would please us to recall how many also praised the work of these women; work which frequently aged them before their time, as some authors had the opportunity to point out. It is our hope that we have provided a small contribution in this respect.
33. A. Mozzillo, *Il giardino ...*

Bibliography

Ackerman, J. S. *La villa. Forma ed ideologia*, Turin 1992.
Alvino, F. *Due giorni a Capri*, Naples 1838.
Alvino, F. and Quaranta, B. *Le antiche ruine di Capri disegnate e restaurate da Francesco Alvino; ed illustrate da Bernardo Quaranta*, Naples 1835.
Amirante, G. *Capri francese, inglese, napoleonica (1806–1816)*, Naples 2011.
Amitrano, M., Cafiero, A. and Fiorentino, C. (eds.), *Conoscere Capri 2. Atti del 2' ciclo di conferenze sulla storia e la natura dell'isola di Capri (Capri–Anacapri, novembre 2003–febbraio 2004)*, Capri 2004.
Andrén, A. *Capri from the Stone Age to the Tourist Age*, Gothenburg 1980.
Anelli, M. 'Sulla presenza di falde di ricoprimento nell'Italia meridionale', *Atti della Società dei naturalisti e matematici di Modena* 70, 1939, pp. 1–13.
Aubert, H. *L'Ile de Capri*, Capri 1927.
Barattolo, F. and Pugliese, A. 'Il Mesozoico dell'Isola di Capri', *Quaderni dell'Accademia Pontaniana* 8, 1987, p. 172.
Barattolo, F., Cinque, A., D'Alessandro, E., Guida, M., Romano, P. and Russo Ermolli, E. 'Geomorfologia ed evoluzione tettonica quaternaria dell'Isola di Capri', *Studi geologici camerti*, volume speciale, 1993, pp. 221–9.
Basilico, A. and Aprea, G. *Omaggio alla venere caprese...*, Capri 2007.
Beloch, J. *Campanien. Geschichte und Topographie des antiken Neapel und seiner Umgebung mit 13 Karten und Plänen, Zweite vermehrte Ausgabe*, Breslau, 1890 [Berlin, 1879].
Bergamo, F. *Statistica medica-topografica-igienica di Capri...*, Naples 1879.
Bergeron, A.W., *Guide to Louisiana Confederate Military Units 1861–1865*, Baton Rouge–London 1989.
Borghese, G.L., *Carlo I d'Angiò e il Mediterraneo. Politica, diplomazia e commercio internazionale prima dei Vespri*, Rome 2008.
Bosellini, A., *Storia geologica d'Italia. Gli ultimi 200 milioni di anni*, Bologna 2005.
Brancaccio, L., Capaldi, G., Cinque, A., Pece, R. and Sgrosso, I. '230Th-238U dating of coral from Tyrrhenian beach in Sorrentine Peninsula (Southern Italy)', *Quaternaria* 20, 1978, pp. 175–83.
Braudel, F., *La Méditerranée et le Monde Méditerranéen à l'Epoque de Philippe II*, Paris 1949.
Breislak, S., *Topografia fisica della Campania*, Florence 1798.
Broccoli, U., *Cronache militari e marittime del golfo di Napoli e delle isole pontine durante il decennio francese (1806–1815)...*, Rome 1953.
Canale, A., *Storia dell'isola di Capri dall'età remotissima sino ai tempi presenti*, Naples 1887.

Bibliography

Cancila, R. (ed.), *Mediterraneo in armi (secc. XV-XVIII)*, Palermo 2007.
Cantone, G., Fiorentino, B. and Sarnella, G., *Capri: la città e la terra*, Naples 1982.
Caputo, V., 'Le lucertole azzurre di Capri', *Almanacco Caprese* 7, 1994, pp. 39–51.
CENSIS, *Alla ricerca di una nuova identità: realtà e problemi dell'isola di Capri...*, Rome 1982.
Cerio, E., *Capri nel Seicento. Documenti e note*, Naples 1934.
Cerio, E., *Guida inutile di Capri*, Rome 1946.
Cerio, E., *L'ora di Capri*, Capri 1950.
Cerio, I., *Relazione sulle condizioni delle scuole a Capri*, manuscript, Capri December 10, 1884.
Cerio. I., *Scritti inediti e materiali di lavoro*, Giulianova 2001.
Chevalley De Rivaz, J. E., *Voyage de Naples à Capri et à Paestum exécuté le 4 Octobre 1845...*, Naples 1846, p. 18.
Ciancio, L., *Le colonne del tempo. Il tempio di Serapide a Pozzuoli nella storia della geologia, dell'archeologia e dell'arte (1750–1900)*, Florence 2009.
Ciuni, R., *Lettere al 'Times' da Capri borbonica...*, ed. E. Mazzetti, Capri 2011.
Colletta, P., *Storia del Reame di Napoli dal 1734 sino al 1825*, Florence 1846.
Coronelli, V.M., 'Isolario descrittione geografico-historica...', in *Atlante Veneto* II, Venice 1696.
Cortese, N., *Lettere e scritti inediti di Pietro Colletta*, Naples 1927.
Cummings, H. S., *Dartmouth College, Sketches of the Class of 1862*, Washington 1884.
D'Argenio, B., Violante, C., Sacchi, M., Budillon, F., Pappone, G., Casciello, E. and Cesarano, M., 'Capri, Bocca Piccola and Punta Campanella. Marine and on-land geology compared', in *Mapping Geology in Italy*, ed. G. Pasquaré, C. Venturini and G. Groppelli, Florence 2004, pp. 36-42.
D'Ayala, M., *Memorie storico-militari dal 1734 al 1815*, Naples 1835.
de Bourcard, F., *Usi e costumi di Napoli e contorni*, Milan 1977 [1853].
De Franciscis, A., *Le statue della Grotta Azzurra nell'isola di Capri*, Naples 1964.
de la Chavanne, C. D., Farjasse, D.D. and Haudebourt Lescot, A.C.H., *L'Italie, la Sicile, les îles Eoliennes, l'île d'Elbe, la Sardaigne, Malte, l'île de Calypso, etc...*, Paris 1835.
De Lorenzo, G., 'L'isola di Capri', *Rendiconti dell'Accademia dei Lincei, Classe di Scienze fisiche*, serie 5, 14, 1907, pp. 853–7.
de Seta, C., in 'L'Italia nello specchio del *Grand Tour*' in *Storia d'Italia*, Annali, V, *Il paesaggio*, Turin 1982.
de Seta, C., *L'Italia del Grand Tour da Montaigne a Goethe*, Naples 1992.

Bibliography

de Seta, C., *Capri*, Turin 1983.
Del Treppo, M. and Leone, A., *Amalfi medioevale*, Naples 1977.
di Stefano, R., *La Certosa di San Giacomo a Capri*, Naples 1982.
Dixon, B.V.B., *A Brief History of H. Sophie Newcomb Memorial College 1887–1919*, New Orleans 1928.
Durante, F., 'Prima e dopo la Grotta Azzurra',in *Capri nell'Ottocento da meta dell'anima a mito turistico,* ed. G. Alisio, Naples 1994.
Fatica, L., 'San Costanzo di Capri: patriarca di Costantinopoli?', *Campania sacra* 23, 1992, pp. 155–62.
Federico, E., 'I Fenici e Capri: messa a punto e prospettiva', in *Almanacco Caprese* 5, 1992, pp. 39–54.
Federico, E. and Miranda, E. (eds.), *Capri antica. Dalla preistoria alla fine dell'età romana*, Capri 1998.
Federico, E., Tafuri, A.and Amitrano, G. (eds.), *Conoscere Capri 1. Atti del 1° ciclo di conferenze sulla storia e la natura dell'isola di Capri (Capri–Anacapri, novembre 2002–aprile 2003)*, Capri 2003.
Federico, E., 'Le Sirene, la morte e il destino di pietra. Impressioni mitiche nel paesaggio naturale', in *Illusione e seduzione*, ed. R. Aragona, Naples 2010, pp. 97–101.
Feola, G., *Rapporto sullo stato attuale dei ruderi Augusto-Tiberiani nella isola di Capri manoscritto inedito del 1830 pubblicato ed annotato dal nipote Ignazio Cerio*, Naples 1894.
Ferranti, L., 'Movimenti "lenti" nell'isola di Capri negli ultimi 124.000 anni', *Conoscere Capri 6. Studi e materiali per la storia di Capri*, Capri 2007, pp. 11–37.
Ferranti, L. and Antonioli, F., 'Misure del solco tirreniano (mis 5.5) nell'isola di Capri: valutazione di attività tettonica durante il Pleistocene Superiore', *Il Quaternario, Italian Journal of Quaternary Sciences* 20(2), 2007, pp. 125–36.
Fiorani, T., *Le dimore del mito. Residenze letterarie a Capri tra Ottocento e primo Novecento*, Naples 1996.
Fiorelli, V., *Una esperienza religiosa periferica. I monasteri di madre Serafina di Dio da Capri alla terraferma,* Naples 2003.
Frederiksen, M. V., *Campania*, ed. N. Purcell, London 1984.
Friedlaender, I., *Capri*, Rome 1938.
Galasso, G., *Il Regno di Napoli*, Turin 1999–2007.
Galasso, G., *Napoli capitale. Identità politica e identità cittadina. Studi e ricerche 1266–1860*, Naples 1998.
Galasso, G., *Una periferia insulare*, now in Id., *Capri insula e dintorni*, Capri 2004.
Gould, S.J., 'Lyell's Pillars of Wisdom' in *The Lying Stones of Marrakech***:** *Penultimate Reflections in Natural History*, New York 2000. (Italian

Bibliography

translation 'Le colonne della saggezza di Lyell', in *Le pietre false di Marrakech, appunti di storia naturale*. Milan 2007, pp. 187–213.)

Green, J. R., S*tray Studies from England and Italy*, London 1876.

Gregorovius, F., *Der Tod des Tiberius*, Hamburg 1851.

Gregorovius, F., *Wanderjahre in Italien. Band 3. Siciliana. Wanderungen in Neapel und Sicilien*, Leipzig 1881.

Hadrava, N., *Ragguagli di varii scavi, e scoperte di antichità fatte nell'Isola di Capri*, Naples 1793.

Hamilton, Ch., 'Peasant wedding in Capri', in *The Cornhill Magazine*, London 1924.

Hull, E., *Volcanoes Past and Present*, London 1892.

Issel, A., 'Le oscillazioni lente del suolo o bradisismi', *Atti R. Università di Genova* 5, 1883, p. 422.

Issel, A., 'Le oscillazioni lente del suolo', *Nuova Antologia* 71, fascicolo 20, 1883, pp. 646–6.

Jezdinsky, F., *Capri, Perla More Stredozemniho* (Capri, Pearl of the Mediterranean), Nemecky Brod 1896.

Karsten, H., 'Zur Geologie der Insel Capri I', *Neues Jahrbuch für Mineralogie Geologie und Paläontologie*, 1895, pp. 139–61.

Kopisch, A., 'Entdeckung der Blauen Grotte auf der Insel Capri', in *Annuario Italia*, ed. A. Reumont, Berlin 1838, pp. 155–210.

Krause, C., *Villa Jovis: l'edificio residenziale*, Naples 2005.

La Cava, P., 'I. Geologia' in 'Statistica fisica ed economica dell'isola di Capri', *Esercitazioni accademiche degli Aspiranti Naturalisti* 2, I, Naples 1840, pp. 11–22.

La Moreaux, P. E., 'History of karst hydrogeological studies', *Proceedings of the International Conference on Environmental Changes in Karst Areas - I.G.U.-U.I.S.- Italy 15–27 Sept. 1991, Quaderni del Dipartimento di Geografia dell'Università di Padova* 13, 1991, pp. 215–29.

Lafon, X., 'À propos des villas de la zone de Sperlonga. Les origines et le développement de la "villa maritima" sur le littoral tyrrhénien à l'époque répubblicaine', in *Mélanges d'Archéologie et d'Histoire de l'École Française de Rome* 93, 1981, pp. 297–353.

Lambeck, K., Antonioli, F., Anzidei, M., Ferranti, L., Leoni, G., Scicchitano, G. and Silenzi, S. 'Sea level change along the Italian coast during the Holocene and projections for the future', *Quaternary International* 232 (1–2), 2011, pp. 250–7.

Landry, S.O., *The History of the Boston Club*, New Orleans 1938.

MacKowen, J.C., *Aromatic Toxins*, New Orleans 1898.

MacKowen, J.C., *Murder as Money Making Art*, Baton Rouge 1901.

Mafrici, M., 'I mari del Mezzogiorno d'Italia tra cristiani e musulmani', in

Bibliography

Storia d'Italia, Annali 18, Guerra e pace, ed. W. Barberis, Turin [2002], pp. 73–121.
Maiuri, A., *Capri. Storia e monumenti*, Rome 1957.
Maiuri, A., 'Grotte ninfei imperiali dell'isola di Capri', *Bollettino d'Archeologia* XXV, 1931.
Maiuri, A., 'La villa augustea di Palazzo a Mare a Capri, *Campania Romana* I, 1938, pp. 115–41.
Mangoni, R., *Ricerche storiche sull'isola di Capri colle notizie più rilevanti sulla vicina regione del cratere,* Naples 1834.
Mazzetti, E., *Capri Ischia e Procida. Dal mito alla metropoli,* Naples 1999.
Melville, H., *Battle-Pieces and Aspects of the War*, New York 1866.
Miele, M., *La Chiesa del Mezzogiorno nel Decennio francese*, Naples 2007.
Millet, F. D., 'Home of the Indolent. The Island of Capri', *The Century Magazine*, Oct. 1898, p. 857.
Mingazzini, P., 'Le grotte di Matermania e dell'Arsenale a Capri', in *Archeologia Classica* VII, 1955.
Mingazzini, P., *Vico Equense (Penisola Sorrentina ed isola di Capri)*, Edizione Archeologica della Carta d'Italia al 100.000, foglio 196, Florence 1931, p. 48.
Moneti, A., 'Le ville di Tiberio a Capri e la villa sotto la Farnesina', in *Rivista d'Archeologia* 15, 1991, pp. 89–96.
Money, J., *Capri, Island of Pleasure*, London 1986.
Mozzillo, A., *Il giardino dell'iperbole. La scoperta del Mezzogiorno da Swinburne a Stendhal,* Naples 1985.
The National Cyclopaedia of American Biography, Vol. IV, New York 1897.
Neudecker, R., *Die Skulpturen-Ausstattung Römischer Villen in Italien*, Mainz am Rhein 1988.
Oppenheim, P., 'Beiträge zur Geologie der Insel Capri und der Halbinsel Sorrent', *Zeitschrift der Deutschen Geologischen Gesellschaft* 42, 1889, pp. 758–64.
Oppenheim, P., *Die Insel der Sirenen von ihrer Entstehung bis zur Gegenwart.Eine populäre Darstellung der physischen und politischen Geschichte der Insel Capri. Mit einer geologischen Karte der Insel Capri,* Berlin 1890.
Ormond, R. and Kilmurray, E., *John Singer Sargent. Figures and landscapes, 1874–1882*, New Haven–London 2006.
Palmieri, L., 'Intorno all'incendio del Vesuvio cominciato il dì 8 dicembre 1861', *Rendiconti dell'Accademia Pontaniana* 10, 1862, pp. 40–61, 72–83.
Parrino, D.A., *Nuova guida de' forastieri, per l'antichità curiosissime di Pozzuoli; delle isole adjacenti d'Ischia, Procida, Nisida, Capri, colline, terre, ville, e città, che sono intorno alle riviere…*, Naples, 1727 [1709].

Bibliography

Raia, P., Guarino, F. M., Turano, M., Polese, G., Rippa, D., Carotenuto, F., Monti, D. M., Cardi, M. and Fulgione, D., 'The blue lizard spandrel and the island syndrome', *Biomed Central Evolutionary Biology* 10, 2010, p. 289–305.

Regione Campania, 'Piano Regionale per la Programmazione delle Attività di Previsione Prevenzione e Lotta Attiva contro gli Incendi Boschivi – Anno 2007', *Bollettino Ufficiale della Regione Campania*, n. speciale del 12.07.2007, p. 154.

Ribaux, A., *Capri (Impressions et souvenirs)*, Paris–Naples 1912.

Romanelli, D., *Isola di Capri. Manoscritti inediti del Conte della Torre Rezzonico, del Professor Breislak e del Generale Pommereul*, Naples 1816.

Rossetti, G. and Vitolo, G. (eds.), *Medioevo Mezzogiorno Mediterraneo. Studi in onore di Mario Del Treppo*, Pisa–Naples 2000.

Rovereto, G., 'L'île de Capri est un lambeau de recouvrement?', *Bulletin de la Société géologique de France* 7, 1907, pp. 162–3.

Ruggiero, M., *Degli scavi di antichità nelle province di Terraferma dell'antico Regno di Napoli, dal 1734 al 1876*, Naples 1888.

San Francisco Daily Supplement, *San Francisco Saturday Evening Post*, Vol. LXIII, Number 132, March 12, 1887.

Santagata, C., *La preistoria a Capri. Cronaca delle ricerche all'epoca di Ignazio Cerio*, Naples 1994

Schettino, A. and Turco, E., 'Tectonic history of the western Tethys since the Late Triassic, *Geological Society of America Bulletin* 123, 1/2, 2011, pp. 89–105.

Secondo, G.M., *Relazione storica dell'antichità, rovine e residui di Capri umiliata al Re*, Naples 1750.

Serrao, E. and Lacerenza, G. (eds.), *Capri e l'Islam. Studi su Capri, il Mediterraneo, l'Oriente*, Capri 1998.

Shelley, M., *Rambles in Germany and Italy in 1840, 1842 and 1843,* London 1844.

Starke, M., *Letters from Italy, between the years 1792 and 1798, containing a view of the Revolution in that country*, London 1800.

Starke, M., *Travels in Europe for the Use of Travellers on the Continent and...*, Paris 1832

Steinmann, G., 'Über das Alter des Appenninkalkes von Capri', *Bericht Naturforschenden Gesellschaft Freiburg* 4, 1889, pp. 48–52.

Trudgill, S. T., Chapter 4. 'Limestone Landforms', 1890–1965, in *The History of the Study of Landforms on the Development of Geomorphology*, ed. T.P. Burt, R.J. Chorley, D. Brunsen, N.J. Cox and A.S. Goudie, Bath 2008, pp.107–25.

Vandyne, M. E., 'Sketches of Capri', *Harper's Monthly Magazine* Vol. LXXVII, n. 457, June 1888, pp. 27–34.

Bibliography

Walther, J., 'Über die Geologie von Capri', *Zeitschrift der Deutschen Geologischen Gesellschaft* 41, 1888, pp. 771–6.
Weber, A., *Fünf Jahre auf Capri…*, Munich 1888.
White, W. B., 'A brief history of karst hydrogeology: contributions of the NSS', *Journal of Cave and Karst Studies* 69, 1, pp. 13–26.
Wreford, H., 'The small communes of South Italy', *Naples and Florence Observer*, November 14, 1868.

Classical Sources
Dio's Roman history: in nine volumes, with a translation by E. Cary, London–Cambridge, Massachusetts 1914–17.
The Geography of Strabo: in eight volumes, with an English translation by H.L. Jones, London–Cambridge, Massachusetts 1917–32.
Pliny the Elder, (*Naturalis historia* III, 6, 82, ed. H. Rackham, Cambridge, Mass. 1947).
Pope, *The Odyssey of Homer*, ed. M. Mack, London–New Haven 1967.
Statius: in two volumes, with an English translation by J.H. Mozley, London–Cambridge, Massachusetts 1961.
C. Suetonius Tranquillus, *The Lives of the Twelve Caesars*, translated by A. Thomson, revised and corrected by T. Forester, London 1876.
Tacitus, *The Histories. The Annals, in four volumes*, with an English translation by C.H. Moore and J. Jackson, London–Cambridge, Massachusetts 1951.
Virgil, *The Aeneid*, translated by C.D. Lewis, Oxford 1986.

Archives
McKowen-Lilley-Stirling Family Papers, Special Collections, LSU Libraries, New Orleans, Louisiana.
Archivio del Centro Caprense Ignazio Cerio, Capri.

Index

Page references for illustrations are in *italics*; those for notes are followed by the note number, e.g. 166n21

Acarnania 163
Agrippa 24, 25, 30–1
Agrippina 24, 27
Alexander 35
Alfonso of Aragon, King of Sicily 44–5
Alvino, Francesco 68–9
Amalfi 42, 179
Anacapri 14
  Barbarossa 42, 45, 118
  Campetiello 66, 99, 154
  and Capri 45, 46–7, 52, 83–4, 179–80
  Caprile 135
  Cocuzza 2
  Damecuta 57, 98–9, 127, 130, 154, 170
  festa of Saint Antonio 83
  Fravicina 119
  geology 153
  Gradelle 66; landing place 98
  Gradola 126, 127, 135, 150n20, 174–5
  Materita Tower 99, 135, 150n20, 154
  Migliara terrace 119, 154
  Monte Solaro 42, 60, 61, 64, 99, 100, 118, 119, 153, 154
  Orico 66, 99
  Parate 172
  population 46, 55, 68, 73
  Pozzo 99
  Punta Campetiello 66, 99, 154
  Punta Capocchia 99
  Punta Carena 99
  Punta Pino 66, 99
  Punta Vitareta 99
  Rio Iacolo 127
  Santa Maria Cetrella 49, 57, 61
  Torre 148n8, 150n20
  Torre della Guardia 99
  Vignolella 127
  walks 119
Anjou dynasty 43–4, 179
Anna, Saint 77
Apennines 152–3, 157n6

appiccico 84–7
Apragopolis 17, 18
Aragon dynasty 44–5
Arcucci, Dr Gennaro 52
Arcucci, Admiral Eliseo 179
Arcucci, Giacomo 43–4, 49, 104, 181
Aromatic Toxins (MacKowen) 134–5, 148n14, 194–5
Augustus 17–18, 24, 26, 28, 29, 33, 172
  and Capri 16–17, 119, 163
  and Tiberius 22, 25, 29, 30
  villas 105, 107, 113, 171

Barbarossa (person) 45–6, 118, 182
Bennett, Sherriff J.B. 142
Bergamo, Dr Ferdinando 192, 193
Bernardo di Serriano 43
bishops 49, 53, 180–1
Blue Grotto *see* grottoes
Boccagiamba, Lieutenant 60
Bonaparte, Joseph 58
Borrelli, Pasquale 129
Bourbons 49, 57–67, 70, 74, 183, 184, *184*
Breislak, Scipione 151

Caesar, Caius 22, 24, 25, 29, 30, 31;
  Julius 28
Caffè Bitter 144, *145*

Caligula 39, 41, 112, 114, 164
Campo Militare 61, 66
Candler, Colonel 135
cannibals 161
Capaccio, Giulio Cesare 46–7, 94
Capri (island)
  ancient history 14–40, 161–5
  description 90–120
  etymology of name 14, 162–3, 165n7
  geology 1–9, 151–6
  habits and customs 75–89, 187–96
  history 41–74, 179–85

207

Index

place names 164, 166–7n24
population 68, 73
sea level, fluctuations in 5, 159n23, 178n26
topography and climate 10–13, 160n28
Capri (town) 14, 90
and Anacapri 45, 46–7, 51–2, 83–4, 179–80
Arco Naturale 112
Bagni di Tiberio (Baths of Tiberius) 91–2, 107, 170–1, 176n10
Cala di Matromania 107–8, 119, 173
Camerelle 105
Castiglione 42, 53, 57, 61, 66, 101–3, 163, 170
Cesina 57
'Cyclopean' wall 16, 118, 163, 166n8, 172, 177n20
Faraglioni 105–7, 156
Grande Marina *see* Marina Grande
Marina Grande 116–18, 127, 169–70; Cimino family 125, 144, 145, 149n20; climate 10; *cloaca* 3, 7, 8, 90, 107, 156, 169, 175n3; geology 156; hotels 54, 126
Marina Piccola 15, 101, and *Sirena* 161, 166–7n24
Monacone 17, 18, 107
Monte San Michele 57, 61, 116, 153, 170
Mount Tiberio 113, 115, 119, 153, 170
Mulo *see* Marina Piccola
Palazzo a Mare 91–2, 107, 170–1, 176n10
Piccola Marina *see* Marina Piccola
population 46, 55, 68, 73
Punta Tragara 107
Punta Masullo 159n24
Salto di Tiberio 21, 113
San Costanzo 49–50, 90, 169, 172, 180
Santa Maria del Soccorso 57, 66
Tiberio 113, 115, 119, 153, 170
Tragara 106, 119, 170
Trasele 92
Unghia Marina 104–5, 170

Villa Jovis 49, 53, 113–15, 119, 170, 171–2, 189
Valentino, via (via Padre Serafino Cimino) 102
Capri (MacKowen) 1–120
map *169*
publication 126–7
review 135
Carthusian monks 43–4, 48, 49, 54, 67, 99, 181–2
Casa Rossa 127, 144, 145–6, *146*, *174*, 175, 178n29
Catherine, Empress of Russia 102
cave-dwellers 15, 161
caves *see* grottoes
Cerio, Edwin *162*, 192
Cerio, Ignazio 15, 118, 158n15, 161, 164, 172, 193
Certosa 70, 104
Charles II of Anjou 43
Charles II of Spain 48
Charles III of Anjou 44
Charles III of Bourbon 49–50
Chervardes, Adjutant 58
Chervet, Captain 57
Chevalley de Rivaz, Jacques Etienne 148n10, 186n14
childbirth 77–8, 192
Christianity 90, 110–11
Cimino, Antonio 125
Cimino, Giulia *see* Maresca, Giulia
Cimino, Maria (Mariuccia) 125,127, 149n20, 192
Ciro, Saint 77–8
Clinton, Louisiana 136
clothing 196
Coleman, Charles Caryl *196*
Colletta, General Pietro 63–5
Commodus 41, 112, 164, 169
coral fishing 56, 74, 182, 188, 190
Corsairs *see* Saracens
Corsican regiment 58–60, 65, 87
Costanzo, Saint 42–3, 46, 180
Crispina 41, 112, 164, 169
Cuma 16, 163
Cummings, Horace Stuart 148n7
Cuomo, Dr Vincenzo 125–6, 130–1, 135, 144, 147n4

208

Index

Dalmasso, Bartolomeo 130
D'Andrea, Signor 113
de Angelis, Doctor Marcello 51
de Bourcard, Francesco 194
Destres, General 58
Dio Cassius 41, 164
Diversi, Emanuele 51
Dixon, Brandt V.B. 134, 149n16
Douglas, Norman vi, 197
Dow, General Neal 122, 135
Dragut 182
Drusus (Tiberius's brother) 22, 24, 27, 28
Drusus (Tiberius's son) 19, 20, 21, 23, 24, 27, 38

education 53, 193
emigration 74, 190
English military presence 57–66, 98, 99, 116, 117, 182–3
Engman, W.F. 135
'epitome of a young Capriote girl, The' (Sargent) *191*

Farace, Luigi 148n8
Federico, Alessio 147n5
Feola, Giuseppe 104, 114, 116, 117, 171, 177n14
Ferdinand IV of Naples 50, 51, 53, 57, 58, 63, 102
fishing 45, 56, 67, 73; coral 56, 74, 182, 188, 190
flora 11
food 82, 194–5
Footnote on Capri (Douglas) vi, 197
forestieri 165, 192, 194
Francesco I of the Two Sicilies 114
Frederick of Aragon 45, 180
Frederick II of Swabia 179
French military presence 57–67, 98, 99, 116, 117, 182–3
Friedlaender, Immanuel 190
Fünf Jahre auf Capri (Weber) 190

Gamboni, Bishop 53, 67
Germanicus 19, 23
Giraldi, Dr Luigi 52, 104
Greeks 14–15, 84, 110, 120, 161, 163, 164, 169–70, 172

Green, John Richard 188
Gregorovius, Ferdinand 10
Gregory, Saint 41
grottoes 1–2, 3, 92, 100, 101–2, 112, 155, 172–3
  'Albergo dei Pescatori' 104
  Blue Grotto 92–8, 168, 174-5, *178 n26*, 187; MacKowen's plans for 127–9, *128*, 132, 134, 135, 138, 150n20; sea divinities 146, 174–5
  Fern Grotto *see* Grotta dell'Arco
  Green Grotto 100
  Grotta dell'Arco 2, 7, 15–16, 118, 161, 162, *162*, 165n2
  Grotta dell'Arsenale 3, 103–4, 173
  Grotta delle Felci *162*, 165n2, 172
  Matromania 107–9, 119, 173
  Red Grotto 100
  stalactites 116
  Turk's Grotto 100
  White Grotto 112
guantiera 194

Haan, Antal 43, 66, 91, 117, 127
Hadrava, Norbert 53–4, 55–7, 114, 169, 173, 177n13, 184–5
Baths of Tiberius 91
Castiglione 102–3
demonstration against governor 51
lighthouse 112
militia review 50
Villa Jovis 113–14, 171
Hamill, Major John 59–60, 66, 99; John and Catherine 66
Hamilton, Charlotte 194
Hamilton, Sir William 102
Herduran, Dr W.B. 135
'Home of the Indolent' (Millet) 190, *196*
Homer 15, 161, 166n21
hotels 54
  Hotel Bristol 126
  Hotel Caesar Augustus 144
  Hotel de France 116
  J.K. Palace Capri Hotel 175n3
  Hotel Metropole 175n3
  Hotel Quisisana 154
  Hotel Villa di Londra 147n5
Howard, Frank T. 132, 134

Index

Irish regiments, traces of 87-8
Irwin, Dr 139
Issel, Arturo 159n23

Jackson, Louisiana 121, *143*
James, King of Sicily 43
Joanna I of Anjou 43–4
Joanna II of Anjou 44
Julia 22, 24, 27, 28, 29, 105
Juvenal 34

Kahir-el-Din 45–6, 118, 182
karstification 155
King, Dr Arthur 134, 135–6, 138, 150n20
King, Carlo Guglielmo 150n20
Kopisch, August 68, 92–3, 94, 175n1

La Cava, Pasquale 151
Ladislaus of Anjou 44
Lamarque, General 58, 62–3, 99
Lamenais, abbé 67–8
Langford, Mary Ann 121
Lavino, abbot 41
lighthouse (*see also* Anacapri, Punta Carena) 23, 41, 112
limestone 1, 11, 151, 152, 160n28
Livia 24, 25–6, 40
  death 38
  murders 20, 21, 29, 30–1
  and Tiberius 25, 27–8, 31–2, 38–9, 164
Livy 16
Lizards, blue 105–6, 156
Lowe, Sir Hudson 57, 58, 59, 61, 62, 63–4, 65, 66, 87, 88, 182–3
Lucilla 41, 112, 164
Lucius 22, 24, 25, 29, 30, 31
Ludovicus 42

MacKowen, John Clay 121–4, *122*, 126–31, 135, *136*, 137–8, 148n8, 149n20
  American Civil War 121–2, 126, 135
  Aromatic Toxins 134–5, 148n14, 194–5
  book collection 131–2, 134, 137, 149n16
  boundary dispute 137, 138
  in Capri 124–31, 137, 187
  Capri 1–120, 126–7, 135, *169*
  death 138–43

and Giulia *see* Maresca, Giulia
  grave 143, *143*
  health 122, 124, 126, 131, 135–6, 137–8
  and Arthur King 135
  medical training 121, 122, 124
  and Axel Munthe 129–30
  return to Louisiana 131, 132, 134–7
  travels in Near East 131
Magenta, Cavaliere Carlo 137
Maiuri, Amedeo 176n10
Maltese regiment 59, 60–1, 64, 87
Mangoni, Rosario 65, 68, 98, 169, 173
Marcellus 22, 24, 25, 26
Marcus Agrippa 24
Maresca
  Armando 144
  Clelia 144
  Flora 144
  Guido 144
  Giulia 125, 127, 134, 135, 138, 144–6, 149–50n20
  Mario 144, 145
  Silvio 144
Martello towers 42
Masgaba 17, 18, 107
Mayer, Emilio 119
Mazzetti, Ernesto 195–6
McKowen
  Alexander Cooper 121
  Christine 124
  John (father) 121, 124
  Sarah *see* Pipes McKowen, Sarah
  Thomas Chalmers 121, 124
  William 121, 124, 127, 136–7, 149–50n20
Melville, Herman 121
Millet, Frank Davis 190, *196*
Mills, Robert Y. 139
Mithraism 107–12, 173
monasteries 41, 43–4, 48, 49, 54, 67, 73–4, 181–2
Monte Cassino 41, 42–3
Montserras, General 58
Mozzillo, Atanasio 187, 197
Munthe, Axel 129–30, 150n20, 178n27

Index

Murat, Joachim 58, 62, 66, 181, 183
Murder as Money Making (MacKowen) 138

Naples 41, 48, 57, 70, 179, 180, 183, 184
Napoleonic Wars 57–66, 99, 116, 117, 182–3, 187
necropolis 172, 177n18
Nerva, Cocceius 23, 34
New Orleans 132, 134, 136, 148n13
New Orleans Medical and Surgical Journal 134–5
Newcomb Memorial College, H. Sophie 134, 137, 149n16
nymphaeum 174–5

Orlandi, Giuseppe 131

Palazzo Inglese 50, 54, 66
Palmieri, Luigi 6–7, 159n25
Panettieri, Captain 59
Parrino, Antonio 48–9, 94, 182
Paul, Jean 10
Peebles, Dr James Martin 137–8
Petagna, Giuseppe 147n5
Petagna, Don Salvatore 147n5
Phoenicians 14, 15 16, 118, 161, 162–3, 172
Pisa, Prudenza (Mother Serafina di Dio) 182
Pietro di Toledo 46
Pike, Dr J.M. 131–2, 134
Pipes, David 138
Pipes McKowen, Sarah 121, 123–4, 137, 139
pirates 49, 50, 182
plague 47–8, 67, 181–2
Pope, Alexander 15, 166n21
Port Hudson 122
poverty 67, 189, 190, 195
Pozzuoli 2–3, 155, 158n21

quarrels 84–7

rainfall 10–11, 160n28
religion 70–3
   Christianity 90, 110–11
   Mithraism 107–12

Renato of Anjou 44–5
Ribaux, Adolphe 190, 192
Robert of Anjou 43
Roger, King (Norman dynasty) 42
Romanelli, Domenico 94, 169
Romano, Giovanni 130–1, 132
Romans 14, 41, 119–20, 161, 164–5, 169, 170
   Augustus 16–18, 163
   Capri (town) 118–19
   First Punic War 172, 177n21
   military camp 172
   Mithraism 108, 110–11
   roads 119
   temple of Jupiter Serapis 2–3
   Tiberius 18–23, 24–40, 106–7, 163–4
   villas 52–3, 104–5, 107, 113–15, 170–2, 174, 176n10
Rossi, Andrea 183
Rubino, Sergio *146*

Sain, Eduard Alexandre 194, *195*
San Costanzo 49–50, 90, 169, 172, 180
San Francesco monastery 43, 66, 117
San Giacomo Charterhouse 181, 185n9
San Michele 57, 61, 116, 153, 170
Santa Maria 113, 115
Saracens 41, 42, 44, 49, 50–1, 99, 101, 182
   and fishermen 48, 56, 100
   San Costanzo 45–6, 180
Sargent, John Singer *191*
Savastano, Salvatore 148n8
Schwartzenberg, Prince 102
Secondo, Don Giuseppe Maria 50
Sejanus 20, 21, 23, 38–9, 170
sellariae 114, 171
Seneca 39
Shannon, Jane 121
Shelley, Mary 188, 189
Shiloh (Battle) 121
Shiloh: A Requiem (Melville) 121
Shurk, Captain 59–60
Sicily 43, 57, 58
Sirena 15, 161, 166–7n24
Sirens 15, 120, 161
Smith, Colonel Hudson 87, 88, 197
Sorrento peninsula 151, *152*, 153, 154

211

Index

Spadaro, Francesco 105
Stanford Restaurant du Louvre 126
Starke, Mariana 68
Statius 41, 112, 164
Stevens, Mr 102
Strabo 14, 16, 169, 172
Strongoli-Pignatelli, Prince 58
Suetonius 166n21, 170
   Augustus 16, 17–18, 30, 163
   Caligula 41
   earthquake 98, 112
   sellariae 114, 171
   Tiberius 19–20, 23, 24–5, 27, 29, 30, 31, 33–4, 36, 37, 38, 39, 52, 106–7
Susino, Captain 59–60
Sylla 35

Teleboi 16, 19, 163
Thomas, Adjutant 58, 60, 62, 66
Thompson, Robert Emerson 137, 138–43, 149n17
Thomson, Alexander 166n21
Thorold, Sir Nathaniel 50
Thrasyllus 17, 92

Tiberius 19–23, 24–40, 163–4
   Capri 18–19, 20, 35, 52, 106–7, 118, 119, 129, 163, 164, 172
   Mithraism 108
   statues 115, 117
   Villa Jovis 113–15, 170, 171
Tischbein, Johann Heinrich Wilhelm 102

Torre del Greco 155
Trippel, Alexander 102
Tyrrhenian notch 155, 159n24
Tyrrhenian Sea 153

Ulysses 15, 161

Vandyne, Mary E. 188, 190, 195
Velpeau, Alfred Armand Louis Marie 122, 147n3
Vespasian 91
Vesuvius 67
Villa San Michele 130
villas 3–5, 52–3, 104–5, 171–2
   Palazzo a Mare 91–2, 107, 170–1, 176n10
vine disease 69, 74
Virgil 163
Vitellius 41, 164
Voit, Carl von 124, 135, 147n4, 148n14

Wall & Laycock Clinton Law Office 137
Water, paucity of 10, 189–90
Weber, August 190
'Wedding on Capri' (Sain) 194, *195*
wine, Capri 69, 73
women 57, 77, 87, 188–90, *189*, *191*, 192, 197, 199n32
   childbirth 77–8, 192
   dress 82–3
Wreford, Henry 129, 189–90, 193
Wurtz, Charles Adolphe 122, 147n3

Notes

Notes

Notes

Notes